View of Hotel Well I
by David Hockney

MICHAEL'S COOKBOOK

MICHAEL'S COOKBOOK

MICHAEL McCARTY

WITH NORMAN KOLPAS

FOOD PHOTOGRAPHY BY RICHARD CLARK
ART PHOTOGRAPHY BY WILLIAM NETTLES

MACMILLAN PUBLISHING COMPANY
NEW YORK
COLLIER MACMILLAN PUBLISHERS
LONDON

Macmillan Publishing Company
866 Third Avenue, New York, N.Y. 10022
Collier Macmillan Canada, Inc.

All of the art that appears in this book is part of Kim and Michael McCarty's private art collection.
The piece that appears on the title page is *View of Hotel Well I* by David Hockney.

Library of Congress Cataloging-in-Publication Data

McCarty, Michael.
    Michael's cookbook.

    1. Cookery, American—California style.
2. Michael's (Restaurant)   I. Kolpas, Norman.
II. Title.
TX715.2.C34M33   1989   641.59794   89-13284
ISBN 0-02-583111-9

Macmillan books are available at special discounts for bulk purchases for sales promotions, premiums, fund-raising, or educational use. For details, contact:

Special Sales Director
Macmillan Publishing Company
866 Third Avenue
New York, N.Y. 10022

10 9 8 7 6 5 4 3 2 1

Printed in the United States of America

DESIGNED BY BARBARA MARKS

TO MY FATHER,
JOHN T. McCARTY,
AND MY MOTHER,
CAROL McCARTY AUSTELL,
FOR THEIR INCREDIBLE GRASP
OF HOW TO THROW
A *GREAT* PARTY.

Harry and Michael
by Kim McCarty

CONTENTS

■

ACKNOWLEDGMENTS

.

I would like to offer a toast (of Krug '59, in magnum) to the following people who have helped make this book possible:

My wife, Kim McCarty, for her loyalty, sensibility, understanding, and love.

My head chef, Martin Garcia, for being the great success story of the kitchen at Michael's.

My pastry chef, Dorte Lambert, for her tireless efforts to perfect our desserts.

Clancy and Chas McCarty, in advance.

Irene Phelps, for being a great assistant and putting up with all my shenanigans.

Phil Reich, for being a winemaster *par excellence* and for having worked with me for fifteen years developing the magical marriage of food and wine.

Norman Kolpas, without whom this book would have been impossible.

Harvey Friend, for keeping all my restaurants running smoothly.

Pam Hoenig and her colleagues at Macmillan, for their faith and support in this project.

And all my fellow American chefs, who continually strive to promote the evolution of New American Cooking.

Back of Head by
Kim McCarty

INTRODUCTION

In 1979, when I was twenty-five years old, I founded Michael's, a restaurant near the beach in Santa Monica, California.

People who came to this new restaurant were knocked out—by the bright, modern setting (actually a ramshackle old Thirties house that we cleaned up and painted a warm, rosy shade of cream); by the lush open-air garden; by the contemporary art collection; by the sharp young waiters; and by the food, which critics labeled with a then-unheard-of term, "California Cuisine."

Actually, I prefer to call my food "Modern American Contemporary French, California Style." And that isn't in any way meant to be facetious. The food I've created at Michael's reflects all these influences, because it's a cuisine that has grown out of my own life and training.

It's American food because *I'm* American, born and raised along the Hudson River in Briarcliff Manor, New York; educated in Pottstown, Pennsylvania; trained in the business and art of gastronomy at the University of Colorado. It's American because it reflects the food I grew up eating—the great American dishes that my parents cooked, from New England clam chowder to Lake Superior whitefish, Hudson River shad roe to New York steak sandwiches, blueberry pancakes to cinnamon layer cake. It's American because I prefer to use American ingredients whenever possible, and to show off the incredible variety of world-class foods now produced in this country—caviars, oysters, cheeses, game birds, lamb, fruits, and vegetables—not to mention outstanding wines from California, the Pacific Northwest, and New York.

My food is also French, because I first acquired a taste for French provincial cooking as a high school exchange student, spending a year with Andover-Exeter School Year Abroad at the University of Rennes in Brittany, where I lived with a local family and learned firsthand the role the foods of that region played in their lives. It's French because, after high school and before college, I lived in Paris and earned degrees in French cooking, wines, and restaurant management at the Cordon Bleu, the Académie du Vin, and the École Hôtelière de Paris. That training gave me a sound foundation in cooking that still prevails in my kitchen—in the stocks, reductions, and sauces, in my refusal to use anything but the finest ingredients available, in the artful presentation of my food, and in the importance I place on the perfect marriage of food and wine.

And yes, the food at Michael's *is* both modern and Californian. Though French cuisine and techniques and American ingredients and traditions may be my starting points, every dish on my menu has a contemporary emphasis on freshness, simplicity, and lightness. Almost all of my recipes are prepared quickly, showcasing the natural quality of the ingredients I use—many of which come from or have been popularized by the innovative food suppliers and cooks of California. My cooking is presented simply, dramatically, with none of the fussiness you find in many fancy kitchens. Even in those dishes that contain butter and cream, I use the light hand that modern sensibilities demand. And my portions are large enough to satisfy guests completely without making them feel uncomfortably full. It's interesting to note, though, that I serve the same size portions today as I first did in 1979. But back then, only kooks jogged, Nautilus was Captain Nemo's submarine, and "aerobics" sounded like a respiratory disease. Funnily enough, as many guests complain today that they get too much to eat at Michael's as complained back then that they weren't getting enough!

In the end, I think that my food and my philosophy of food and entertaining is now best defined as New Modern American Cooking—and creative American chefs throughout the country will tell you the same thing about what's happening in their own kitchens.

■

In order to understand my approach to food, you must experience it. That's the purpose of this book—to offer, as much as possible on the printed page, the experience of cooking and dining at Michael's, right down to the art collection that surrounds my guests. On the pages that follow, I'll share with you the key lessons I've learned about the basics of great cooking; how to seek out and consistently find the finest ingredients and how to plan and throw a great party, with great food, in your own home. Phil Reich, who puts together the wine list at Michael's, will offer his insightful, no-nonsense advice on how to select and serve the perfect wines with my food—or with anyone's food, for that matter.

And then you'll get to the recipes—more than 160 recipes and variations, virtually all of the dishes that have been or currently are on the menu at Michael's. As much as possible, the recipes have been written not just to direct you step-by-step but to teach you the principles behind my cooking as you prepare each dish. The photographs accompanying the recipes have been deliberately taken as tight closeups—not just because I think great ingredients well prepared are inherently beautiful, but also because I hope you can learn something

from seeing *exactly* how the recipes should look when they've been cooked and presented properly. And where appropriate, each recipe includes a wine suggestion from Phil Reich that explains why a particular wine or wines are best suited to that particular dish.

The recipes are organized in course-by-course menu order. First are hors d'oeuvres, a selection of light, bite-sized little finger foods specifically designed to be passed with drinks as guests mingle, to excite appetites before the meal proper begins. If you like, though, you can certainly choose to serve one or more of the hors d'oeuvre recipes as a sit-down first course.

Next come the appetizers, an array of knife-and-fork first courses to serve once your guests are seated. Soups, though a separate category, are also intended as first-course alternatives to the other appetizers. You'll find that many—though not all—of my soups are cream based in the classic French manner, simply because those are the kind of soups I and my guests seem to prefer; but they all emphasize fresh, high-quality ingredients, enhanced rather than overwhelmed by the cream, and they make a great, refreshing start to a meal.

My pasta recipes are topped with a wide variety of ingredients, from spring vegetables to grilled seafood, sautéed sweetbreads to a selection of great American caviars. They're based on freshly made angel hair pasta, which is usually tossed with a light Chardonnay cream sauce that is excellent with white wines. Depending on the occasion, you can serve any of these pastas as a first course, a second course before the main course, or as a main course itself.

The same range of options applies to my salads, which many of my lunchtime guests enjoy as main courses. These salads incorporate many different kinds of toppings—wild mushrooms, crayfish and fresh mozzarella, lobster and foie gras, chicken breasts stuffed with goat cheese, grilled lamb tenderloins, and so on. All of them have as their base an assortment of fresh, tender, baby salad leaves, though you can feel free to substitute whatever high-quality fresh leaves, of whatever size, are available to you.

Seafood, poultry, and meat recipes get separate chapters. Your choice of main course will, naturally, depend on your own preference in foods, and on the overall composition of your menu and choice of wines.

We serve brunch at Michael's every Saturday and Sunday, and I've gathered together some of my favorite dishes for that meal into a separate chapter. Naturally, the emphasis here is on eggs, pancakes and French toast, and sandwiches. A number of my appetizers, soups, pastas, and salads also make appearances on the brunch menu, so feel free to choose from those chapters when you plan your own weekend meals.

Finally, there's a slew of desserts. You'll find recipes here to suit any taste and occasion, from fresh fruit and simple, quickly prepared recipes to ice creams, sorbets, and cookies to a selection of cakes and pastries that combine classic French concepts and techniques with modern Californian taste and presentation.

ENTERTAINING

The main reason I decided to become a restaurateur was that I love to entertain people, to show them a really wild time. And when things are going right at a party or in a restaurant—great food and great service with the right mix of people in the perfect setting—nothing beats it.

My wife, Kim, and I entertain a lot at home, too, and we pay attention to the same details there that I do at Michael's. Yet many people don't realize that the same basic principles apply whether you're cooking for 6 people in your own kitchen or 150 at a restaurant. If you just give some careful thought and preparation to the same elements I concern myself with every day, you'll find it easier to throw a truly memorable bash.

Start off with the setting; after all, you've got to have a stage before you put actors on it, and I always like to think of dining as a form of theater. At Michael's, we've created a simple, contemporary environment with a lot of attention to the little details: golden lighting that comforts guests and makes them look great, cream-colored walls, a well-

manicured garden. The art on the walls is part of that overall aesthetic statement—beautiful, stylish, and sophisticated. We put the finest, simplest furnishings and settings in the dining room: plush alpaca, natural wood, and chrome Breuer chairs; Christofle silver; white Villeroy and Boch plates; and *lots* of flowers. And, just on the basis of this environment alone, some of our guests feel they've had the best meal in the world!

Of course, a restaurant is a very controlled environment, and I hardly expect you to duplicate my dining room in your own home. The main point is that I pay attention to the little details, and you ought to do the same. Give some thought, first of all, to *where* in your home you entertain. It doesn't always have to be at the dining room table. Even in the restaurant, we have a number of different environments that suit themselves to different kinds of occasions—the informal garden, the quieter main dining room, and large and small private rooms upstairs for more formal or intimate parties. Depending on the occasion, you might want to serve your meal on your own patio, or on a table set up by a window that offers a particularly nice view, or very informally on the coffee table in the living room. Don't let yourself be limited by convention.

Music too can play a part in helping you set your scene. At the restaurant, we usually play light, contemporary jazz, at a volume that's not too obtrusive. Choose some sounds that go with your own setting, and with the occasion. At home, for example, whenever Kim and I do a clambake on the patio, I like to play reggae. Nothing gives you a better rhythm for popping those clams into your mouth!

Whatever the setting and occasion, don't think you have to serve your food on plain white china as we do in the restaurant. We use it there because it goes best with the setting. Go with what *you* have, and what best suits your own home and the kind of party you're planning. I love it when we dine at friends' homes and they pull out great old china that they've inherited, or some funky collection of plates they picked up in a flea market somewhere. Feel free to alter the presentations you see on any of the dishes in this book to make them

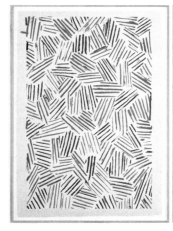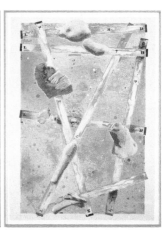

Untitled by Jasper Johns

look their best on whatever plates you're using.

Give some careful thought to the mix of people you're inviting. Though I have no great control over who comes to the restaurant on any particular night, some evenings seem to have a fairly elegant mix of people, while at other times it's a really wild scene; better yet, on some evenings we get both together. Think about the personalities of your guests, and whether they'll get along well and strike the sparks that make for a great time; plan who sits next to whom accordingly. And try to aim for the right number of people for the food you're cooking and the overall style of party you're after. In other words, if you want to cook a complicated, formal menu, don't invite an army!

You've got to plan your foods to suit the occasion and the number of guests. Not surprisingly, most guests at my restaurant order just three courses: some kind of appetizer or other first course; a main course of seafood, poultry, or meat; and a dessert. And they're perfectly satisfied. So why do so many people who entertain at home feel they have to go all out with some five- or seven-course extravaganza, and wind up exhausted and unable to enjoy their own party? After all, when you're entertaining at home, more likely than not it's *you* who play the role of waiter. Don't make things difficult for yourself.

Of course, there may very well be an occasion when you *want* to serve that many courses—when you want to show off a progression of great wines, for example, or simply when you really want to celebrate some special, formal occasion. When I'm doing a formal meal, I serve an hors d'oeuvre course before guests are seated, or the moment they sit down; then I like to serve one of my pastas, followed by a salad, then a main course of meat or poultry; and then dessert. Naturally, I give special attention to the balance of ingredients in the different courses—taking care not to repeat ingredients from one course to the next, and to observe a progression from lighter to more filling dishes. And, when I'm cooking such a meal at home, I plan the menu carefully to make sure there are enough simple dishes—or dishes I can prep well in advance —so that I'm not spending the entire evening in the kitchen.

But on so many other occasions you can entertain in much simpler style, with three courses or less. If you're serving a casual brunch, for example, all you've got to do is prepare a little fresh fruit salad to start, and then follow it with an omelet, or a pasta topped with grilled salmon or swordfish, or perhaps a chicken and goat cheese salad. End the brunch with some fresh berries or a quickly made berry compote served over vanilla ice cream, and you'll have knocked your guests out with a meal they won't stop talking about. The best part of it is, you'll have been free to enjoy it all just as much as they did.

A GUIDE TO INGREDIENTS

Ultimately, what's going to knock your guests' socks off is the quality and simplicity of what they're eating.

One of the comments I hear again and again about the food at Michael's is the impeccable quality of my ingredients. The implication always seems to be that certain restaurants have some secret access to ingredients ordinary home cooks could never dream of buying.

I'm going to let you in on my secret. And that is, there *is* no secret! In today's world, no matter where you live, you can find the best-quality food products in all their variety. What you've got to do—what I and other food professionals take the time to do—is to *look* for the best, to take the trouble to learn where the best items of whatever kind can be found near your home.

That may mean calling your friends, or combing the Yellow Pages, or reading the food section of your newspaper and city magazine, or even asking the maître d' or waiter at your favorite restaurant to tell you where they buy certain items. Do some exploring and testing. If you come up with the names of four butchers who reputedly have the best lamb in town, for example, buy one lamb chop from each of them and—keeping track of which chop came from which shop—grill them all for the same meal and have a lamb tasting. Let your tastebuds tell you which butcher has the best lamb. You can do the same with steak, or salmon, or the vegetables and lettuces for your salads.

When you've located a supplier whose products show he's committed to quality, don't be afraid to make demands on him. Let him know what specific ingredients you've been looking for but haven't been able to find; a good supplier will probably have the contacts to get it for you, and should be happy to help a regular customer who shows a real interest in quality. And the surprising thing is, you'll find you don't really pay all that much more for the best than you would for lesser quality, though the enjoyment you'll derive from cooking and eating a dish composed of the finest ingredients available is so much greater.

That said, let me offer you some of my own observations on the ingredients you'll find throughout this book. But remember: all the written explanations and all the books in the world are no substitute for actually getting out there, looking for the food, and then bringing it home to cook and taste. That's the real way to learn about quality.

OILS, FATS, AND CONDIMENTS

Olive oil. We always use olive oil that is labeled "extra-virgin," which is extracted on a first pressing from olives without the use of heat or chemicals. Extra-virgin oil has the purest, cleanest flavor for dressings and marinades. The color of extra-virgin oil may vary from pale yellow-green to deep dark-green, depending on the olives that were used and how the oil was filtered; the darker the oil, the more pronounced and fruity its flavor, and different oils from different parts of the world show almost as much variety as wines. I prefer to use a dark-green, rich, and full-flavored oil from the Lago del Garda region of Italy. Do some sampling and find one that suits your own tastes. Store your oil airtight in a cool, dark place to keep its flavor fresh.

Walnut oil. Rich, dark walnut oil has the distinctive flavor of the nuts from which it is extracted. We sometimes use it in salad dressings, and more often to sauté ingredients, such as wild mushrooms, sweetbreads, and pine nuts, that are complemented by its flavor. Walnut oil goes rancid fairly quickly, so buy it in small quantities and store it airtight away from light and heat.

Beef suet. For french frying potatoes and my Maui Onion Rings, I like to use beef suet, which gives a rich flavor and incomparable crispness. You can buy packages of already rendered suet in most supermarkets. If you're concerned about cholesterol, you can certainly substitute vegetable oil for the suet.

Butter. We use only unsalted—"sweet"—butter at Michael's, and that's the kind of butter called for in every recipe in this book. Sample the various brands of unsalted butter available in your area and find one that pleases you. Land O' Lakes is a good brand that's available nationwide.

Pepper. Only white peppercorns, freshly ground, are used at Michael's; they have a gentler, less assertive flavor than the black. Any good supermarket spice section will have jars of whole white peppercorns, and pepper grinders can be purchased inexpensively from kitchenware stores.

Vinegars. We use two different kinds of vinegar predominantly at the restaurant. Balsamic vinegar, a red wine vinegar that is aged in oak and develops a rich, complex flavor, is wonderful in salad dressings. Sherry wine vinegar has the distinctive flavor of good, dry sherry, and appears in both dressings and sauces. You'll find both kinds of vinegar in well-stocked supermarkets or in gourmet shops.

VEGETABLES

Baby vegetables. Michael's has been one of the restaurants responsible for the popularizing in recent years of baby vegetables—yellow squash, acorn squash, zucchini, all with their blossoms still attached, along with baby carrots, beets, and turnips. In spite of jokes made about these tiny vegetables, we really do serve them for one simple reason: not only are they beautiful, they taste great. It's surprising to see how many produce wholesalers and retailers are now making these little vegetables available to the public nationwide; seek them out at good supermarkets or produce stands, and ask for them if you don't see them. But if you can't find them, feel free to substitute the smallest, freshest, best-quality vegetables you *can* locate; they don't have to be baby vegetables to taste or look good.

Baby salad leaves. Just as we garnish our entrée plates at Michael's with baby vegetables, so are our salads presented on a foundation of baby leaves: clusters of mâche or lamb's lettuce; bitter arugula; tender, yellow-green limestone lettuce; purple leaves of radicchio. You're more likely to find such a variety of young leaves at a well-stocked supermarket or a good greengrocer. But the variety of tastes and colors is more important than the size of the leaves; seek out whatever supplier offers the best selection of good, fresh salad leaves of whatever kind to give that range of sensations to your salads.

Mushrooms and truffles. Ordinary white domestic mushrooms are so commonplace now that it's amazing to realize that, as recently as the late 1950s, most people could only buy them canned—an example of how enterprising produce merchants and public demand can alter our eating habits. Though wild mushrooms—yellow, trumpet-shaped chanterelles; pale, succulent oyster mushrooms; dark, meaty shiitakes; intense, honeycomb-textured morels—are a delicacy to most people, they too are growing in popularity and are becoming much more widely available, but all are subject to seasonal fluctuation. You can now even get the most prized denizens of the mushroom world, truffles, almost anywhere when they're in season—mid-fall to early spring for black truffles, early fall to early winter for white. It's just a question of locating local suppliers who get them in or can order them for you. Black truffles have a wonderfully heady, musky aroma and flavor; the white, equally aromatic, are sometimes described as having peppery or garlicky overtones. When our truffles arrive at the restaurant, we keep them fresh by storing them buried in a bowl or large jar of dry Italian arborio rice in the refrigerator; this has the added benefit of giving wonderful flavor to the rice, which can be used to make a great risotto. Just before shaving or slicing the truffles, we give them a quick rinse to remove any surface dirt. Though the truffles are relatively expensive, a little goes a long way, and they're one of those seasonal specialties that you really don't want to miss.

Onions. The onion of choice at Michael's—for sauces and stocks, grilled or stewed in butter for garnishes, and even batter-coated and deep-fried as onion rings—is a brown-skinned Maui onion from Hawaii, which has a wonderfully sweet, mild yet distinctive flavor. Good substitutes are other sweet, brown-skinned onions such as those from Vidalia, Georgia, or Walla Walla, Washington; if neither is available, you can substitute a good sweet red onion or, in a pinch, the mildest, sweetest-tasting brown-skinned onion you can find.

Tomatoes. Tomato concasse—peeled, seeded, chopped, and seasoned tomatoes—is a favorite garnish at Michael's, and its success depends entirely on the tomatoes we use. Select vine-ripened tomatoes that are firm and deep red in color.

Ahi tuna. As deep red as a superb piece of beef, ahi—or bluefin—tuna is to my taste the finest tuna of all. But if it's unavailable, most good fishmongers will have some sort of fresh tuna on hand that you can substitute; just be sure that it is *absolutely* fresh—"off the fin."

Caviars. One of cuisine's greatest luxuries, caviar adds a touch of elegance as a garnish for many of the seafood dishes at the restaurant. At the ultimate end, we'll use the three classic grades of imported sturgeon caviar—beluga, sevruga, and osetra. I prefer the Persian caviars over Russian, because they have a cleaner, more briny flavor. But almost as elegant, and certainly more affordable, are the great American caviars now widely available in good supermarkets and gourmet shops: bright pink salmon caviar, golden caviar from whitefish, and black American sturgeon caviar.

Clams. I like to use the sweet, tender little Manila clams that are now being farmed in Dabob Bay on the coast of Oregon. If you can't get hold of them, substitute other small, fresh clams such as littlenecks or Ipswich, or larger clams such as quahogs, cut into bite-sized strips.

Crayfish. Like tiny freshwater lobsters, crayfish are prized for their sweet, tender, bite-sized pieces of tail meat. The best crayfish come from either the Sacramento River delta in California or the Mississippi delta in Louisiana. You can buy them live from a good fishmonger.

John Dory. These elegant little white-fleshed, delicate fish are flown in fresh from New Zealand and widely available here; ask your fishmonger to order you some. We buy baby John Dory weighing about 1 pound each whole, which yield 2 fillets of about 3½ ounces each—one fillet the perfect size for an appetizer, two just right for a main course.

Lobsters. Almost any really good fishmonger now will have a tank of live lobsters on hand, and whether you use New England or West Coast lobsters, it's the live freshness that's essential. Go for lobsters on the small side, to be served as individual portions—1½-pounders for main courses, or lobsters weighing in at no more than 1 pound, called "chicken" lobsters, as appetizers.

Oysters. At Michael's, we celebrate the great range of oysters now farmed on the Pacific Coast—the once almost-extinct little Olympia Bays from Washington, the great French-style Belons from Bodega and Tomales bays in California, Northwestern Portuguese oysters, Japanese-style kumomotos, and many others. But don't restrict your search for oysters to this list. Airfreight makes it possible to buy fresh oysters almost anywhere in the country; we certainly get great Gulf and East Coast oysters here in California. Check with your local fishmongers to see what varieties they get in, and treat yourself to an oyster tasting to check them out and decide on your own favorites.

There's a lot of talk today about the possible danger of eating raw shellfish from polluted waters. I approach the problem by dealing only with the most reputable fishmongers or oystermen, and if there's even the slightest doubt, I don't buy the shellfish. I also follow a very simple principle when making my purchases: if the shellfish smells even slightly suspect, I won't touch it.

Pompano. Pompano is an elegant little fish from Florida that we buy in small, baby sizes of about 1 pound each, which yields 2 fillets—a main-course serving. It's available fresh, via airfreight, at good fishmongers all over the country.

Salmon. At different times of the year, we get in different varieties of fresh salmon—Norwegian, Scottish, Pacific Northwest, Alaskan. Though I prefer the Norwegian salmon, which has a finer taste and texture, I'll go with whatever is the freshest available.

Scallops. With the exception of our scallop-and-goat-cheese pasta, for which tiny bay scallops make an attractive presentation, I serve the largest jumbo sea scallops I can find—at least 1 inch in diameter and ¾ inch thick. Fresh sea scallops are widely available. I also recommend the medium-sized cape scallops.

Shad roe. Shad roe—the whole roe sacks of spawning shad—are one of the great spring delicacies that we always serve at Michael's during the brief month or so that they're available. Though they're one of the few seafood items that aren't bad when bought frozen, the fresh roe is still far superior and

Hotel Acatlan: First Day by David Hockney

can be purchased from really good fishmongers; ask your local one to let you know when he expects it in. A whole shad roe comes in two separate, self-contained lobes, and you've got to be careful not to break a lobe or it will fall apart during cooking.

Shrimp. We serve the largest fresh shrimp we can find at Michael's—giant Alaska spot prawns, Texas gulf shrimp, or Santa Barbara shrimp. Which of these or other varieties is available will depend on where you are and when you're ordering them; just ask your fishmonger for the largest jumbo shrimp he can get.

Snapper. A case in point on the widespread availability of fresh fish: We serve fresh red snapper, which is flown in by our suppliers from either Florida or New Zealand. Ask your fishmonger for the baby ones, weighing about 1 pound each, and have him fillet them for you into 2 fillets each, which will give you one main-course serving. If only larger snappers are available, adjust your order accordingly.

Softshell crabs. Between May and October, blue crabs molt their hard shells and become what is known as "softshell crabs." These are a great seasonal delicacy that I love to serve as an appetizer, or in double or triple portions as a main course. Go for the really tiny softshell crabs, which are known as "roaches." They'll be live when you buy

them, and you can have the fishmonger clean them for you if you like. If not, clean them by first cutting off the face section of each crab, which will kill them; then gently pry up the shell flap from the back, scrape off the gills, and remove the sand receptacle near the mouth area. Wash the crabs and pat them dry before cooking.

Swordfish. This great, meaty fish is now widely available. Be sure to get fresh, not frozen, swordfish, and buy fillet steaks that have a good, clean, pale pinkish-white color to them.

Whitefish. The best whitefish comes from the deep, clean, clear, and cold waters of Lake Superior—a moist, pure-flavored, delicate fish that's so perfect it can be eaten virtually plain. Today, Lake Superior whitefish is flown fresh all over the country; insist on fresh, not frozen, whitefish.

POULTRY

Chicken. I don't hold with all this business about free-range chickens that roam the farmyard eating whatever happens their way. The flavor of a chicken *is* determined by what it eats, but the important thing is not that it's free-range but simply that it's fed with good grains rather than commercial processed chicken feed. Ask your butcher what his chickens have been fed on, and let your taste buds be the final judge as to whether a particular chicken is good.

Duck. Our duck breasts, as meaty and red as a good steak, come from American-raised Muscovy, Pekin, or Mallard ducks. A good butcher should be able to get them for you, but feel free to substitute whatever good, meaty duck breasts you can find.

Foie gras. The rich, buttery liver of specially fattened geese or ducks is one of the great delicacies of the table. I prefer American duck foie gras to the more traditional goose foie gras of French cuisine; the former has a richer, earthier, more rustic flavor. Ask your butcher to order American duck foie gras for you.

Quail. I serve tender little baby quail, which weigh about ¼ pound each. Ours are farm-raised in the Acton Valley north of Los Angeles, but they're also raised all over the country. If you have trouble ordering them from your butcher, your best bet for finding good quail is to go to an Oriental market. Have the butcher bone them out for you, leaving them whole with only the leg and wing bones remaining.

Rabbit. Not strictly poultry, the meat of rabbit is usually included in this category because its taste and texture is more akin to chicken than meat. Farm-raised rabbit is fairly widely available at good butcher shops.

Squab. We serve baby squabs weighing about ½ pound each, boned out except for the leg and wing bones. Look for huge, plump, meaty breasts on the birds, which will tell you they've been fed and raised properly.

MEATS

Beef. Dry-aged New York steaks are the beef of choice at Michael's. Good steaks are widely available, but you've really got to go to a top-notch butcher who'll have the best, properly aged beef with the meatiest flavor and texture. It's worth organizing a steak taste-off, to judge where the best ones come from in your area.

Lamb. We serve California lamb at Michael's, but good lamb is now available virtually everywhere all the time. It bears repeating, though, that you should try lamb from several different reputable butchers near you, and decide which offers the best lamb to your taste.

Pork. Pork tenderloins have a delicacy of taste and texture far removed from the world of hams and bacon, which makes them a truly elegant meat to serve.

Sweetbreads. Sweetbreads, the common term for the veal thymus gland, are a great delicacy, with a smooth, creamy texture and a distinctive flavor whose mildness surprises people who've shied away from this meat. Most good butchers will carry sweetbreads. Look for ones that seem moist and firm, without any major blemishes or discolorations. You'll clean the sweetbreads at home as part of the recipe preparations, parboiling them and peeling off their membranes.

Veal. Buy the best, whitest milk-fed veal you can find, available from high-quality butchers nationwide.

DESSERTS AND BAKING

Berries. Fresh raspberries, blackberries, boysenberries, ollalaberries, blueberries, and strawberries are favorite dessert items at Michael's. Modern international airfreight keeps many of these berries in constant supply virtually year round. Check with your best local produce market to see what's available, and let the best-quality fresh berries determine what fruit desserts you'll prepare.

Chocolates. We use the highest quality imported chocolate for the desserts at Michael's. For bittersweet chocolate, we use Valrhona Caraque or Tobler Tobamera, chocolates with high cocoa butter content and a good bitter edge; melted, they give rich flavor and a glossy sheen to desserts. Valrhona Superior or Tobler Velma chocolates are more semisweet, lower in cocoa butter, and more brittle in consistency; they're especially good for chocolate chips. By all means substitute other chocolates that may be more readily available to you; Lindt, in particular, is a good line.

Flour. Regular, all-purpose flour is all you'll need for our baking recipes. In this book, we give volume measures in cups for aerated flour—that is, flour that has been shaken from the bag or from a spoon into the measuring cup. We also give weight measures for flour—in pounds and ounces—that, for those who have kitchen scales, is a useful cross-check.

CHEESES

We always have a selection of cheeses on hand to offer guests after their main course. We serve them with freshly toasted walnut bread, and present the cheeses arrayed on a marble slab that sets them off beautifully and also keeps them a touch cooler than room temperature. Unlike some fancy restaurants, we don't go all out to overwhelm people with dozens of different cheeses. Instead, I like to present a few really select cheeses at the peak of ripeness, and the variety will change with whatever is available from our supplier—creamy or aged goat cheeses, creamy Bries and Camemberts and Port Saluts, cheddars, Swiss cheeses, blue cheeses from French Roquefort to Italian gorgonzola to such great American blue cheeses as Maytag. More and more of the cheeses we get in are actually produced in America—and that includes goat cheeses, Swiss, gorgonzolas, and even Bries and Camemberts.

Since there are so many different great cheeses available—literally hundreds—rather than following any specific recommendations from me, your best bet is to find the best cheese shop in your area and start educating yourself firsthand—go in and really look at the cheeses, ask questions, taste little samples if possible, and bring home a few at a time to try with your family and friends with some wine after dinner. Eventually, you'll arrive at your own ideal selection.

METHODS

The whole secret behind the cooking at Michael's is time-saving simplicity. Virtually every dish we serve is made fresh to order in under 20 minutes.

What we do spend time on, which makes the final speed of preparation and delicious results possible, are our stocks and sauces, for which you'll find the basic recipes in Chapter 2. A good stock that has simmered for hours, extracting every last bit of flavor from its ingredients, will go a long way toward making your sauces taste fabulous. And you can make stock in large quantities, and refrigerate or freeze it to have immediately on hand.

The key cooking method at the restaurant, which bears some discussion here, is grilling. A lot of home kitchens today now include indoor grills, and even more people have good barbecues, so it's likely you'll be able to duplicate the results I get. Just be sure to build up a really intense heat, and grill the food fairly close to the heat—about 3 inches away —so it sears quickly and seals in its juices.

If you don't have a grill, you can still get good results with your home broiler. The important thing to remember in this case, though, is *not* to preheat the broiler tray while you're heating up the broiler. Put the food on the cold tray, and then place the tray about 3 inches from the heat; you want the food to cook from the direct heat of the broiler rather than frying on the hot broiler tray.

I've given approximate cooking times for all the recipes in this book, including grilled foods. But bear in mind that stoves vary in the intensity of the heat they deliver, and you should learn to be aware of your own stove's characteristics and to let your eyes, ears, nose, and tongue tell you—as much as the clock—when a particular dish is ready.

When I'm grilling at home, I have an even more foolproof method of making sure the food I'm cooking is done just right. I always cook an extra little "taster" portion of the same thickness as the meat, poultry, or seafood I'm serving. When I think the food just might be done, I slice off a little piece of the taster to make sure.

The secret behind the smoothness and sheen of the sauces at Michael's lies in the straining. The best tool for the job is a fine-meshed conical sieve known as a chinoise, available in most good cookware stores.

And it's worth mentioning a few special items you may need to create some of my desserts. For melting chocolate, it helps to have a double boiler, which prevents the chocolate from scorching when it's heated. You'll find an assortment of stainless steel cake rings essential for making some of my more elaborate cakes. For decorating them, you'll need a small piping bag with a fine writing tip.

Liquids by
Ed Ruscha

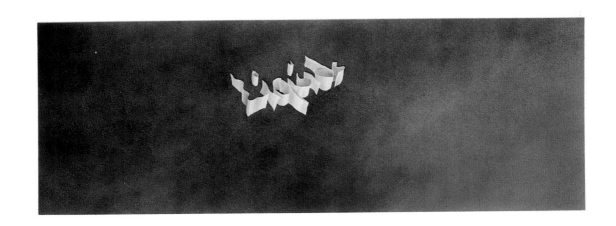

CHAPTER ONE

WINE AND CUISINE

Ever since Michael's opened in 1979, the restaurant's wine list has been under the expert direction of Philip Reich. Here, Phil offers his own observations on how he matches wine with my cooking, along with guidelines on how to select and serve wines in your own home.

．

Until the mid-to-late 1970s, if you talked at all about matching wines and foods, you were primarily talking about *French* wines and *French* cuisine. The French have had at least a 500-year jump on the rest of the world in the art of adapting their wines to the foods they cooked and ate, and adapting their foods to the wines they produced. But Michael McCarty was, to my mind, the first person to develop a California cuisine that specifically showed off the wines of California.

American wines, as a rule, are bigger, bolder, and fresher tasting than their European counterparts—a result of soil, climate, and winemaking methods. And Michael's cooking, with its emphasis on absolutely fresh, big-flavored American ingredients—quickly cooked to maintain and enhance their naturally intense flavors—is a natural match for such wines. The French wines that do work are the biggest, richest ones. These happen to be the finest of the French wines, but they are also the most extravagantly priced of all wines.

MAKING THE MATCH

These principles apply to greater or lesser degrees when I'm selecting wines to go with Michael's

cooking. Throughout the recipe chapters in this book, you'll find wine recommendations wherever appropriate. For each recipe, I explain the main characteristics that are being matched—in the food and the wine. I give several different wine options, starting with ideal matches—wines that may tend to be costlier and less widely available—and ranging through to other, appropriate wines that you're likely to find easily at a reasonable price.

The basis for these recommendations is the concept that wines may be matched with foods on two separate levels. One is simply to pay attention to the *flavor* links between individual ingredients and the characteristics of specific wine varieties. On a second, somewhat more abstract level, you can actually match wines to the *structure* of a particular recipe, its method of preparation, the sauce, and so forth—pairing, for example, delicately flavored and textured dishes with delicate wines; fresh, lively dishes with crisp, tart wines; hearty dishes with big, full-bodied wines; and so on.

In a general way, you can choose a wide range of "appropriate" wines—in effect, designating which wine varieties will go well with the food you're serving. This is the source, more or less, of the old "white with fish and poultry, red with meat" maxim, since white wines as a general rule are lighter like fish and poultry, reds more robust like meat.

But when you go beyond the general to deal with flavors and structure of individual wines, it's actually possible, through experience, to arrive at a few "ideal" wines, perfect matches in which all the elements of a dish and a wine interact—the tartness or mellowness of the food intermingling with that of the wine, the richness of a sauce carrying over into the wine's own texture, the hints of an herb or spice in the seasoning recurring in the wine's aftertaste, the freshness of the ingredients matched by the equal freshness of the wine. On such a basis, that old maxim about whites and reds no longer applies as emphatically, since we begin to see how certain lightly structured red wines may go very well with chicken, perhaps, or even some richer seafoods; and a duck breast, as meaty as a steak, could call for a big red wine.

Such a wide range of interactions opens up other possibilities. You can aim for a harmonious combination—the kind of classical approach just described—in which the wine and the food display similar tastes and textures. Or, alternatively, you can aim for contrast, choosing a wine for particular characteristics that aren't present in the food—tartness as a refreshing foil for rich, fatty foods, for example.

ADAPTING RECIPES TO COMPLEMENT THE WINE

With such possibilities in mind, in very special cases you can even adapt certain recipes to better highlight outstanding wines you may have picked to serve with them. At its most basic, that may mean simply substituting Pinot Noir for the Cabernet Sauvignon in Michael's Cassis Sauce when you want to pour a Pinot Noir with that dish.

As a more complex example, you may want to serve a really spectacular old wine with one of Michael's salads—say a very well aged French white Burgundy with the Salade Classique. Rather than risk letting the vinegar in the salad dressing fight with the wine, you can replace the vinegar with flat champagne, boiled until it reduces to the same intensity as vinegar, about one quarter of its original volume. You'll get the illusion of the vinegar without any of the acetic acid, and you'll show off the wine very well.

To show off a very rare old red or white wine with a main course, you should try to match its

levels of acidity and oxidation in the sauce. Start the sauce with a younger bottle of the same wine variety. Add to it, ¼ teaspoon at a time, champagne vinegar (to add acidity) and either dry sherry (for old white wines) or dry madeira (for old reds) to add an oxidized flavor; stop when your taste tells you you've matched the wine you'll be drinking. Then prepare the sauce following its recipe. If you want, you can even make a too-old wine taste younger by making the sauce slightly *more* acidic and oxidized.

PLANNING THE WINES FOR A MENU

First the basics—how much wine to serve, and what kind of glasses to serve it in. A standard fifth-size wine bottle holds 24 ounces of wine—six glasses, or five if you're pouring a little more generously —and we generally figure on a glass to a glass and a half per person for each course. For a dinner of more than one course, you can count on pouring at least half a bottle of wine—three glasses—per person. A really long, multicourse dinner lasting four or five hours will call for up to a full bottle's worth of wine for each person present. And if we're serving dessert wines, we pour only half or a third as much as the other wines, since these are meant more for sipping and savoring; most dessert wines come in half-bottles, giving you just the right amount you'll need for a dinner party.

Of course, you should change wineglasses for each different wine you pour. Long, narrow flutes are a must for champagne, since they hold the bubbles in longer; whatever you do, don't pour champagne into those wide, shallow glasses, which will make it go flat in no time. We're not real sticklers on the shape of the glasses you use for the rest of the wines in a meal, just as long as they have bowls that are bigger in the middle than at the top, so that the wine has room to develop its bouquet, which the narrower top holds in; are large enough so that you fill them by no more than a third to a half, again so that the wine has a large surface area from which its bouquet can develop; and are clear, so you'll be able to appreciate the wine's color. We don't use different glasses for whites and reds. But we do tend to serve lighter or sweeter wines in smaller glasses, and bigger wines, white *or* red, in bigger glasses.

Following the general principles outlined in the previous section, it makes sense that—just as the courses of a meal progress from simpler, lighter tastes and textures to more robust and complex dishes—the wines you choose to serve will generally follow the same pattern of progression as your menu: from champagnes and light, white wines; to heavier, more serious whites; to light red wines; to heavier, more complex reds; and finally to sweet dessert wines.

But there's a lot of flexibility in that pattern, just as there's a lot of flexibility in how you go about choosing the foods you want to serve. And the important thing to remember is that, one way or another, you can bend the rules. There's nothing in the world stopping you from serving red wines before white, if there's a good reason. There's logic, for example, in serving a light young Beaujolais—a red wine—with your appetizers, and then moving on to a robust Chardonnay. Your own taste buds and experience will suggest endless other possibilities.

When you have enough guests to make it practical, it's also very interesting sometimes to serve more than one wine—a white *and* a red—with the same course, using the principles I've discussed for finding the common denominator that matches both wines with the food. You'll find certain wine suggestions in this book where I've given both white and red options for a dish—Michael's Grilled Chicken Breasts with Black and White Truffles, for example.

One course of the menu for which I don't suggest wines is soup. As a general rule, people aren't sipping their wine while they're sipping their soup; you've already got enough liquid there in the bowl. People who want wine with their soup will usually be finishing what was poured for the course before. And while the soup is being served is a good time to pour the wine that will accompany the next course, to give it a little more time to breathe and develop its flavor and aroma in the glass.

And, as already suggested, we seem to be defying convention at Michael's by actually recommending wines with our salads, since conventional European wisdom suggests that the vinegar in salad dressings destroys wine. But there are two good reasons for doing what we do. One is that Michael's salads aren't in any way conventional; the lettuces and the dressings usually form a background for some kind of main ingredient—seafood, poultry, or meat—that calls for wine to accompany it. And, getting back to the point that Michael's food is adapted to American wines, those we serve are fresher, bigger, and more powerful than most European wines, and have room for the edge of acidity in a salad.

You'll also find that I've recommended wines for certain desserts—particularly fruit desserts—that are nicely complemented by some of the late-harvest wines that are available. Dessert is the only course where I feel wine is optional. A dinner can be made to seem lighter and more casual without them, or more opulently luxurious with them.

To conclude, let me add a note here on drinking temperatures. Wine can't get colder in your glass; it can only get warmer. I like my white wines, and particularly champagnes, colder than most wine connoisseurs do—well iced in an ice bucket. And generally, the lighter the wine, the colder it should be. Even red wines should be served cooler than most people think. The often-repeated rule that reds should be at room temperature came from an era before central heating. *Cool* room temperature—that is, a proper wine cellar temperature in the low 60s—is best for red wines, even the biggest ones. I'd suggest placing a red wine that's been at warm room temperature in the refrigerator for twenty minutes to half an hour before you open and pour it.

A SURVEY OF CALIFORNIA WINES

To help you in your own wine selections, this brief survey covers the main California varietal wines we serve at Michael's.

Sparkling wines. California sparkling wines are

Olympic Torso Plaques by Robert Graham

growing closer and closer to the style and elegance of French Champagnes. Such great French Champagne houses as Moët et Chandon, Mumm, and Roederer are now producing excellent sparkling wines right here in California, though Schramsberg remains the ultimate. Serve them with hors d'oeuvres, salads, or seafoods.

Chardonnay. This is generally considered to be the best white wine in California, with big body and elaborate flavor. Styles of Chardonnay break down into three fairly distinctive categories. Most popular and definitive are the robust wines with a big, buttery flavor and pronounced oak from the casks they're aged in—wines like Mount Eden, Chalone, and Mayacamas, which are best to drink after about two years of aging and have the staying power to last ten years or longer. You can serve these with chicken, veal, or quail, and with darker-meated fish like tuna, salmon, and swordfish; they're also great, surprisingly, with grilled meats.

Another style of Chardonnay puts an emphasis on fruitiness, developing a lush, juicy quality that is sometimes compared to apples; they're best enjoyed young, no more than two to two and a half years old. Chateau St. Jean and Heitz are good examples. They're great with seafood or poultry, and dishes with lots of vegetables.

Some Chardonnays—such as Grgich Hills, Acacia, and Sonoma-Cutrer—manage to combine these two styles. For the first three years or so, you enjoy it for its fruity qualities; then, as it ages, you can drink it for the robust varietal characteristics.

A third style of Chardonnay is made with grapes picked a little underripe. This produces the lightest, leanest Chardonnays of all, lighter in alcohol than the others. Iron Horse, Sterling, and Trefethen are good examples. They go well with Michael's pastas, with salads, grilled seafood, and poultry.

Sauvignon Blanc. Also known as Fumé Blanc, Sauvignons are generally lighter and crisper than Chardonnays, and they tend to work better as a wine to be enjoyed at lunch with salads, pastas, seafood, or poultry; or you can serve them as a first-course wine when you're planning to serve a big Chardonnay with your main course. Some Sauvignon Blancs—such as those from Grgich Hills, Mayacamas, and Matanzas Creek—are being produced in a big, buttery, oaky style; these can be enjoyed at one to three years of age. Lighter, fruitier Sauvignons that show off the wine's characteristic grassy, figlike flavors—Iron Horse, Brander, Chateau St. Jean, and Mondavi, for example—can be drunk when they are brand-new.

Vin Gris. These so-called blush wines are based on red-skinned grapes—Zinfandel, Cabernet Sauvignon, or Pinot Noir—but made in the style of white wines, with the skins being left in contact with the wine for no more than a day or so as opposed to the two to three weeks they'd remain in contact for red wine. The best Vin Gris is dry, with a lightness and delicacy that highlights its characteristic berrylike aroma and flavor. They're best drunk young, chilled like a white wine, and served at midday with sandwiches or salads featuring meat or poultry; they're also excellent with seafood, particularly salmon and shrimp, that have a complementary edge of sweetness. Some good examples of Vin Gris are made by Edna Valley, Bonny Doon, and Caymus.

Cabernet Sauvignon. These wines are dark, full-bodied, dry, and elegant, with rich characteristic undertones of black currants. The biggest Cabernets—like those from Ridge, Diamond Creek, Mount Eden, and Mayacamas—are very ripe-flavored, brawny, and oaky, with a high alcohol content; they're ready to drink after three to four years, and will age well for eight to ten years or more. A lighter, fruitier style of Cabernet is made by such vineyards as Robert Mondavi, Iron Horse, and Clos Pegase; these can be enjoyed younger, at two to four years of age. All Cabernets are spectacular with beef or lamb, and with quail, squab, or duck.

Many of the better producers are blending Cabernet Sauvignon with the other traditional grapes of the Bordeaux blend—Merlot and Cabernet Franc. This gives the wine increased softness and complexity. A remarkable number of these rank among California's finest Cabernets—Jordan, Phelps Insignia, Rubicon, Mondavi-Rothschild's Opus One, Dominus, Stag's Leap, and Clos du Val.

Pinot Noir. This elegant wine has a refined, almost ethereal quality, with mild, lingering flavors. Makers like Mount Eden, Chalone, and Calera are producing Pinots that are big, robust, with plenty of oak, that should be aged for three to seven years or longer. Others, like Acacia, Iron Horse, and Bouchaine, make lighter Pinot Noirs that you can enjoy for their freshness when young but that develop more body and character as they age. Pinots are classic wines to serve with beef, and their delicacy makes them well suited to veal or pork. The lighter styles are also surprisingly good with shrimp and scallops. Pinot Noirs, even more than Cabernets, show off complexity of flavors in really elaborate dishes; a Cabernet might smother nuances that a Pinot Noir will display fully.

Zinfandel. Zinfandel is a spicy, generously flavored wine, more fun-loving, simpler, and less elegant than a Cabernet Sauvignon or Pinot Noir. Lighter styles of the wine, such as those from Joseph Phelps and Louis Martini, can be drunk young—one and a half to three years. Bigger, oak-aged Zinfandels—Ridge and Mayacamas, for example—have a brawny structure and a higher alcohol content that allows them to age well. Zin-

fandel is terrific with lamb, squab, or duck; and, incidentally, it's the ultimate wine to drink with great pizza.

Merlot. This wine is still developing in California, and the best ones—such as those from Stag's Leap and Clos du Val—have soft, gentle flavors and medium body, and can age for some three to six years. Serve with beef, veal, or chicken.

Petite Sirah. Petite Sirah is a peppery, robust, fairly simple wine—great to pour at a party, with casual foods like barbecue. They'll take four to eight years of aging. Some good examples are Ridge and Joseph Phelps.

Dessert wines. This is a vastly intricate field, one that's growing popular among California winemakers. Chateau St. Jean and Joseph Phelps, for example, are making late-harvest Rieslings with rich, honeyed flavors comparable to their best German counterparts. Bonny Doon produces what they call "ice wines"—late-harvest wines made from spicy Muscat Canelli grapes, as well as from Gewürztraminer and Grenache. Fortified wines—ports and muscats—are another big area of development, with some wonderful examples in particular coming from Andrew Quady. In general, desserts featuring fruits and nuts go best with these kinds of wines.

FRENCH WINES

Although we've been emphasizing the appropriateness of American wines for Michael's food, the matches work not so much because of the Americanness of the wines or ingredients, but because the recipes are designed to work with wines, period. Any recipe in this book will work with French wines, and almost always the French wine that works best is one that is made from the same grape variety as the California wine we recommend. In most cases we have given these suggestions with the recipe and the difference it will make at your table will simply be one of style—the French wine, a bit lighter and gentler than a California wine, will offer a more subtle match with the food, emphasizing quiet harmonies rather than dramatic flavors. The choice is yours, and should depend on the kind of experience you would like. And the choice is yours both for the wine you drink and the wine you use for cooking.

The climate of France, generally cooler than California's, tends to produce wines with less fully ripe grape flavors, and these, coupled with the lower sugar content that comes with less ripeness, bring out a whole different set of flavors which are shown off in the lighter alcohol content of the wines. The warm California climate gives the winemakers both riper flavors and more alcohol in their wines, with some loss of subtlety.

Just as French chefs devised a whole repertoire of cooking techniques that are, in effect, transparent mediums to convey the nuances of flavors of their ingredients, so have French winemakers evolved techniques that are transparent to minute differences of character in their ingredients, the grapes. In California, on an ever-increasing scale, the best winemakers have found French winemaking techniques to be the ones that best bring out the characteristics they want in their wines. This similarity of both technique and intent provides the best wines of both regions with related structures and flavor balances.

The main way to think about differences between French and California wines as they apply to your use of them is to think of the difference between *finesse* and *power*. The finesse of French wines can be considered in two ways, the more familiar being the qualitative one of elegance, but it should also be thought of as a difference in *texture*—finesse as fine-ness, as, for example, in woven cloth. That finer texture can make a telling difference in the overall effect of a dish.

Our final recommendation for an ultimate food-wine experience is not simply to match the grape variety of the sauce-wine with the wine you are drinking. Go further. Cook with a wine of the same variety *and from the same region* as the wine you are drinking. The effect, with even the simplest dishes, is truly orchestral. It need not be expensive either; with a fine Medoc from your cellar, use a little Bordeaux Superieur; for a fine white Burgundy, make the sauce with an inexpensive Macon. The resonances of flavor between sauce and wine will show both at their best. Those "marriages" of wine

and food that are the aim of cooks and connoisseurs are made successful by starting with as much compatibility of the components as can be managed, and you can do a surprising amount of that management in the kitchen.

Briefly and simply, Michael's recipes tend to work best with the wines of four grapes: Chardonnay and Sauvignon Blanc among the whites, and Pinot Noir and Cabernet Sauvignon among the reds. In a French context this translates into two regions: the whites and reds of Burgundy in eastern France (made of Chardonnay and Pinot Noir) and the whites and reds of Bordeaux in western France (made of Sauvignon Blanc and Cabernet Sauvignon, each traditionally blended with other grapes in Bordeaux). Both these regions have long been recognized as producing the finest French wines of all, and those of the best producers have set quality standards that winemakers of other countries either respect and emulate or ignore at their own peril.

WINE REVOLUTION IN ITALY

A number of Italian winemakers, still only a few, have broken with long-standing traditions in Italy to make wines that employ a combination of newly planted French grape varieties and a combination of French and Californian winemaking techniques. These will make an exciting area of exploration over the years ahead, and this new Italian-international style works well with the recipes in this book. Again, look first to wines made of Chardonnay, Sauvignon Blanc, Cabernet, and Pinot Noir. The leading quality producers are presently Angelo Gaja in the Piemonte and Maurizio Zanella of Ca'del Bosco in Lombardy. The list will undoubtedly grow longer in the years ahead.

THE NEW AUSTRALIAN WINES

The new international style, combining French and California methods, and emphasizing freshness and quality, has begun to come out of Australia as well, with Chardonnays and Cabernets showing particularly well. So far we have noted the wines of Rosemount in the upper Hunter Valley, Taltarni in the Barossa Valley, Redbank in Victoria, and Cullens in Western Australia as having the qualities we look for in the wines we choose for our food: unique individuality, strength, complexity, and harmony.

WINE BOOKS FOR COOKS

It is possible to cook successfully with only a casual acquaintance with wines, but the more familiar you are with them, the more it will be reflected in your cooking confidence. Wine continues and amplifies the taste experience of food because, like a completed dish, it is a complex of flavors whose effects come from the variety of causes introduced by human processing of the ingredients.

We've tried to cover the key ways that wine interacts with food, but the intricacies of wines require books of their own, and many exist. There is one single book that covers wine in great detail, and always with regard to its relationship to food. That is *The World Atlas of Wine* edited by Hugh Johnson. Johnson is the author or editor of several other wine books, all of which are helpful, but if you own only one book on wine, this is the one you should have.

For good guidance through the intricacies of French wines, a series of separate books published by Faber and Faber of London, each authored by a specialist Master of Wine, offers reliable information, updated in new editions every few years. For skillful discussion of the pleasures and esoterica of great wines and old wines, see Michael Broadbent's *The Great Wine Book*.

In Italy, America, and Australia, the whole field of wine is undergoing such rapid change that the best book on the subject will probably be the one published most recently.

A NOTE ON AFTER-DINNER DRINKS

There are times when the style of meal you're serving and the sense of occasion will call for an after-dinner drink. We offer several at Michael's worth mentioning.

Cognacs and Armagnacs—rich, aromatic, and complex in flavor—are a wonderful, reflective way to end an evening's meal, sipped from a snifter that allows you to swirl the liquor, warm it with your hands, and develop its aroma. There's some confusion in the difference between Cognac and Armagnac, but it's simply explained. Cognacs, basically, are blended by their manufacturers to give a consistent product, year after year; a fifty-year-old Cognac from a particular maker will taste pretty much the same whether it was bottled one year ago, or five, or ten. Armagnacs, on the other hand, are vintage products; so any particular year from a producer will differ from those Armagnacs produced in other years, and the Armagnac will go on aging and developing in its bottle, like a vintage wine.

Cognac producers, as a result, develop very distinctive house styles. Hine, for example, produces very robust, oaky Cognacs. Hennessey's have plenty of body and a fairly light, fruity quality. The best Cognacs from Courvoisier are really marvelous—very oaky and pungent. Rémy Martin's appeal is the mildness, gentility, and roundness of flavor and body that come with aging.

Armagnacs tend to function more like a cottage industry, so we tend to rely more on the exporter than on any one house. The best Armagnacs we've found in this country have come from an exporter called Darroze, who for years has specialized in putting together Armagnacs for use in the three-star restaurants of France.

A fairly new development in California is that some distillers are now making brandies using the Cognac and Armagnac methods. One in particular is, I find, getting truly remarkable results here: Germain-Robin, owned by a native of the Cognac region.

Other after-dinner drinks of particular note are the new fresh fruit eaux-de-vie now being produced in California, particularly those by St. George. And Bonny Doon is now offering fortified fruit wines—strawberry, blueberry, raspberry, and blackberry "infusions"—that are, in effect, very elegant examples of a classic European-style fruit liqueur. They're well worth seeking out.

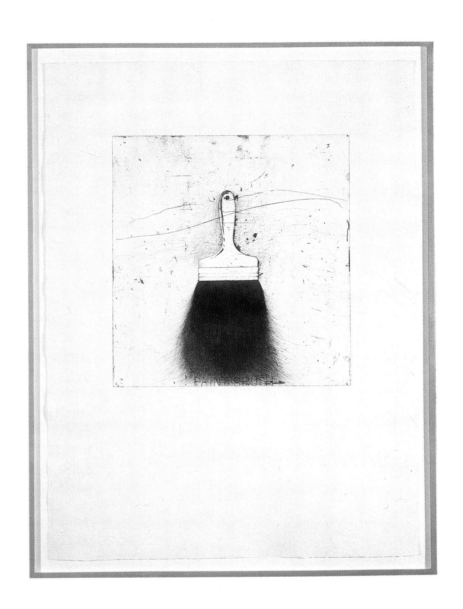

CHAPTER TWO

BASIC RECIPES AND TECHNIQUES

Red Beard by Jim
Dine

BASIC
PREPARATIONS

·

STOCK

·

FOR 2 TO 3 TO QUARTS

5 pounds chicken, squab, duck,
    rabbit, veal, or lamb bones
1 tablespoon unsalted butter
1 large yellow onion, peeled and cut
    in half
1 cup dry red wine
2 cloves garlic, unpeeled
1 tablespoon whole white peppercorns
2 bay leaves
2 carrots, coarsely chopped
½ stalk celery, coarsely chopped
2 sprigs fresh thyme
½ bunch fresh tarragon
½ bunch fresh basil

STOCK IS THE SINGLE MOST IMPORTANT ELEMENT OF MAKING GREAT sauces. The stock-making procedure is virtually the same whether you're making chicken, squab, duck, rabbit, veal, or lamb stock—the only difference being that, for chicken stock only, you do not roast the bones.

The stock will keep for almost a week covered in the refrigerator. You can also freeze the stock in ice-cube trays, then store the ice cubes in plastic freezer bags for several months.

In a pinch, you can use a good-quality canned chicken or meat clear broth to substitute for homemade stock. Many gourmet markets now also carry specially-made stocks for cooking; they are usually found in the freezer section.

For chicken stock, leave the chicken bones unroasted. For the other stocks, put the bones in a roasting pan and roast them in a 325°F oven until deep golden brown, 1½ to 2 hours.

While the bones are roasting, melt the butter in a heavy skillet over medium to low heat and sauté the onion halves until caramel-brown all over, 15 to 20 minutes per side.

When the bones are ready, add them to a large stockpot with the onion. Place the roasting pan over medium heat, add the wine, and stir and scrape to dissolve the glaze in the pan; then add the wine to the stockpot. (For chicken, omit the wine.)

Put all the remaining ingredients in the stockpot and add enough water to cover them. Bring the water to a boil over medium heat, skimming the surface constantly, then reduce the heat and simmer, skimming frequently, for about 5 hours.

Pour the stock through a double thickness of cheesecloth to remove the solids. Discard them. Let the stock cool to room temperature, then refrigerate until cold. Lift or scrape off any fat from the surface of the stock before using. Stock may then be stored in the freezer.

CLARIFIED BUTTER

•

FOR ABOUT ¾ CUP

1 pound (4 sticks) unsalted butter,
cut into cubes

BUTTER CLARIFIED OF ITS MILK SOLIDS HAS A LIGHTNESS AND PURITY OF taste, and can be heated to a higher temperature without burning than straight butter. Though you can use plain melted butter in any recipe, clarified butter simply gives better results.

The clarified butter can be stored, covered, for up to a week in the refrigerator.

In a saucepan, melt the butter over medium to low heat.
When all the butter is melted, use a spoon to skim off the froth from the top. Then carefully and gently pour off the clear butter into a bowl, stopping before any of the milky solids on the bottom leave the pan. Discard the solids.

BASIC MARINADE

•

FOR 2½ TO 3 CUPS

1 cup extra-virgin olive oil
6 medium-size cloves garlic,
    unpeeled, bashed
½ medium-size Maui, Walla Walla,
    Vidalia, or sweet red onion,
    sliced
1 medium-size carrot, coarsely
    chopped
1 bunch parsley, leaves only, coarsely
    chopped
1 bunch fresh basil (about 12 leaves),
    coarsely chopped
Cracked white pepper, to taste

I USE THIS MARINADE TO GIVE EXTRA FLAVOR AND TENDERNESS TO DUCK, squab, or pork. If you're marinating quail or rabbit, add ¾ cup of Sauvignon Blanc or Chardonnay to the ingredients listed below.

Combine all the ingredients and pour over the poultry or meat to be marinated.

SIMPLE SYRUP

·

FOR ABOUT 4½ CUPS

3¼ cups water
1¼ cups granulated sugar

THIS IS AN ESSENTIAL INGREDIENT IN DESSERTS, FROM PASTRIES TO SORbets. It may be refrigerated for a month or longer in a covered container.

In a saucepan, combine the water and sugar and bring to a boil, stirring as the sugar dissolves.

As soon as the mixture boils, remove it from the heat. Let it cool to room temperature, then refrigerate in a covered container.

BUTTERCREAM

·

FOR ABOUT 2 CUPS

¼ cup plus 1 teaspoon granulated sugar
¼ cup plus 1 teaspoon cold water
4 large egg yolks
12 tablespoons (1½ sticks) unsalted butter, cut into ½-inch cubes, at room temperature

THE CLASSIC FOUNDATION FOR CAKE FILLINGS.

In a saucepan over medium to high heat, bring the sugar and water to a boil and continue boiling until it reaches 217°F to 220°F on a candy thermometer, about 8 to 10 minutes.

Meanwhile, whisk the egg yolks in the bowl of an electric mixer on high speed until they're creamy and a light yellow color, about 10 minutes.

As soon as the sugar syrup is ready, with the mixer still running on high speed, pour the syrup into the egg yolks, taking care to avoid splatters. Continue beating until the mixture is cool, about 10 minutes.

A piece at a time, gradually whisk in the soft butter. The finished buttercream should look thick, shiny, and smooth. Transfer to a bowl, cover with plastic wrap, and store in the refrigerator until ready to use, for up to a week.

Large Bright Blue by
Richard Diebenkorn

PASTRY CREAM

■

FOR ABOUT 2 CUPS

2 cups milk
6 large egg yolks
½ cup plus 2 teaspoons granulated
    sugar
1 vanilla bean, split lengthwise
¼ cup (1¼ ounces) pastry flour

THIS CLASSIC PASTRY PREPARATION IS AN ESSENTIAL INGREDIENT IN THE fillings of my Heath Bar (see pages 200–201) and Millefeuille (see page 210).

In a medium-size saucepan, bring the milk to a boil over high heat. Meanwhile, put the egg yolks in a mixing bowl with the sugar and, with a wire whisk, whisk them together until light creamy yellow in color, about 2 minutes. With the tip of a small, sharp knife, scrape the insides of the vanilla bean into the mixture; whisk it in just until combined. Then add the flour and whisk just until incorporated.

As soon as the milk boils, slowly whisk half of it into the egg mixture. Then pour the contents of the bowl back into the saucepan with the remaining milk and whisk continuously over medium heat until thick, 3 to 4 minutes.

Place a sieve over a bowl and pour the mixture through, pressing it through with a rubber spatula. Cover the surface of the pastry cream with waxed paper to keep a film from forming, and let stand at room temperature for 30 minutes. Then refrigerate until cool, at least 1 hour. The pastry cream will keep in the refrigerator, covered, for up to 1 week.

CRÈME ANGLAISE

■

FOR ABOUT 4 CUPS

4 cups milk
1 vanilla bean, split in half
    lengthwise
8 large egg yolks
1¼ cups granulated sugar

In a medium-size saucepan, bring the milk and vanilla bean to a boil, stirring frequently to prevent scorching.

In a bowl, using a wire whisk, beat the egg yolks and sugar together until creamy and light yellow, 2 to 3 minutes. Whisking continuously, slowly pour in the boiling milk.

Return the mixture to the saucepan and stir continuously with a wooden spoon over low heat until thick enough to coat the spoon, 30 seconds to 1 minute.

Pour the crème anglaise through a fine-mesh sieve into a stainless steel or glass container and let it cool to room temperature before storing, covered, in the refrigerator. It will keep for up to 1 week. Stir any skin that forms on the surface back into the crème anglaise before serving.

GANACHE

■

FOR 2 TO 2½ CUPS

½ pound bittersweet melting
    chocolate, such as Valrhona
    Caraque, or Tobler Tobamera,
    broken into pieces
½ cup heavy cream
3½ tablespoons unsalted butter, cut
    into pieces

THE BASIS OF CHOCOLATE TRUFFLES (SEE PAGES 234–235) AS WELL AS various pastry and cake fillings, this rich chocolate paste is good enough to eat by itself.

Put the chocolate in the top of a double boiler over barely simmering water. As the chocolate melts, stir with a wire whisk to help it meet smoothly and evenly.

In a small saucepan, bring the cream to a boil. Whisking the melted chocolate continuously, pour in the cream.

When the cream and chocolate are blended, remove the mixture from the heat. Add the butter and whisk until melted and blended in. Set the mixture aside to cool to room temperature before using. The ganache can be kept up to 1 month, covered, in the refrigerator.

PRALINE POWDER

■

MAKES ABOUT 2 CUPS

½ pound hazelnuts
¼ cup water
1 cup granulated sugar

A FAVORITE FLAVORING FOR CAKE AND PASTRY FILLINGS, THIS IS ALSO great just sprinkled over ice cream.

Preheat the oven to 350°F. Spread the hazelnuts on a baking sheet and roast them until their skins darken and crack, about 10 minutes. Let them cool to room temperature, then rub them between your hands to remove the skin.

In a medium-size saucepan, bring the water and sugar to a boil, then continue boiling until mixture reaches a light caramel color and becomes thick and opaque, about 8 to 10 minutes.

Immediately pour in the hazelnuts and take the pan from the heat. Stir constantly with a wooden spoon until the sugar crystallizes, about 1 minute.

Return the pan to medium-high heat, stirring until the sugar becomes liquid again and then turns a dark caramel color, 5 to 10 minutes.

Immediately pour the mixture out on a baking sheet and let it cool until hard.

Break the praline into pieces and put in a food processor. Process until pulverized. Store in an airtight container.

BASIC TECHNIQUES

·

ROASTING JALAPEÑO PEPPERS

·

WHEN ROASTING HOT CHILI PEPPERS SUCH AS JALAPEÑOS, BE VERY CAREful not to touch your eyes or any cuts after handling them, as their volatile oils can burn badly. Wash your hands very thoroughly with soap and water.

To roast the peppers, char their skins evenly over a direct gas stove flame or on top of an electric burner, about 2 minutes for jalapeños, longer for larger peppers.

Peel off the charred skins under cold running water; then cut the pepper open, pull off their stems, and remove the seeds and white membranes.

GRILLED PEPPERS

·

GRILLED BELL PEPPERS, PARTICULARLY RED AND YELLOW ONES, ARE A favorite garnish for my salads and pastas.

To grill peppers, preheat the grill or broiler until very hot. Slice the peppers in half through the stem. Cut out the stems, seeds, and white membranes, and slice each half vertically into 3 pieces. Drizzle the skin sides of each piece with olive oil and sprinkle with salt and white pepper.

Grill the peppers with their skins facing the heat just until the skins begin to blister and char slightly. They are ready to serve at this point, without peeling.

DOUBLE-BLANCHED GARLIC

•

DOUBLE-BLANCHING WHOLE GARLIC CLOVES REMOVES THEIR SHARP edge, leaving the garlic mild and sweet yet still full-flavored.

To double-blanch garlic, peel the cloves, put them in a small saucepan, and cover with cold water. Bring the water to a boil. Drain the garlic. Cover with cold water again, bring to a boil, and drain once more.

PULVERIZED ALMONDS

•

TO PULVERIZE ALMONDS, PUT BLANCHED ALMONDS IN A FOOD PROCESSOR fitted with the metal blade. Pulse the machine just until the almonds are finely chopped.

Roman Notes #2 and #3 by Cy Twombly

SAUCES
AND DRESSINGS

·

BEURRE BLANC

·

FOR ABOUT 2 CUPS

½ cup champagne vinegar
1 cup California Chardonnay
2 tablespoons finely chopped shallots
3 tablespoons heavy cream
½ pound (2 sticks) unsalted butter,
    chilled and cut into ½-inch cubes
1 tablespoon fresh lemon juice
Salt and freshly ground white pepper

THIS IS ONE OF THE CLASSIC SAUCES OF THE FRENCH KITCHEN, ADAPTED here with the addition of California Chardonnay.

Since beurre blanc is, like mayonnaise, an emulsion—in this case, a thick but delicate blend of butter, wine, and vinegar—pay careful attention to the constant stirring and the heat, to ensure the sauce doesn't separate.

For a beautiful rose-colored beurre rose, substitute a Sauvignon for the Chardonnay and red wine vinegar for the champagne vinegar.

In a small, heavy, nonaluminum saucepan, boil the vinegar and Chardonnay with the shallots over high heat until only about 1 tablespoon of the liquid is left, 10 to 15 minutes.

Stir in the cream with a whisk and continue cooking for about 1 minute. Then reduce the heat to medium and, whisking constantly, add the butter a few cubes at a time, adding more butter as each new addition melts and blends into the sauce. If the sauce begins to simmer, lift it from the heat. When all the butter has been incorporated, whisk in the lemon juice and season to taste.

To keep the beurre blanc warm, set the saucepan inside a bowl or larger pan of hot but not boiling water.

CABERNET CASSIS SAUCE

•

FOR ABOUT 1½ CUPS

¾ cup Cabernet Sauvignon
¼ cup black currants
2 tablespoons cassis syrup
2 cups poultry or lamb stock (see
    page 22)
1 clove double-blanched garlic (see
    page 28)
2 fresh basil leaves
1 teaspoon unsalted butter, chilled
Salt and freshly ground white pepper

THIS IS ONE OF THE GREAT SAUCES FOR MEAT AND POULTRY AT MICHAEL'S, the perfect bridge to an outstanding California Cabernet Sauvignon. If you want to serve a Pinot Noir or a French red Burgundy or Bordeaux with the dish, substitute that wine for the Cabernet Sauvignon in the sauce. Likewise, you can also use red currants and red currant syrup in place of the black currants and cassis.

Be sure to buy a high-quality cassis syrup, available in most wine and liquor shops or gourmet markets; black currant liqueurs are not acceptable substitutes.

In a small, heavy, nonaluminum saucepan, boil the Cabernet with the black currants and cassis syrup over high heat until the liquid has reduced by three quarters to a thick syrup, 5 to 7 minutes.

Add the stock and simmer over medium heat, skimming the surface frequently, until the sauce is thick enough to coat the back of a spoon and has reduced to about 1½ cups, 10 to 15 minutes. Add the garlic and basil and swirl in the butter until thoroughly incorporated.

Strain the sauce through a fine-mesh sieve and return it to the pan to warm through gently. Season to taste with salt and pepper.

To keep the sauce warm, set the saucepan inside a bowl or larger pan of hot but not boiling water.

CHARDONNAY CREAM SAUCE I (FOR SEAFOOD)

•

FOR ABOUT 2 CUPS

¼ medium-size Maui, Walla Walla,
    Vidalia, or other sweet red
    onion, thinly sliced
½ medium-size carrot, peeled and
    coarsely chopped

ONE OF THE MOST POPULAR SAUCES AT MICHAEL'S, AND THE PERFECT bridge between my seafood dishes and great California Chardonnays.

Put the onion, carrot, and mushrooms in a small, heavy, nonaluminum saucepan. Cover the pan and cook over low heat until the onion is transparent, about 10 minutes.

Add the wine, fish bones or trimmings, parsley, and thyme. Raise the heat to medium to high and bring the liquid to a gentle boil. Then remove the pan from the heat and set it aside for about 15 minutes.

Strain out and discard the solids from the liquid and return the liquid to the pan. Add the shallot and bring the liquid to a boil over

*2 medium-size white mushrooms,
    thinly sliced*
¾ cup California Chardonnay
*2 ounces white-fleshed fish bones
    (such as John Dory or red
    snapper), scallop trimmings, or
    shrimp or lobster shells*
2 or 3 stems fresh parsley
1 small sprig fresh thyme
1 medium-size shallot, finely chopped
2 cups heavy cream
Salt and freshly ground white pepper
Fresh lemon juice

high heat; continue boiling until only about 2 tablespoons of liquid are left, 5 to 7 minutes. Then add the cream, reduce the heat slightly, and simmer until the sauce is thick and reduced by about a third, 7 to 10 minutes more. Season to taste with salt, pepper, and a little lemon juice.

In a food processor, or with a hand-held blender, process the sauce until smooth, 1 to 2 minutes. Strain it through a fine-mesh sieve and return it to the pan to warm through gently. Adjust the seasonings to taste.

To keep the sauce warm, set the saucepan inside a bowl or larger pan of hot but not boiling water.

CHARDONNAY CREAM SAUCE II (FOR POULTRY, MEAT, OR VEGETABLES)

■

FOR ABOUT 2 CUPS

¾ cup California Chardonnay
1 medium-size shallot, finely chopped
2 cups heavy cream
Salt and freshly ground white pepper
Fresh lemon juice

I USE THIS VERSION OF CHARDONNAY CREAM SAUCE WITH NONSEAfood pastas and main courses.

In a small, heavy, nonaluminum saucepan, boil the Chardonnay with the shallot over high heat until only about 2 tablespoons of liquid are left, 5 to 7 minutes. Then add the cream, reduce the heat slightly, and simmer until the sauce is thick and reduced by about half, 7 to 10 minutes more. Season to taste with salt, pepper, and a little lemon juice.

In a food processor, or with a hand-held blender, process the sauce until smooth, 1 to 2 minutes. Strain it through a fine-mesh sieve and return it to the pan to warm through gently. Adjust the seasonings to taste.

To keep the sauce warm, set the saucepan inside a bowl or larger pan of hot but not boiling water.

RASPBERRY
SAUCE

■

FOR ABOUT 1½ CUPS

6 cups fresh raspberries
½ cup (more or less) Simple Syrup
    (see page 24)

In a processor, puree the raspberries.
    Pour the puree into a very fine-mesh sieve and press it through with a rubber spatula. Discard the seeds.
    Stir together the raspberry puree and the syrup to taste. Chill the sauce in a covered bowl in the refrigerator.

CARAMEL
SAUCE

■

FOR ABOUT 1½ CUPS

½ cup water
½ cup granulated sugar
6 tablespoons heavy cream
4 tablespoons (½ stick) unsalted
    butter, cut into pieces

In a small saucepan, boil the water and sugar over high heat until the mixture turns a dark caramel color, 7 to 10 minutes.
    Put a whisk in the pan to keep the mixture from boiling over and, being careful of any steam rising from the pan, pour in the cream; then immediately add the butter. Let the sauce simmer until thick and bubbly, about 1 minute more.
    Remove the pan from the heat and let the sauce cool to room temperature. Then transfer it to a bowl or other storage container and refrigerate, covered.

JALAPEÑO-
CILANTRO-
LIME SALSA

•

FOR ABOUT 1 CUP

2 jalapeño peppers, roasted, peeled,
    seeded, and finely chopped (see
    page 27)
2 tablespoons chopped fresh cilantro
    leaves
1 cup extra-virgin olive oil
Salt and freshly ground white pepper
2 limes, cut in half

I USE THIS SPICY, TANGY SEASONING ON SALADS, HORS D'OEUVRES, AND
the sandwiches I serve at brunch.

In a bowl, stir together the jalapeños, cilantro, and olive oil. Season
to taste with salt and pepper.

Just before serving, squeeze the limes into the mixture and stir
well. (The lime juice will turn the cilantro brown if added any earlier.)

4 People in Beach Chairs by Kim McCarty

BALSAMIC VINAIGRETTE

■

FOR 1 CUP

⅓ cup balsamic vinegar
⅔ cup extra-virgin olive oil
Fresh lime juice
Salt and freshly ground white pepper

AN INCREDIBLY SIMPLE DRESSING THAT SHOWS OFF THE MELLOW, RICH, complex flavor of balsamic vinegar.

Put the vinegar in a mixing bowl and, whisking continuously, gradually pour in the olive oil. Season to taste with a little lime juice, salt, and pepper.

TOMATO-CILANTRO-JALAPEÑO VINAIGRETTE

■

FOR ABOUT 6 CUPS

4 medium-size tomatoes (red or
    yellow)
2 tablespoons chopped fresh cilantro
    leaves
1 jalapeño pepper, roasted, peeled,
    seeded, and finely chopped (see
    page 27)
1 cup extra-virgin olive oil
¼ cup sherry wine vinegar
Juice of 1 lime
Salt and freshly ground white pepper

THIS SALAD DRESSING COMBINES THE SWEETNESS OF RIPE TOMATOES with the heat of jalapeños and the tang of sherry wine vinegar and lime juice.

Bring a large saucepan of water to a boil and prepare a large bowl filled with water and ice cubes.

With a small, sharp knife, cut the stem ends and cores of the tomatoes; cut a shallow X on the bottom of each tomato. Boil the tomatoes until their skins are loose, about 40 seconds. With a slotted spoon, transfer them to the ice-water bath.

After about 1 minute, remove the tomatoes from the ice water and peel off their skins. Cut them in half through their stem ends. Remove their seeds with your finger, then cut the flesh of the tomatoes into ¼-inch dice.

In a bowl, stir together the diced tomatoes with the rest of the ingredients, seasoning them to taste. Chill in the refrigerator for at least 30 minutes before serving.

BREADS
AND PASTRY

■

WALNUT BREAD

■

FOR 1 LOAF

¾ cup water

¼ cup milk

¾ ounce fresh cake yeast (available in the refrigerated section of most supermarkets)

2¼ cups plus 2 tablespoons (1 pound) all-purpose flour

½ cup plus 2 tablespoons (3 ounces) rye flour

1 tablespoon granulated sugar

1 tablespoon salt

2 cups coarsely broken walnuts

1 tablespoon malt syrup (available in supermarket baking sections)

2½ tablespoons unsalted butter, melted

CUT INTO ¼-INCH SLICES AND TOASTED, THIS BREAD IS EXCELLENT with hors d'oeuvres, appetizers, and egg dishes. It's also a perfect partner for serving cheese with wines. Wrapped in plastic wrap, it will keep for 4 to 5 days in the refrigerator.

In a small saucepan, heat the water and milk to 115°F on a cooking thermometer.

Put the yeast in the bowl of an electric mixer (or a food processor with the metal blade), add the hot liquid, and whisk until the yeast dissolves. With the mixer on low speed, mix (or pulse) in the flours, sugar, and salt just until incorporated. Add the walnuts and mix until they are incorporated, then mix in the malt syrup.

Cover the mixing bowl with a damp towel (or, if using the processor, remove the dough to a bowl and cover) and leave it at warm room temperature until the dough doubles in volume, about 1 hour. Punch down the dough, cover again, and let it rise once more, 45 minutes to 1 hour more.

Lightly butter the inside of an 11½ × 3½ × 3-inch metal loaf pan. Roll the dough into a log shape that will fit into the pan and place it inside. Leave the loaf in a warm place until the dough rises to the top of the pan, 20 minutes.

Meanwhile, preheat the oven to 375°F.

Brush the top of the loaf with the melted butter and bake it until dark brown, 1 to 1¼ hours. Unmold onto a wire rack to cool before slicing and serving.

BRIOCHE

.

¾ cup milk

½ ounce fresh cake yeast (available in the refrigerated section of most supermarkets)

4¼ cups (1¼ pounds) all-purpose flour

4 large eggs

¼ cup granulated sugar

4 teaspoons salt

½ pound (2 sticks) plus 3 tablespoons unsalted butter, at room temperature, cut into ½-inch pieces

1 large egg yolk

¼ teaspoon heavy cream

THIS CLASSIC BREAD, RICH WITH BUTTER AND EGGS, IS A PERFECT COMplement to many of the hors d'oeuvres and appetizers at Michael's, and it makes spectacular French toast. Unlike the French, who bake brioche in large or small round loaves, we prepare ours in rectangular sandwich-style loaves, which facilitates slicing and serving.

In a small saucepan, heat the milk to 115°F on a cooking thermometer. Pour the milk into a mixing bowl, add the yeast, and whisk until the yeast dissolves. Whisk in ¾ cup of the flour.

Pour the remaining flour on top of the yeast mixture and, without stirring, leave the bowl uncovered in a warm place until the yeast mixture just begins to show through the top of the flour, anywhere from 10 to 30 minutes, depending on the temperature and humidity.

Put the eggs in the bowl of an electric mixer fitted with the dough hook (or in a processor with the metal blade), and mix briefly until smooth. Add the yeast-flour mixture, sugar, and salt, and mix on slow speed (or pulse) just until combined; increase the speed to medium (or process continuously) and mix just until the dough forms a ball that pulls away from the sides of the bowl. Add the butter and continue mixing until it is completely incorporated and the dough reforms a ball or climbs up the dough hook or blade.

Cover the bottom of a small sheet cake pan with parchment paper. Empty the dough into the pan and spread it out; cover with another sheet of parchment paper. Leave the dough in the refrigerator overnight.

Butter the inside of an 8½ × 4½ × 2½-inch ovenproof glass loaf pan. Roll the dough into a log shape that will fit into the pan and place it inside. Leave the loaf in a warm place until the dough rises to the top of the pan, 45 minutes to 1 hour.

Meanwhile, preheat the oven to 375°F.

When the loaf has risen, beat together the egg yolk and cream and brush it over the top of the loaf. Bake until the loaf is a golden brown, about 30 minutes. Unmold onto a wire rack to cool before slicing and serving.

WALNUT BREAD

BRIOCHE

FEUILLETAGE AND FEUILLETÉS

■

1½ cups plus 1 tablespoon (7⅓
    ounces) all-purpose flour
1 tablespoon plus 2 teaspoons (½
    ounce) pastry flour
½ pound (2 sticks) unsalted butter,
    chilled and cut into pieces
5 tablespoons ice water
½ large egg yolk
½ teaspoon salt

MAKING GREAT PUFF PASTRY—THE CLASSIC FRENCH FEUILLETAGE—IS the Ph.D. of pastry-making. But after years of research, we've come up with a pretty foolproof technique. Just be sure to follow the steps carefully, and not to cheat on any of the chilling, folding, or turning of the dough.

We use feuilletage at Michael's to make our Feuilletés—puff pastry cases for appetizers as well as desserts.

Put two thirds of the all-purpose flour, all the pastry flour, and 3 tablespoons of the butter in a food processor with the metal blade. In a cup, stir together the ice water, egg yolk, and salt. With the processor running, pour in the water mixture, then pulse continuously until the pastry just comes together in a ball.

Empty the pastry onto a large sheet of plastic wrap; wrap it up and, through the plastic, shape the pastry into a rectangle ½ inch thick and about 5 by 4½ inches. Refrigerate the pastry overnight.

The next day, remove the chilled pastry from the refrigerator, unwrap it, and place it on a floured work surface. Put the remaining flour and butter in the processor and pulse until it just reaches a coarse, gravelly texture. Empty it onto a large sheet of plastic wrap; wrap it up and, through the plastic, shape it into another rectangle ½ inch thick and about 5 by 4½ inches. Chill in the refrigerator for about 30 minutes.

With a rolling pin, roll out the pastry from the previous day to a rectangle about 11½ inches long by 5 inches wide. Unwrap the chilled butter-flour mixture and place it on the bottom half of the pastry rectangle, with an even edge of pastry around it; fold the top half of pastry over it and pinch the edges of the pastry to seal it in.

Rotate the pastry 90 degrees counterclockwise, so the sealed edges are at top, bottom, and left. Beginning at the center, roll it out again top to bottom, stopping short of the sealed edges, to a length of 11 inches and a width of 5 inches, with a narrow end nearest you. Fold the pastry in thirds, rotate 90 degrees counterclockwise again, and roll out once more. Then fold both narrow ends inward to meet at the center, and fold in half once more to make 4 layers. Wrap the pastry in aluminum foil and refrigerate for 45 minutes.

Remove the pastry from the refrigerator, unwrap it, and place it on a floured surface with the opening of the folds on the right, like a book. Roll out the pastry top to bottom to a length of 11 inches and a width of 5 inches, with a narrow end nearest you. Fold the narrow ends inward to meet at the center and fold in half once more, as you did in the previous step. Rewrap in foil and refrigerate for 30 minutes more.

Repeat the rolling procedure. Refrigerate for 1 hour.

Remove the pastry from the refrigerator, unwrap it, and roll it out to a ¼-inch-thick rectangle about 10 inches wide and 6 inches wide. At this point, the feuilletage may be wrapped airtight and refrigerated or frozen.

FOR FEUILLETÉS (PUFF PASTRY CASES)

Preheat the oven to 350°F.

With a pastry cutter or large, sharp knife, cut the sheet of feuilletage (defrosted if previously frozen) into 8 rectangles, each 2½ by 3 inches.

Place the rectangles of pastry on a baking sheet lined with parchment paper. Bake for 20 to 25 minutes, until well risen and golden.

COUPES

■

FOR 18 TO 20 COUPES

6 tablespoons granulated sugar
6 tablespoons (1¾ ounces) all-
    purpose flour
2 large egg whites
3½ tablespoons unsalted butter,
    melted

WE USE THESE CRISP, DELICATE COOKIE CUPS AS CONTAINERS FOR ICE creams and fresh fruit desserts.

In a mixing bowl, stir together the sugar and flour. Make a well in the center.

Pour the egg whites and the melted butter into the well. Vigorously stir with a mixing spoon until the mixture forms a smooth batter. Cover the bowl and refrigerate for 30 minutes. Then let the batter rest at room temperature for 1 hour.

Preheat the oven to 350°F.

Lightly butter and flour a rimless baking sheet or the back of a baking sheet with a rim. Use a 6-inch cake ring or pot lid to lightly stamp circles in the prepared surface. Pour ¼ cup of the batter into each circle and swirl the batter with the back of a spoon to fill each circle. Bake until the edges of each circle are golden brown but the centers are still light.

To shape the coupes, use a spatula to remove the circles one at a time, quickly pressing them into a medium-size fluted Charlotte mold; work fast, because the coupes harden very quickly—in less than 20 seconds—when removed from the baking sheet. Store the coupes in an airtight container.

PÂTE SUCRÉE

■

MAKES ENOUGH FOR 4 TART SHELLS

5⅓ cups (1½ pounds) all-purpose
    flour
¾ cup granulated sugar
1 pound (4 sticks) unsalted butter,
    chilled and cut into 1-inch cubes
3 large egg yolks
3 tablespoons heavy cream

A CLASSIC PASTRY FOR TART SHELLS AND CERTAIN COOKIES. ONE QUAR-
ter of the recipe—about 10 ounces—will make a shell for one of the
fresh fruit tarts starting on page 186, and I give instructions below
for making the shell. You can easily divide the recipe if you like,
though the pastry stores well for weeks in the freezer.

Put the flour and sugar into the bowl of an electric mixer fitted
with the dough hook. With the machine running on low, add
the butter; mix until the ingredients resemble cornmeal, about 10
minutes. (You can also process the ingredients in a food processor
with the metal blade.)

Meanwhile, whisk together the egg yolks and cream until smooth.

Turn up the mixer speed to medium (or turn on the processor)
and add the egg yolk–cream mixture; as soon as the dough comes
together, in just a few seconds, stop the machine. Divide the dough
into 4 equal pieces; gather each piece into a ball, wrap it in plastic
wrap, and chill in the refrigerator for 1 hour before using. Securely
wrapped, the dough may be stored in the refrigerator for several days
or in the freezer for several weeks.

FOR A PASTRY SHELL

Remove one ball of the pâte sucrée from the refrigerator and let it
warm and soften at room temperature for about 30 minutes.

On a cool, floured surface, pound it with a rolling pin to flatten
it out to a circle, then roll it out to a circle about 11 inches in diameter
and about ⅛ inch thick.

Gently roll the pastry around the rolling pin, then unroll it carefully into a 10-inch fluted tart ring with a removable bottom. Gently
press the pastry into the bottom and sides of the pan and trim the
edges. Refrigerate for about 1 hour before using.

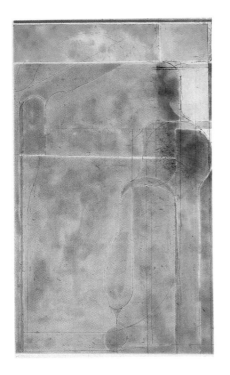

Large Light Blue by
Richard Diebenkorn

GARNISHES

·

MAUI ONION CONFIT

·

FOR ABOUT 2 CUPS

1 medium-size Maui onion, very
    thinly sliced
2 tablespoons water
½ pound (2 sticks) unsalted butter,
    cut into 1-inch pieces
Salt and freshly ground white pepper
Fresh lemon juice

THIS IS ONE OF MY ALL-TIME FAVORITE GARNISHES—THE SWEETNESS of Maui onions melting together with the richness of butter. If you can't get Mauis, buy Vidalia or Walla Walla onions; or make it with the sweetest red onions you can find.

Put the onion, water, and 1 piece of butter in a small, heavy saucepan. Cover the pan and cook over low heat until the onions are cooked through but not too soft, 10 to 15 minutes. Carefully pour off all liquid from the pan.

Still over low heat, stir in a few pieces of butter at a time, with a wooden spoon, until all the butter has melted and been incorporated into the onions. Season to taste with salt, pepper, and a little lemon juice.

To keep the confit warm, set the saucepan inside a bowl or larger pan of hot but not boiling water.

COOKED WILD RICE

·

FOR 1 CUP

⅓ cup wild rice
1 cup water
1 thick strip lean smoked bacon
1 teaspoon unsalted butter
Salt and freshly ground white pepper

THE NUTLIKE TASTE OF WILD RICE MAKES IT AN EXCELLENT GARNISH FOR dishes featuring quail, sweetbreads, or lamb.

Put the wild rice and water in a small saucepan. Bring the water to a boil, reduce the heat to a bare simmer, cover, and cook until the rice is tender, 1 to 1¼ hours.

While the rice is cooking, sauté the bacon until golden brown and crisp, then drain on a paper towel. Cut the bacon crosswise into thin julienne strips and set them aside.

When the rice is done, gently stir in the butter with a fork until melted; season to taste with salt and pepper. Just before serving, toss the rice with the bacon strips.

TOMATO CONCASSE

■

FOR ABOUT 2 CUPS

4 medium-size tomatoes (red or
   yellow)
1 cup extra-virgin olive oil
¼ cup sherry wine vinegar
½ medium-size shallot, finely
   chopped
2 tablespoons julienne of fresh basil
Salt and freshly ground white pepper

GOOD, RIPE TOMATOES, PEELED, SEEDED, AND CHOPPED, ARE A FAVORITE ingredient and garnish of mine. Sometimes I'll use them unseasoned in a recipe, but more often, I'll toss them with herbs, seasonings, olive oil, and vinegar, particularly when they're an element in one of my salads.

Bring a large saucepan of water to a boil and prepare a large bowl filled with water and ice cubes.

With a small, sharp knife, cut out the stem ends and cores of the tomatoes; cut a shallow X on the bottom of each tomato. Boil the tomatoes until their skins are loose, about 40 seconds. With a slotted spoon, transfer them to the ice-water bath.

After about 1 minute, remove the tomatoes from the ice water and peel off their skins. Cut them in half through their stem ends. Remove their seeds with your finger, then cut the flesh of the tomatoes into ¼-inch dice.

Put the diced tomato in a bowl with the olive oil, vinegar, shallot, and basil. Season to taste with salt and pepper and stir well. Cover and chill in the refrigerator for at least 30 minutes.

SIDE DISHES

∎

SHOESTRING POTATOES

∎

FOR 6 SERVINGS

Rendered beef suet or vegetable oil for deep frying
2 large baking potatoes (about 1 pound total), peeled
Salt

I LOVE TO SERVE THESE ULTRA-CRISP, LIGHT POTATO STRINGS WITH grilled quail, and they're a great side dish for other poultry, meats, or seafood.

The French hand-operated slicing device known as a mandoline (perhaps because you work it with a strumming motion of the wrist and arm) is the best way I know to cut the thin shoestrings. Some food processors, though, do have very thin blades that will do a good job.

Though I prefer the flavor of potatoes fried in beef suet, you can use any good deep-frying oil.

In a deep-fryer or large, deep, heavy skillet, heat at least 4 inches of suet or vegetable oil to a temperature of 375°F on a deep-frying thermometer.

While the fat is heating, cut the potatoes into matchstick-thick shoestring strips. Carefully add them to the hot fat and fry until light golden brown, about 2 minutes.

Remove the potatoes with a wire skimmer and drain them well on paper towels. Toss with a light sprinkling of salt before serving.

VEGETABLE MOSAICS/THE VEGETABLE ENTRÉE PLATE

•

FOR 6 SERVINGS (OR 2 VEGETARIAN
MAIN COURSES)

6 baby zucchini, with blossoms if
   available
6 baby yellow squash, with blossoms
   if available
6 baby acorn squash, with blossoms if
   available
6 baby carrots, peeled
6 large broccoli florets
3 to 4 dozen small snow pea pods,
   trimmed
4 baby turnips, peeled, stems
   trimmed down to ¼ inch, each
   turnip cut into 6 wedges
4 baby beets, peeled, stems trimmed
   down to ¼ inch, each beet cut
   into 6 wedges
4 tablespoons (½ stick) unsalted
   butter, melted
1 teaspoon Grand Marnier
¼ teaspoon sesame oil

THE TOP HALF OF EVERY ENTRE PLATE AT MICHAEL'S IS DECORATED WITH an array of baby vegetables, arranged in an artful, overlapping pattern. We also serve an entrée plate completely covered with this vegetable design, for vegetarian guests who request it.

Every plate has a slightly different arrangement, depending on the vegetables available and on the whim of whoever prepared the garnish. The choices of vegetable include baby yellow squash, acorn squash, and zucchini, with blossoms still attached, if possible; baby carrots; baby beets and turnips; snow peas; and broccoli florets.

You can still prepare the vegetables even if baby ones aren't available. Just seek out the smallest, best-quality vegetables you *can* find, and slice and arrange them in the same way.

Use the quantities and instructions below as only the most general of guidelines, letting the fresh produce you find and your own fancy guide you in the final preparation.

If the zucchini, yellow squash, or acorn squash still have nice blossoms attached, leave them whole. With a mandoline (a hand-operated slicing device) or a small, sharp knife, cut the other squash and the carrots at a 45-degree angle into wafer-thin slices—about ¹⁄₁₆ inch thick.

Bring a large pot of water to a boil. One variety at a time, blanch the vegetables until cooked al dente—about 3 minutes for broccoli florets, 1½ to 2 minutes for snow peas or turnips, 1 minute for sliced carrots and whole baby zucchini or squash, 15 to 30 seconds for sliced zucchini or squash. Cook any beets last, for 5 to 6 minutes, so they don't discolor the other vegetables.

Distribute the butter between 3 small skillets or saucepans (4 if you're including beets). Put the carrots into one pan with the Grand Marnier; put the broccoli in another with the sesame oil; put beets in a third; and put the remaining vegetables in the fourth pan. Toss the vegetables with the butter over low heat for about 30 seconds, just until heated through, and season with salt and pepper.

Arrange the sliced vegetables and the snow peas in neat overlapping patterns, starting at one point on the top left-hand side of the plate and fanning wider as the design moves toward the right; see any of the main-course photographs in this book for inspiration. Place the whole baby vegetables, wedges of turnip or beet, and broccoli florets at the right-hand side of the design.

For main-course vegetable plates, cover the entire plate with a neat symmetrical design of vegetables, placing the larger pieces along the bottom and center vertical third of the plate and fanning the sliced vegetables and snow peas on either side.

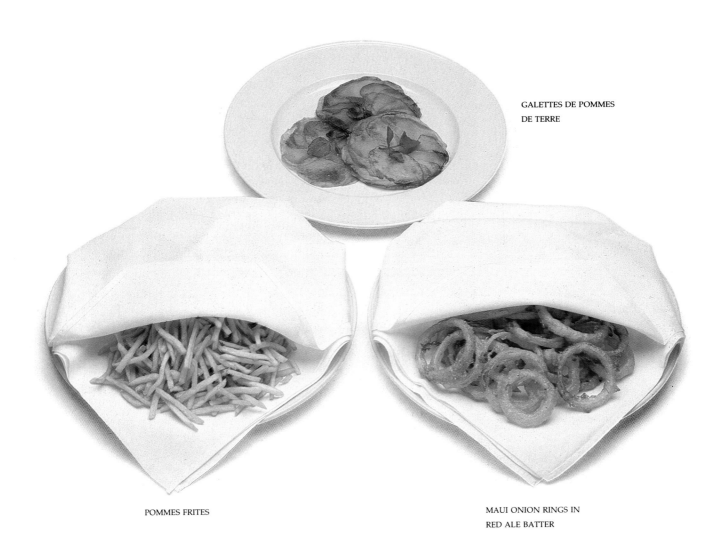

GALETTES DE POMMES
DE TERRE

POMMES FRITES

MAUI ONION RINGS IN
RED ALE BATTER

POMMES FRITES

Rendered beef suet or vegetable oil for deep-frying
3 pounds frozen french fries
Salt

BELIEVE IT OR NOT, GOOD-QUALITY BULK FROZEN POTATOES CUT INTO ¼-inch-thick fries are your best bet for dependable French-style *pommes frites*. We use a brand called Mor-Fries, from Wesson Oregon.

Fry the potatoes in beef suet or any good deep-frying oil.

In a deep-fryer or large, deep, heavy skillet, heat at least 4 inches of suet or vegetable oil to a temperature of 375°F on a deep-frying thermometer.

Add the potatoes to the hot fat—in batches, if necessary, to prevent crowding—and fry them until golden brown, 3 to 5 minutes.

Drain the potatoes on paper towels and sprinkle lightly with salt before serving.

GALETTES DE POMMES DE TERRE

6 medium-size baking potatoes (about 3 pounds total)
¼ cup clarified butter (see page 23)
Salt and freshly ground white pepper
Fresh watercress sprigs

THESE LITTLE POTATO CAKES ARE A TERRIFIC SIDE DISH FOR POULTRY and meat entrées.

Wash and peel the potatoes and cut them thinly crosswise into round slices about ⅛ inch thick.

For each potato cake, place a slice of potato on a work surface. Then, using that slice as the center of the cake, arrange 8 or so more slices around it, overlapping in a circular pattern and with the edge of each slice touching the very center of the first potato slice.

In a large skillet, heat the butter over medium-to-high heat. Season the potato cakes with salt and pepper and, with a spatula, carefully transfer them one at a time to the skillet, taking care not to overcrowd it. Let the cakes fry undisturbed for about 30 seconds, then gently shake the skillet and move the cakes slightly with the spatula to prevent them from sticking, and fry about 1 minute more, until the undersides of the cakes are golden brown.

With the spatula, carefully flip each cake with a quick turn of the wrist. Fry the cakes for about 1½ minutes more, until their other sides are golden brown. Keep them warm in a low oven while you fry any remaining cakes. Garnish with watercress before serving.

MAUI ONION RINGS IN RED ALE BATTER

■

FOR 6 SERVINGS

6 medium-size Maui onions, peeled
Rendered beef suet or vegetable oil for
    deep frying
3 cups all-purpose flour
3 tablespoons cornstarch
½ teaspoon salt
½ teaspoon freshly ground white
    pepper
2 bottles, 12 ounces each, ale,
    preferably Killian's red

THE SUMMER OF THE 1984 LOS ANGELES OLYMPICS, I GOT A PHONE call from the *L.A. Times* Food Section asking if I planned to serve any special Olympic dishes at Michael's. Thinking of my friend Robert Runyon, who designed the logo for the '84 games, I jokingly told the *Times* I was going to make the Olympic rings out of Maui onions.

Then it hit me that that wasn't a bad idea. Those sublimely sweet onions would make great onion rings. (If you can't get Mauis, substitute Vidalias from Georgia, Walla Wallas from Washington, or the mildest, sweetest red or brown onions you can buy.) To complement their flavor, the batter is made with rich red Killian's ale, which also gives it a pale brown color; you can substitute any good-quality bottled ale.

The key to a batter that fries up light and crisp is adding just the right amount of cornstarch: too little and the batter will be cakey, too much and it will absorb fat during frying. Beef suet, with its distinctive flavor and high frying temperature, is the ultimate choice for cooking the onion rings. It's available in most supermarkets. Why compromise?

Cut the onions crosswise into ¼- to ⅜-inch slices and separate them into rings. Don't discard the centers of the slices; they'll fry up into delicious, crisp little nuggets.

Put the suet in a deep-fryer or a large, heavy skillet; there should be enough fat when melted to give a depth of at least 4 inches. Heat the suet to 375°F on a deep-frying thermometer.

While the suet is heating, put the flour, cornstarch, salt, and pepper in a large mixing bowl. Pour in the ale, beating with a wire whisk just until the batter is smooth.

When the suet is hot, dredge the onion rings by hand in the batter and carefully drop the rings into the fat, adding just as many rings at one time that can float without crowding on the surface of the fat.

Fry the onion rings, turning them once with a wire skimmer, until golden brown, 3 to 5 minutes. Remove them with the skimmer, drain on paper towels, and serve at once while you cook the remaining batches.

Blue Surround by
Richard Diebenkorn

CHAPTER THREE

HORS D'OEUVRES AND APPETIZERS

NEW POTATOES WITH AMERICAN CAVIARS

■

FOR 6 SERVINGS

6 small red new potatoes
Rendered beef suet or vegetable oil for
*   deep frying*
6 tablespoons sour cream
1 medium-size shallot, finely chopped
Salt and freshly ground white pepper
¼ cup Lake Superior (golden) caviar
2 tablespoons chopped fresh chives

WINE SUGGESTION

CALIFORNIA CHAMPAGNE—ANY GOOD
BLANC DE NOIRS OR BLANC DE BLANC,
SUCH AS THOSE FROM SHRAMSBERG OR
IRON HORSE—IS A NATURAL. OR USE A
REALLY WELL-BALANCED, FRESH-TASTING,
AND FULL-FLAVORED CHARDONNAY
SUCH AS ONE FROM GRGICH HILLS,
CHATEAU MONTELENA, OR SONOMA-
CUTRER.

THIS IS A PERFECT, ELEGANT HORS D'OEUVRE TO SERVE WITH CHAMPAGNE. For large parties, make them in small batches and keep sending them out to your guests while the potatoes are still warm.

The excellent domestic American caviars are so reasonably priced compared to imported varieties that this recipe is not as extravagant as it seems. I use either all of one kind of caviar, such as the golden caviar listed below, or a number of different kinds of caviars—salmon, trout, and American sturgeon.

Cut each potato in half. With a sharp-edged pointed teaspoon or a small melon-baller, scoop out each potato half to leave a shell about ¼ inch thick.

In a deep-fryer or heavy skillet, heat the suet or oil to 375°F on a deep-frying thermometer. Fry the potato shells until golden brown, 2 to 3 minutes. Drain well on paper towels. (If you prefer, you may brush the shells lightly with oil and bake them in a preheated 475°F oven for about 15 minutes.)

Stir together the sour cream and chopped shallot. Season to taste with salt and pepper.

Spoon the sour cream mixture into the potato shells. Top each potato with a teaspoon of golden caviar. Garnish with a sprinkling of chives. Serve immediately.

DUCK LIVER MOUSSE ON WALNUT TOAST

■

FOR 6 SERVINGS

3 tablespoons walnut oil
12 medium-size duck livers, trimmed
6 medium-size shallots, finely
    chopped
1 tablespoon fresh thyme leaves
¼ cup Calvados
¼ cup Cognac
¾ cup walnut halves
10 tablespoons (1¼ sticks) unsalted
    butter
1 firm red apple, peeled, cored, and
    thinly sliced
¾ cup granulated sugar
Salt and freshly ground white pepper
3 slices Walnut Bread, each ¼ inch
    thick (see page 35), cut into
    quarters to make 12 rectangles
2 tablespoons chopped fresh chives

WINE SUGGESTION
THE COMBINATION OF THESE RICH,
NUTTY, FRUITY FLAVORS CALLS FOR A
GOOD, DRY CALIFORNIA
GEWÜRZTRAMINER—ONE WITH
GENEROUS FRUITINESS AND SPICE BUT
WITHOUT EXCESSIVE SWEETNESS;
CLAIBORNE & CHURCHILL OR JOSEPH
WELLS ARE FINE. YOU COULD ALSO SERVE
A GOOD ALSATIAN GEWÜRZTRAMINER OR
RIESLING, SUCH AS THOSE FROM HUGEL
OR TRIMBACH.

DUCK LIVER, APPLE, SHALLOTS, CALVADOS, COGNAC, AND BUTTER ARE combined here to make a perfect cocktail appetizer. A butcher shop that carries good poultry should be able to supply you with duck livers.

Serve any extra mousse with endive spears and walnuts.

In a large skillet, heat the oil over moderately high heat until very hot. Add the livers and sauté them for about 3 minutes. Add the shallots and thyme and sauté a few seconds more, then transfer the mixture to the bowl of a food processor.

Add the Calvados and Cognac to the skillet and stir and scrape with a wooden spoon to deglaze the pan. Pour the juices over the livers.

Place the walnut halves on a baking sheet and toast in a preheated 350°F oven for about 10 minutes, stirring occasionally.

In a separate skillet, melt the butter over low heat. Add the apple slices and sauté until they begin to soften. Then add the sugar and continue cooking, stirring occasionally, until the apples are caramel-brown in color, 7 to 10 minutes.

Add the apples and all but 12 of the walnut halves to the livers in the processor. Process until finely pureed.

Press the puree through a very fine sieve. Season to taste with salt and pepper, then pack the mixture into a terrine. Let the mousse cool to room temperature, then chill it in the refrigerator for at least 1 hour.

Preheat the broiler and toast the walnut bread on the broiler tray until evenly browned, turning the rectangles over once.

Spread the mousse generously on the toast rectangles. Top each with a walnut half and dip an end into the chopped chives.

SHRIMP ON LETTUCE LEAVES WITH JALAPEÑO-CILANTRO-LIME SALSA

■

FOR 6 SERVINGS

12 Santa Barbara shrimp, shelled and
    deveined
1½ tablespoons clarified butter (see
    page 23)
Salt and freshly ground white pepper
1 head Bibb lettuce, separated to get
    12 perfect leaves
6 tablespoons Jalapeño-Cilantro-Lime
    Salsa (see page 33)

TRADITIONALLY, HORS D'OEUVRES HAVE ALWAYS FEATURED SOME SORT of meat or have included some sort of bread or pastry. I created this recipe, as well as the ahi one that follows, in an effort to offer new hors d'oeuvres that are lighter and more refreshing.

Use Santa Barbaras or other large, plump shrimp for this hors d'oeuvre.

Preheat the grill or broiler until very hot.
    Brush the shrimp with the melted butter and season lightly with salt and pepper. Grill them about 1½ minutes per side.

Arrange the lettuce leaves on a serving platter or plates and place a shrimp at the center of each leaf. Spoon the salsa over each shrimp and serve immediately.

SHRIMP ON LETTUCE
LEAVES

NEW POTATOES WITH
AMERICAN CAVIARS

DUCK LIVER MOUSSE ON
WALNUT TOAST

AHI ON LETTUCE LEAVES WITH GINGER AND LIME

■

FOR 6 SERVINGS

AHI ON LETTUCE
LEAVES WITH GINGER
AND LIME

1 tablespoon balsamic vinegar

1 teaspoon freshly grated ginger

½ lime, juiced

Salt and freshly ground white pepper

3 tablespoons extra-virgin olive oil

12 ounces fresh raw ahi tuna, well
    chilled

1 small head Bibb lettuce, separated
    to get 12 perfect leaves

1 each small red and yellow bell
    peppers, top and bottom cut off,
    seeded and grilled (see page 27),
    cut into ⅛-inch-wide strips

2 tablespoons chopped fresh chives

FOIE GRAS SAUTÉ ON
WALNUT TOAST

THIS IS A PERFECT LITTLE FINGER FOOD, WITH EACH PIECE OF FISH—RAW, like Japanese sashimi—served inside a small lettuce leaf.

Start with a beautiful piece of ahi tuna (or the best, freshest tuna of any variety you can find)—it must be absolutely fresh—bloodred, firm, and moist. The combination of ginger and lime with the rich fish is a clear knockout.

WINE SUGGESTION

THE STRONG, SPICY FLAVORS OF A MEXICAN-INFLUENCED DISH SUCH AS THIS CALL FOR A FULL-BODIED, OAKY, DRY CALIFORNIA FUMÉ BLANC SUCH AS THOSE FROM GRGICH HILLS OR MATANZAS CREEK. YOU COULD ALSO SERVE A WHITE RHÔNE WINE SUCH AS CONDRIEU OR HERMITAGE.

In a small mixing bowl, stir together the vinegar and ginger. Stir in the lime juice, and salt and pepper to taste. Gradually whisk in the olive oil.

Thinly slice the tuna into 12 equal pieces. Arrange the lettuce leaves on a serving platter or plates and place a piece of tuna at the center of each leaf. Cross a red and yellow pepper strip on top of each piece of tuna.

Spoon the dressing over the tuna and sprinkle each piece with chopped chives.

FOIE GRAS SAUTÉ ON WALNUT TOAST

■

FOR 6 SERVINGS

3 slices Walnut Bread, each ¼ inch
   thick (see page 35), cut into
   quarters to make 12 rectangles
6 ounces fresh duck foie gras,
   trimmed and cut into 12 slices
   (about 2 × 1 × ⅓ inches)
Salt and freshly ground white pepper

WINE SUGGESTION
ANY REALLY GOOD WINE WILL TASTE
ABSOLUTELY WONDERFUL WITH THIS, BUT
IT'S A NATURAL FOR A REALLY GREAT
BRUT OR BLANC DE NOIRS CHAMPAGNE
LIKE LOUIS ROEDERER CRISTAL. IT'S ALSO
GOOD WITH A BIG, BUTTERY-FLAVORED
CHARDONNAY WITH A GOOD BALANCE
OF ACIDITY, CRISPNESS, LUSHNESS, AND
FRESHNESS—GRGICH HILLS, CHATEAU
MONTELENA, AND SONOMA-CUTRER ARE
GOOD CHOICES.

THIS HORS D'OEUVRE IS ONE OF THE PUREST EXAMPLES OF MY BELIEF that simple cooking shows off ingredients at their natural best. Slices of fresh foie gras are seared extremely quickly in a hot skillet, placed on fingers of toasted walnut bread, seasoned with salt and white pepper, and served immediately.

The simple preparation belies the wonderfully complex results. You get three distinctly different but complementary flavors—the nuttiness of the toast, the rich, earthy taste of the foie gras, and the sharp accent of the pepper. There are the contrasting textures of the crunchy crusts and the juice-soaked centers of the toast squares, and that of the crisp surface and incomparably smooth interior of the liver. And the colors combine in a strikingly subtle interplay of earth-toned beiges and browns.

As always, I prefer the excellent duck fois gras from New York, which has a richer, earthier taste than goose fois gras. No fat is needed to sauté the buttery liver, which exudes its own sauce in the brief time it cooks.

Preheat the broiler and toast the walnut bread on the broiler tray until evenly browned, turning the rectangles once.

While the bread is toasting, heat a large skillet over moderately high heat. When the skillet is hot, add 6 slices of foie gras. Cook them quickly, until lightly browned, no more then 30 seconds per side, turning them with a metal spatula. (Do not overcook the foie gras; it will turn bitter.)

The instant the foie gras is done, transfer each slice to a piece of walnut toast. With a teaspoon, quickly spoon up the juices from the skillet and lightly moisten each slice of foie gras with some of the juices. Sprinkle lightly with salt and white pepper and serve them immediately while you prepare the second batch.

MICHAEL'S RAW OYSTER PRESENTATION

■

FOR 6 SERVINGS

12 each of three different types of fresh oysters, scrubbed
12 slices, each ¼ inch thick, Walnut Bread (see page 35)
2 lemons, quartered lengthwise into 4 wedges each

WINE SUGGESTION
THE FINE, FLINTY FLAVOR OF A GOOD CALIFORNIA BLANC DE BLANCS CHAMPAGNE IS A PERFECT COMPLEMENT TO THE CLEAN, BRINY FLAVORS OF THE OYSTERS; CHOOSE A SCHRAMSBERG, SCHARFFENBERGER, OR IRON HORSE. YOU CAN ALSO SERVE A FUMÉ BLANC OR SAUVIGNON BLANC WITH A FLINTY, GRASSY FLAVOR AND FAIRLY HIGH ACIDITY, SUCH AS THOSE FROM IRON HORSE OR BRANDER.

ONE OF THE MAIN PROBLEMS WHEN WE OPENED THE RESTAURANT WAS getting oysters to serve on the half shell; there were really no West Coast oysters to be found on a commercial basis. In the past few years, however, there has been a big renaissance in the cultivation of oysters in California and the Pacific Northwest. Whole businesses blossomed, and now there is a whole new range of oysters to choose from, all with entirely different tastes and textures than those you find on the East Coast—Olympia Bays from Washington, which had been almost extinct; Belons, which couldn't be found here at all but are now farmed in Bodega and Tomales bays in California; Northwestern Portuguese oysters, called kumomotos; and so on.

As a result, we decided that a selection of fresh oysters on the half shell would become a permanent part of our menu—a classic presentation on a bed of crushed ice. We serve them either in individual platters at table, with a Cristofle silver oyster fork—cupped like a spoon—along with wedges of lemon and triangles of walnut toast; or we pass them as an hors d'oeuvre before guests sit down. For a large party you can set up an oyster bar, with all the oysters arranged on a mound of ice and someone opening them continuously; have plenty of lemon wedges, as well as chopped shallots for those who want to sprinkle a little on top.

Fold a towel several times and use it to get a firm grip on an oyster, holding the mollusk in the palm of your weaker hand, with the flatter half of the shell up and the hinged lip of the oyster facing upward toward you. Carefully force the blade of a good, sturdy oyster knife through the hinge, prying the two halves of the shell apart. Cut all around the edge of the shells to remove the top half.

Move the knife beneath the oyster to cut through the membranes and free it completely from the shell. Leave it in the lower half of the shell, taking care not to lose any of the oyster liquid, and place the shell on a large tray. Continue with the remaining oysters, then cover them with plastic wrap and chill for at least 30 minutes.

Fill individual shallow soup plates or a large, shallow serving platter with a 1-inch-thick layer of crushed ice. Carefully arrange the oysters on the bed of ice.

Toast the walnut bread slices in a toaster or broiler until golden. Put them in a folded napkin to keep warm.

Place the lemon wedges around the sides of each plate of oysters and serve immediately with the walnut toast.

GRAVLAX WITH MUSTARD DILL MAYONNAISE

•

FOR 6 SERVINGS

1½ pounds salmon, cut from the
    thickest part and filleted
12 bunches fresh dill, finely chopped
⅓ cup each salt, freshly ground
    white pepper, and granulated
    sugar
Mustard Dill Mayonnaise (recipe
    follows)
6 small fresh dill sprigs
1 large lemon, thinly sliced, slices
    cut in half
12 slices Brioche (see page 36),
    toasted

WINE SUGGESTION
THIS IS VERY GOOD WITH A REASONABLY
MATURE CALIFORNIA CHARDONNAY,
TWO, THREE, OR FOUR YEARS OLD, WITH
A SLIGHT TO MODERATE BUTTERINESS.
TRY ACACIA, CHAPPELLET, OR JORDAN.
OR SERVE A GOOD CHAMPAGNE SUCH AS
TAITTINGER OR SCHRAMSBERG.

WHEN I RETURNED TO AMERICA FROM PARIS IN 1974, I STOPPED IN NEW York and ate at George Lang's Cafe des Artistes. That was where I first tasted gravlax. Lang prepared this cured, thinly sliced salmon in the traditional Scandinavian way—using aquavit to moisten the fish during curing, and serving it with a sweet mustard dill sauce.

I've come up with a more American/French version, omitting the aquavit and dressing the sliced salmon with creamy French-style mayonnaise flavored with Dijon mustard and fresh dill. It's a terrific first course—light, clean, and delicate—and goes great with champagne or white wine. It also makes a wonderful hors d'oeuvre served on toasted fingers of brioche.

Place the salmon, flesh side up, on a work surface. With your fingertips, carefully feel for the tiny bones extending from the thickest part of the fillet; with tweezers, pull out the bones.

With a small, sharp knife, score the skin side of the salmon fillet just deep enough to break the skin in diagonal lines about 1 inch apart.

Stir together the chopped dill, salt, pepper, and sugar. Spread half of this mixture in the bottom of a shallow baking dish or pan just large enough to hold the salmon.

Place the salmon, skin down, inside the dish. Spread the remaining dill mixture on top, packing it evenly around the sides of the fillet.

Cover the salmon fillet with a large sheet of plastic wrap, pressing the plastic down against the salmon and the dill mixture that surrounds it. Place a large sheet of aluminum foil on top, and bring it up to the rim of the dish, crimping to seal it.

Place another baking dish, just small enough to fit inside the first, on top of the covered salmon fillet. Place several kitchen weights or large water-filled jars or crocks inside the second dish to weigh it down and keep the salmon submerged in its juices while it cures.

Leave the salmon to cure in the refrigerator for at least 48 hours and no longer than 72 hours.

To serve the gravlax, unwrap it and remove the salmon fillet from the pan. Brush off the dill mixture and place the fillet on a carving board. With a long, sharp knife, held almost parallel to the surface of the fillet, cut the salmon into long, tissue-thin slices. Cover each chilled serving plate with a layer of salmon slices. Spoon a line of mustard dill mayonnaise across the center of each plate and garnish the sauce with a dill sprig. Place 4 half-slices of lemon around each plate. Serve with toasted brioche.

MUSTARD DILL MAYONNAISE

■

FOR ABOUT 1½ CUPS

1 large egg yolk
1 tablespoon Dijon mustard
1 tablespoon champagne vinegar
1 cup peanut oil
1 to 2 teaspoons fresh lemon juice
½ tablespoon water, optional
1 bunch fresh dill, leaves finely
    chopped
Salt and freshly ground white pepper

THIS MAYONNAISE SAUCE IS EASIEST TO MAKE IF ALL THE INGREDIENTS and utensils are at room temperature before you start.

In a medium-size mixing bowl, whisk together the egg yolk, mustard, and vinegar until smooth and light yellow in color.

Whisking continuously, pour in the oil in a very slow, steady stream, increasing the flow slightly as the mayonnaise begins to thicken.

Stir in lemon juice to taste and, if the sauce seems too thick, the water. Stir in the dill and season to taste with salt and white pepper.

SEAFOOD TERRINE WITH TWO SAUCES

■

FOR 6 SERVINGS

2¼ pounds fresh wall-eyed pike fillets
1 teaspoon salt, or to taste
1 teaspoon freshly ground white
    pepper, or to taste
2¼ cups heavy cream
2 bunches watercress, stems
    discarded, 12 sprigs reserved
5 tablespoons unsalted butter, at
    room temperature
2 ounces thin French-style green
    beans (haricots verts), trimmed
6 ounces freshly cooked shelled
    lobster meat
1½ cups Tomato Concasse (see page
    42)
1 cup Watercress Mayonnaise (recipe
    follows)

SOPHISTICATED, DELICATE, LIGHT, AND DELICIOUS—THIS IS ONE OF THE greatest cold appetizers on the face of the planet. I always loved the classic pike mousselines of Fernand Point, and they were the inspiration for this lighter version—without all the classic French complication like pâte à choux and eggs. All you need is good, fresh wall-eyed pike, enriched with cream and a little butter. Fresh lobster adds contrast to the pike mixture; you can substitute an equal amount of salmon, sea or bay scallops, shrimp, John Dory, or snapper if you like.

I serve the terrine with complementary sauces—a Tomato Concasse with lots of fresh basil, and a light Watercress Mayonnaise. It's a knife-and-fork appetizer, served without bread.

Start the terrine a day in advance, and complete its preparation the morning before you plan to serve it, allowing sufficient time to chill it.

Put the pike in a food processor with the metal blade and process until pureed. Add the salt and pepper and pulse to blend. With the machine running, slowly pour in half the cream, stopping when it is thoroughly blended.

With a rubber spatula, press the puree through a fine-mesh sieve. Put it in a stainless-steel or glass bowl, cover with plastic wrap, and chill in the refrigerator overnight.

The next morning, whip the remaining cream with a wire whisk or electric beater until soft peaks form. With a rubber spatula, gradually fold the whipped cream into the fish mixture until smoothly blended.

Bring a medium-size saucepan of lightly salted water to a boil. Add the watercress leaves and, as soon as the water returns to a boil, drain well. Finely chop the watercress.

Coat the bottom and sides of a 1½-quart ovenproof glass loaf pan with 2 tablespoons of butter. Line the bottom of the pan with the watercress. Put about a third of the pike mixture in the bottom of the pan; use a rubber spatula to pack it down and eliminate air pockets and to smooth its surface.

Neatly place half the French beans lengthwise on top of the pike layer; cover them with a ½-inch layer of the pike mixture. Arrange the lobster meat lengthwise along the center third of the loaf pan. Then cover with another ½-inch layer of the pike mixture and arrange the remaining beans on top.

Pack and smooth the remaining pike mixture in the loaf pan. Melt another 1 tablespoon butter in a small saucepan and brush it evenly over the surface of the terrine.

Preheat the oven to 325°F.

Put 2 cups of water in a metal baking pan larger than the loaf pan. Bring the pan of water to a boil over medium heat. Place the loaf pan in the baking pan and bring the water back to a boil.

Fold a sheet of heavy aluminum foil to make a tent that fits over the terrine. Puncture a few holes in the foil and rub the remaining 2 tablespoons butter on one side. Place the tent, buttered side down, over the terrine. Carefully transfer the terrine, inside its water bath, to the oven; bake for 1 hour, then remove from the oven.

Let the terrine cool in its water bath for about 1 hour. Transfer the terrine to the refrigerator to chill for several hours.

To unmold the terrine, fill the sink with hot water and dip the loaf pan in it for a few seconds to loosen the sides. Invert a platter over the pan; holding the platter and pan securely together, invert them and lift off the pan.

With a very sharp knife, cut the terrine crosswise into ½-inch-thick slices. Serve on chilled plates with the concasse on one side and the watercress sauce on the other. Garnish with watercress sprigs.

WATERCRESS MAYONNAISE

■

FOR ABOUT 2 CUPS

2 *bunches watercress, stemmed*
1 *large egg yolk*
1 *tablespoon Dijon mustard*
1 *tablespoon champagne vinegar*
1 *cup peanut oil*
1 to 2 *teaspoons fresh lemon juice*
½ *tablespoon water, optional*
Salt and freshly ground white pepper

THIS MAYONNAISE SAUCE IS EASIEST TO MAKE IF ALL THE INGREDIENTS and utensils are at room temperature before you start.

Bring a medium-size saucepan of lightly salted water to a boil. Add the watercress leaves and, as soon as the water returns to a boil, drain well. Finely chop the watercress.

In a medium-size mixing bowl, whisk together the egg yolk, mustard, and vinegar until smooth and light yellow in color.

Whisking continuously, pour in the oil in a very slow, steady stream, increasing the flow slightly as the mayonnaise begins to thicken.

Stir in lemon juice to taste and, if the sauce seems too thick, the water. Stir in the watercress and season to taste with salt and white pepper.

FEUILLETÉ OF ASPARAGUS WITH BEURRE BLANC

■

FOR 6 SERVINGS

6 Feuilletés (see pages 38–39)
1½ cups Beurre Blanc (see page 29)
¼ cup Beurre Rose (see page 29), optional
3 dozen baby asparagus spears, trimmed to the length of the feuilletés
2 tablespoons chopped fresh chives

WINE SUGGESTION
SERVE A LIGHT, CRISP CHARDONNAY SUCH AS A TREFETHEN, ROBERT MONDAVI RESERVE, OR CLOS PEGASE.

WHEN FRESH ASPARAGUS—EITHER GREEN OR WHITE, JUMBO OR BABY—comes into season, this is an absolutely spectacular, elegant way to present it.

If you bake the feuilletés well in advance and they've turned cold, split and warm them in a 350°F oven for about 10 minutes before you fill and serve them.

Prepare and bake the feuilletés and set them aside.

Prepare the beurre blanc—and, if you like, the beurre rose—and keep warm.

Bring a large saucepan of lightly salted water to a boil. Add the asparagus and boil them until just tender, about 3 minutes. Drain well.

Split each feuilleté in half. Put a bottom half on each heated serving plate. Place the asparagus on top. Spoon the beurre blanc over the asparagus and around the feuilleté. If you like, spoon a little beurre rose onto the beurre blanc on the plate and use the tip of a small knife to swirl it into a decorative pattern. Scatter the chives over the sauce and place the top halves of the feuilletés on top of the asparagus.

FEUILLETÉ OF SCALLOPS
WITH SPINACH AND
BEURRE BLANC

FEUILLETÉ OF SALMON
WITH SPINACH AND
BEURRE BLANC

FEUILLETÉ OF SCALLOPS OR SALMON WITH SPINACH AND BEURRE BLANC

■

FOR 6 SERVINGS

6 Feuilletés (see pages 38–39)
1½ cups Beurre Blanc (see page 29)
¼ cup Beurre Rose (see page 29),
    optional
2 bunches spinach, leaves stemmed,
    ribbed, and thoroughly washed
4 tablespoons (½ stick) unsalted
    butter
Salt and freshly ground white pepper
12 giant sea scallops (1 to 1¼
    pounds), or 1¼ pounds salmon
    fillet, cut into 6 equal pieces
2 tablespoons clarified butter (see
    page 23)
2 tablespoons chopped fresh chives

WINE SUGGESTION
THE RICHNESS OF THIS COMBINATION
WOULD OVERWHELM ANYTHING BUT A
BIG, WELL-AGED FRENCH WHITE
BURGUNDY SUCH AS A CORTON-
CHARLEMAGNE OR ONE OF THE
MONTRACHETS, OR A BIG, BUTTERY
CALIFORNIA CHARDONNAY WITH
SLIGHTLY LOWER THAN NORMAL
ACIDITY, SUCH AS CHALONE, WOLTNER,
OR FORMAN.

IMAGINE A SCALLOP OR SALMON SANDWICH—GREAT BIG SEA SCALLOPS or rich, bright pink salmon fillets, grilled and served on a bed of spinach inside a crisp, buttery feuilleté. This dish has that perfect combination of tastes and textures to get a meal off to a great start.

If you bake the feuilletés well in advance and they've turned cold, split and warm them in a 350°F oven for about 10 minutes before you fill and serve them.

Prepare and bake the feuilletés and set them aside.

Prepare the beurre blanc—and, if you like, the beurre rose —and keep warm.

Preheat the grill or broiler until very hot.

Bring a large saucepan of lightly salted water to a boil. Add the spinach and, as soon as the water returns to a boil, drain well. Return the drained spinach to the pan and, over low heat, stir it several times with the butter, and season with salt and pepper to taste.

Brush the scallops or salmon with the clarified butter and season with salt and pepper. Grill the scallops about 1 minute per side or the salmon for about 4 minutes per side, until firm but still moist inside; halfway through the cooking on each side, rotate the seafood 90 degrees to give it crosshatched grill marks.

Split each feuilleté in half. Put a bottom half on each heated serving plate. Place a dollop of spinach on top, and then two scallops or a piece of salmon. Spoon the beurre blanc over the scallops and around the feuilleté. If you like, spoon a little beurre rose onto the beurre blanc on the plate and use the tip of a small knife to swirl it into a decorative pattern. Scatter the chives over the sauce and place the top halves of the feuilletés on top of the scallops.

SHAD ROE WITH MAUI ONION CONFIT AND LARDONS

■

FOR 6 SERVINGS

1½ cups Maui Onion Confit (see
    page 41)
3 slices, each ¼ inch thick, smoked
    slab bacon, as lean as possible
¼ cup extra-virgin olive oil
4 tablespoons clarified butter (see
    page 23)
3 whole shad roes, each separated
    into 2 separate sacks
Salt and freshly ground white pepper
1 bunch watercress, stems discarded

WINE SUGGESTION

POUR A REALLY BIG CHARDONNAY,
YOUNG OR OLD, WITH PLENTY OF OAK,
GOOD FRUIT, AND BUTTER—SUCH AS
CHALONE OR RIDGE.

GROWING UP IN NEW YORK STATE, I DEVELOPED A REAL TASTE FOR SHAD roe, a seasonal delicacy of the spring, when the shad are spawning. It's impeccable—very rich, like any caviar. Sautéed whole as it comes in the roe sack, medium-rare, it's meaty and satisfying; in an odd way, comparable to the experience of eating a really good cheeseburger.

Whole shad roe comes in two separate, self-contained lobes. Be careful not to break up an individual lobe, or the roe will fall apart. Shad roe has a very short season—about a month in spring, the exact time varying from year to year. And though frozen shad roe isn't bad, and can be purchased from good seafood shops or markets, it's worth it to keep an eye out for that moment when the fresh roe is available. When it is, I think it's something you should really indulge in and eat every day; for that reason, I've devised the following three recipes to showcase it.

Be careful not to overcook the roe. You want to sauté it fast, crisp on the outside, with a line of almost cold roe running through the middle; longer cooking will turn it mealy and unappetizing.

In this recipe the Maui confit and crisp lardons complements the shad roe's rich, sweet, satisfying flavor.

Prepare the confit and keep it warm.

On a preheated grill or in a skillet over medium heat, cook the bacon until golden, about 2 minutes per side. Drain on paper towels. Cut the bacon crosswise into thin julienne strips.

In a large skillet, heat the olive oil and butter together over medium heat. Season the shad roe with salt and pepper and sauté until golden brown, 2 to 3 minutes per side.

Place a shad roe on each heated serving plate. Spoon the onion confit alongside the roe and sprinkle with bacon. Garnish each plate with watercress.

SHAD ROE WITH POMMERY MUSTARD CREAM SAUCE AND BASIL

■

FOR 6 SERVINGS

1½ cups Pommery Mustard Cream
    Sauce (recipe follows)
¼ cup extra-virgin olive oil
4 tablespoons clarified butter (see
    page 23)
3 whole shad roes, each separated
    into 2 separate sacks
Salt and freshly ground white pepper
3 tablespoons julienne of fresh basil
1 bunch watercress, stems discarded

SINCE I LIKEN THE SENSATION OF PROPERLY COOKED SHAD ROE TO A good burger, it seemed logical to serve it with a mustard sauce, which complements its meatiness.

See the note on page 63 regarding the importance of cooking shad roe medium-rare.

Prepare the mustard cream sauce and keep it warm.

In a large skillet, heat the olive oil and clarified butter together over medium heat. Season the shad roe with salt and pepper and sauté until golden brown, 2 to 3 minutes per side.

Place a shad roe on each heated serving plate. Spoon the sauce alongside the roe and sprinkle with basil. Garnish each plate with watercress.

WINE SUGGESTION

TO GO WITH THIS RICH COMBINATION, POUR A GREAT BLANC DE NOIRS CALIFORNIA CHAMPAGNE SUCH AS SCHRAMSBERG, IRON HORSE, DOMAINE MUMM, OR DOMAINE CHANDON.

POMMERY MUSTARD CREAM SAUCE

•

FOR ABOUT 2 CUPS

THIS IS A VARIATION ON MY CHARDONNAY CREAM SAUCE II, WITH THE addition of whole-grain Pommery-style mustard.

¾ cup California Chardonnay
1 medium-size shallot, finely chopped
2 cups heavy cream
2 tablespoons Pommery mustard
Salt and freshly ground white pepper
Fresh lemon juice

In a small, heavy, nonaluminum saucepan, boil the Chardonnay with the shallot over high heat until only about 2 tablespoons of liquid are left, 5 to 7 minutes. Then add the cream, reduce the heat slightly, and simmer until the sauce is thick and reduced by about a third, 7 to 10 minutes more. Whisk in the mustard and season to taste with salt, pepper, and a little lemon juice.

SHAD ROE WITH MAUI
ONION CONFIT AND
LARDONS

SHAD ROE WITH GIANT
CAPERS AND LEMON
BUTTER

SHAD ROE WITH GIANT CAPERS AND LEMON BUTTER

■

FOR 6 SERVINGS

½ pound (2 sticks) unsalted butter,
    cut into cubes
1 lemon, halved and seeded
Salt and freshly ground white pepper
¼ cup extra-virgin olive oil
4 tablespoons clarified butter (see
    page 23)
3 whole shad roes, each separated
    into 2 separate sacks
¼ cup giant Spanish capers, drained
1 bunch watercress, stems discarded

THE TART, RICH LEMON BUTTER AND THE SWEET, TANGY GIANT SPAN-
ish capers offer an excellent contrast to the richness of shad roe.

See the note on page 63 on the importance of cooking shad roe
medium-rare.

In a small saucepan, melt the butter over low heat. Squeeze in the
juice of the lemon and season to taste with salt and pepper.

In a large skillet, heat the olive oil and clarified butter together
over medium heat. Season the shad roe with salt and pepper and
sauté until golden brown, 2 to 3 minutes per side.

Place a shad roe on each heated serving plate. Spoon the lemon
butter over and alongside the roe and sprinkle with capers. Garnish
each plate with watercress.

WINE SUGGESTION

TO COMPLEMENT THE TART
ACCOMPANIMENTS, SERVE A CRISP
YOUNG CHARDONNAY OR FUMÉ BLANC
FROM IRON HORSE, CLOS PEGASE, OR
CHIMNEY ROCK.

JOHN DORY WITH GOLDEN CAVIAR

■

FOR 6 SERVINGS

1½ cups Chardonnay Cream Sauce I
(see pages 30–31)
6 whole baby John Dory, skinned and
filleted, bones reserved
3 tablespoons clarified butter (see
page 23)
Salt and freshly ground white pepper
1½ tablespoons American golden
(whitefish) caviar
2 tablespoons chopped fresh chives

JOHN DORY IS AN ELEGANT FISH WITH VERY LIGHT, DELICATE WHITE flesh that goes perfectly with the Chardonnay Cream Sauce and golden caviar. Baby John Dory, flown in fresh from New Zealand and now widely available in the United States, are the perfect size for an appetizer.

Prepare the sauce and keep it warm.
Preheat the grill or broiler until very hot.
Brush the John Dory fillets with the butter and season them with salt and pepper. Grill them for about 1½ minutes per side, until browned but still very moist in the center.
Spoon the sauce into the center of each heated serving plate. Place two John Dory fillets side by side on each plate. Spoon the caviar on top of the fillets. Garnish with chives.

WINE SUGGESTIONS
SERVE A FAIRLY LIGHT CHARDONNAY
THAT WILL GO WITH THE SAUCE BUT NOT
OVERPOWER THE FISH—SAY A
TREFETHEN, ACACIA "CARNEROS,"
ROBERT MONDAVI RESERVE, OR CLOS
PEGASE.

SOFTSHELL CRAB WITH GIANT CAPERS AND BEURRE BLANC

■

FOR 6 SERVINGS

¾ cup Beurre Blanc (see page 29)

¼ cup all-purpose flour

Salt and freshly ground white pepper

6 baby softshell crabs (2 to 3 ounces
    each)

4 tablespoons clarified butter (see
    page 23)

Shoestring Potatoes (see page 43)

3 tablespoons giant Spanish capers,
    drained

1 bunch watercress, stemmed

SOFTSHELL CRABS, SAUTEED AND EATEN SHELL AND ALL, ARE ONE OF the world's great delicacies. When you're buying them, ask for ''roaches''—the term for the really tiny ones—which have the finest flavor and texture. Beurre blanc and capers are classic accompaniments for their rich, sweet flavor.

Though you can use any capers for this recipe, the very best ones are the giant capers from Spain, which have a sweet flavor that complements the crabs and the sauce.

You can ask your fishmonger to clean the crabs for you, but if you buy them live, they're easy to clean. Put each crab on your work surface and, with a sharp knife, cut off the face section. Then lift off the shell to expose the gills and sand receptacle; cut or scrape them out. Rinse the crabs and pat them dry before cooking.

This recipe can also be served as a main course, with three or four little crabs to the serving.

Prepare the beurre blanc and keep it warm.

Spread the flour, seasoned with salt and pepper, on a plate. Turn the crabs in the flour to coat them lightly but evenly.

In a medium-size skillet, heat the clarified butter over medium to high heat until very hot. Add the crabs upside down and sauté them for 1½ minutes; with tongs, turn them and sauté them, for 1½ minutes more, until crisp and golden brown.

While the crabs are sautéing, deep-fry the shoestring potato garnish and stir the capers into the beurre blanc.

Place a crab on the bottom half of each heated serving plate and spoon the beurre blanc with capers around it. Mound the shoestring potatoes on the top half of the plate. Garnish with sprigs of watercress.

SOFTSHELL CRAB WITH GINGER AND LIME

■

FOR 6 SERVINGS

¼ cup all-purpose flour
Salt and freshly ground white pepper
6 baby softshell crabs, (2 to 3 ounces
    each), cleaned (see page 68)
4 tablespoons clarified butter (see
    page 23)
Shoestring Potatoes (see page 43)
1 lime, halved
2 tablespoons freshly grated ginger
1 bunch watercress, stemmed, or 2
    tablespoons chopped fresh
    cilantro leaves

THE SAUCE FOR THESE SOFTSHELL CRABS WAS INSPIRED BY SOME OF THE seafood dishes served by Michael Chow of the Mr. Chow restaurants.

Spread the flour, seasoned with salt and pepper, on a plate. Turn the crabs in the flour to coat them lightly but evenly.

In a medium-size skillet, heat the clarified butter over medium to high heat until very hot. Add the crabs upside down and sauté them for 1½ minutes; with tongs, turn them and sauté about 1½ minutes more, until crisp and golden brown.

While the crabs are sautéing, deep-fry the shoestring potato garnish.

With the tongs, remove the crabs from the skillet and place a crab on the lower half of each heated serving plate. Remove the skillet from the heat and squeeze the lime juice into the skillet; stir and scrape with a wooden spoon to deglaze the pan deposits, then stir in the ginger and immediately spoon the lime-ginger sauce over the crabs. Mound the shoestring potatoes on the top half of each plate. Garnish with sprigs of watercress or the chopped cilantro.

WINE SUGGESTION
A REALLY YOUNG CHARDONNAY WITH
LOTS OF OAK, ACIDITY, AND ALCOHOL—
SAY, ONE FROM MATANZAS CREEK,
SINSKEY, OR GRGICH HILLS—GOES GREAT
WITH THE GINGER AND LIME. THE GINGER
SEEMS TO MAKE THE WINE TASTE LIKE IT
WILL AFTER IT HAS AGED A FEW YEARS.

FOIE GRAS SAUTÉ WITH SHERRY WINE VINEGAR SAUCE

■

FOR 6 SERVINGS

3 medium-size shallots, finely
    chopped
1 cup sherry wine vinegar
½ cup duck stock (see page 22)
2 tablespoons heavy cream
Salt and freshly ground white pepper
36 medium-size spinach leaves,
    washed, stemmed, and blanched
    in boiling water
12 ounces fresh duck foie gras, sliced
    into 6 thick slabs
Chopped fresh chives

THE RICH, SWEET SHERRY WINE VINEGAR SAUCE SERVES AS THE PERFECT bridge between a fine wine and the buttery duck liver.

In a medium-size saucepan over moderate to high heat, boil the shallots in the vinegar until just a few tablespoons of vinegar remain, about 10 minutes.

Add the stock and cream to the pan, reduce the heat slightly, and simmer until the sauce is thick enough to coat a spoon, 5 to 7 minutes more. Season to taste with salt and pepper and keep the sauce warm.

Arrange the spinach leaves at the top of 6 heated appetizer plates.

Heat a heavy dry skillet over high heat. Lightly season the foie gras slices with salt and pepper, then add them to the pan and sear them quickly, about 30 seconds per side, so that they remain rare.

Place a slice of foie gras at the bottom of each plate and spoon the sauce around it. Sprinkle with chives.

WINE SUGGESTION
THIS ONE DEMANDS A REALLY GREAT
BRUT OR BLANC DE NOIRS CHAMPAGNE
LIKE LOUIS ROEDERER CRISTAL, OR A BIG,
BUTTERY CALIFORNIA CHARDONNAY
WITH GOOD ACIDITY, LUSHNESS, AND
FRESHNESS EVENLY BALANCED—GRGICH
HILLS, CHATEAU MONTELENA, AND
SONOMA-CUTRER, FOR EXAMPLE.

LOBSTER WITH BELUGA CAVIAR

■

FOR 6 SERVINGS

1½ cups Chardonnay Cream Sauce I
    (see pages 30–31)
6 live lobsters, 1 pound each
3 tablespoons clarified butter (see
    page 23)
Salt and freshly ground white pepper
3 tablespoons beluga or American
    sturgeon caviar

_____

WINE SUGGESTION
THE VERY BEST CALIFORNIA
CHARDONNAYS—SUCH AS THOSE FROM
MOUNT EDEN, STONY HILL, WOLTNER, OR
CHALONE—WILL BE SHOWN OFF
SPLENDIDLY WITH THIS APPETIZER.

ONE-POUND BABY LOBSTERS, KNOWN AS "CHICKEN" LOBSTERS, ARE THE perfect size for this elegant, sophisticated first course. It's not elaborate, it doesn't take a long time to prepare, yet it really makes a spectacular statement. It's great for special occasions like New Year's Eve or Christmas Eve—anytime you really want to do something classically correct.

Prepare the sauce and keep it warm.

Preheat the grill or broiler until very hot.

Meanwhile, put about 8 inches of water in a very large pot big enough to hold all the lobsters at once. Bring the water to a full boil. Add all the lobsters and boil them for 2 to 3 minutes.

Carefully remove the lobsters from the pot. Put each lobster on its back, legs up, and with a heavy, sharp knife, split it in half lengthwise. Hit each claw with a heavy mallet to crack it slightly. Remove the claw meat and the two halves of tail meat from each lobster.

Brush the lobster tails and claws with the butter and season them with salt and pepper. Grill or broil them until they are just cooked through but still moist, about 1 minute per side; halfway through the cooking on each side, rotate the pieces of lobster 90 degrees to give them crosshatched grill marks.

Arrange the lobster tails and claws on each heated serving plate. Ladle the sauce over them and garnish with caviar.

Chinese Mr. Hyde by
Charles Garabedian

CHAPTER FOUR
SOUPS

CALIFORNIA GAZPACHO

.

FOR 6 SERVINGS

6 cups tomato juice
1 each medium-size red and yellow
    tomato, peeled, seeded, and
    finely chopped (or 2 red
    tomatoes)
1 medium-size cucumber, seeded and
    finely diced
1 medium-size Maui onion, finely
    diced
½ each medium-size red and yellow
    bell pepper, stemmed, seeded,
    and finely diced
½ jalapeño chili, stemmed, seeded,
    and finely minced
½ bunch fresh cilantro, stemmed and
    finely chopped
1 medium-size garlic clove, finely
    chopped
1 lime, juiced
¼ cup extra-virgin olive oil
¼ cup Cabernet vinegar or white
    wine vinegar
Salt and freshly ground black pepper
3 tablespoons sour cream
6 small sprigs fresh cilantro

WHEN I WAS A KID, MY MOM USED TO MAKE THE GAZPACHO OUT OF *THE New York Times Cookbook.* I always liked the way the cool tomato soup had all those fresh little goodies in it. I've adapted my memories of that childhood gazpacho into the somewhat more fiery version here. The key to it, I feel, is to start with really impeccable ingredients; since you don't cook gazpacho, the soup has nothing to hide. Use a rich, high-quality tomato juice as your base; I like the Sacramento brand. If Maui onions aren't available in your area, Walla Walla, Vidalia, or a good sweet red onion will do.

In a large mixing bowl, combine the tomato juice with all the vegetables, the lime juice, olive oil, and vinegar. Cover and chill for several hours in the refrigerator. Season to taste with salt and pepper.

Ladle the soup into chilled serving bowls. Spoon a dollop of sour cream into each bowl and top with a sprig of cilantro.

CUCUMBER DILL SOUP

▪

FOR 6 SERVINGS

2 tablespoons unsalted butter

1 medium-size Maui onion, thinly
  sliced

3 medium-size cucumbers, peeled,
  halved lengthwise, seeded, and
  cut into chunks

2 bunches fresh dill, stemmed, 6
  small sprigs reserved

6 cups heavy cream

3 tablespoons sour cream

THIS IS ONE OF THE FEW COLD SOUPS—ALONG WITH VICHYSSOISE AND gazpacho—that I really like. The fresh, icy green taste of the cucumbers is enriched by cream, enhanced by the sweet flavor of Maui onion, and perfumed with fresh dill. You may substitute a Walla Walla, Vidalia, or a good sweet red onion if Maui onions aren't available in your area.

It's a genteel soup, a simple, elegant statement in white on white, and for me it conjures up images of Gatsby-style summer parties on well-manicured lawns.

Serve the soup ice cold, in chilled bowls.

Melt the butter in a small saucepan or skillet over moderate heat. Add the onion and sauté it until transparent, 3 to 5 minutes.

Put the onion, cucumbers, dill, and heavy cream in a blender or food processor and puree them together.

Pass the pureed soup through a fine-mesh sieve over a large mixing bowl, pressing with a rubber spatula, to give it a smooth, even consistency. Cover the bowl with plastic wrap and chill the soup in the refrigerator for several hours.

Half an hour before serving the soup, place soup bowls in the freezer to chill. Serve the soup in the chilled bowls, and garnish each serving with a dollop of sour cream and a sprig of dill.

CALIFORNIA GAZPACHO

CUCUMBER DILL SOUP

LEEK AND POTATO SOUP

•

FOR 6 SERVINGS

THIS IS ONE OF THE CLASSIC FRENCH COUNTRY SOUPS. SERVED HOT, AS below, it's wonderfully satisfying on a cold winter's day; chilled in the refrigerator, it is absolutely stunning in summer.

4 tablespoons (½ stick) unsalted
    butter
3 medium-size leeks, white parts
    only, halved lengthwise,
    thoroughly washed, and cut
    crosswise into ¼-inch pieces
3 cloves garlic, peeled and coarsely
    chopped
Salt
3 large baking potatoes (about 1½
    pounds total), peeled and cut
    into ½-inch pieces
1 cup water
6 cups heavy cream
Freshly ground white pepper
2 tablespoons chopped fresh chives

In a medium-size saucepan over medium heat, melt the butter. Add the leeks, garlic, and a pinch of salt and sauté, stirring frequently, until the leeks are soft but not yet browned, about 10 minutes.

Add the potatoes and water. Bring to a boil, then simmer until the potatoes have cooked through, 10 to 15 minutes more.

Add the cream and bring to a boil. Puree the mixture in a processor, then press it through a fine-mesh sieve. Return to the pan, warm it through, and season to taste with salt and pepper.

Serve in heated soup bowls, garnished with chives.

DEFINITIVE CORN CHOWDER WITH JALAPEÑO PEPPERS

■

FOR 6 SERVINGS

8 cups heavy cream
3 tablespoons unsalted butter
1 medium-size Maui onion, thinly
    sliced
1 medium-size clove garlic, finely
    chopped
6 medium-size ears corn, kernels
    removed
½ fresh jalapeño pepper, roasted (see
    page 27), peeled, seeded, and
    finely chopped
1 each medium-size red and yellow
    bell pepper, roasted (see page
    27), peeled, seeded, and diced
½ lime, juiced
3 tablespoons sour cream, optional
6 small sprigs fresh cilantro

WHEN I WAS STUDYING COOKING IN PARIS, IT SURPRISED ME TO LEARN that the French think of corn as pig feed and never eat it. I grew up on yellow summer sweet corn during my family's summers in Rhode Island and Wisconsin, and white corn while I was living in Illinois. I have great memories of the creamed corn my mom always served at Thanksgiving.

Cream and corn are a perfect match, and with this soup I've tried to take an old-fashioned, fairly pedestrian chowder and give it French refinement. The base of the soup is a classic French-style vegetable puree, blended with a reduction of heavy cream and flavored with sautéed onions. (Substitute a Walla Walla, Vidalia, or a good sweet red onion if Maui onions aren't available in your area.) Whole kernels of corn give it a chowder's trademark chunkiness. And the corn-and-cream combination is shown off in sharp relief by an addition I was introduced to by the Hispanics on Michael's kitchen staff—a lively seasoning of jalapeño peppers, lime juice, and cilantro.

This soup is superb when made with the white corn grown in the Midwest instead of the yellow sweet corn.

In a medium-size saucepan, bring the cream to a boil, then reduce the heat and simmer briskly until it reduces by one quarter, about 10 minutes.

Meanwhile, melt 2 tablespoons of the butter in a medium-size skillet over moderate heat. Add the onion and garlic and sauté just until soft, about 5 minutes. Add two thirds of the corn kernels and the jalapeño, and continue sautéing until the kernels are al dente, 3 to 5 minutes.

Put the reduced cream and the corn mixture into a processor or blender and puree smoothly. Press the soup through a fine-mesh sieve and return it to the saucepan.

In the skillet, melt the remaining butter over moderate heat and sauté the remaining corn kernels until al dente. Stir them into the soup with the roasted peppers and heat the soup through over low to moderate heat. Stir in the lime juice.

Ladle the soup into heated serving bowls. Garnish each serving with a dollop of sour cream, if you like, and a sprig of cilantro.

CREAM OF ASPARAGUS SOUP

•

FOR 6 SERVINGS

YOU CAN MAKE THIS CLASSIC SOUP WITH EITHER WHITE OR GREEN AS-paragus.

8 cups heavy cream
4 tablespoons (½ stick) unsalted
 butter
1 small Maui, Walla Walla, Vidalia,
 or sweet red onion, chopped
3 medium-size cloves garlic, chopped
3 pounds asparagus, ends trimmed,
 tips cut off and set aside, stalks
 cut into ½-inch pieces
Salt and freshly ground white pepper
½ each red and yellow bell peppers,
 roasted (see page 27), peeled,
 seeded, and cut into strips for
 garnish, optional

In a saucepan, bring the cream to a boil and simmer briskly until it reduces by about a third, about 15 minutes.

Meanwhile, melt half the butter in a large skillet over medium heat. Add the onion and garlic and sauté, stirring frequently, until they are soft and transparent but not browned, about 10 minutes.

Bring a large pot of water to a boil and blanch the asparagus tips for about 2 minutes; remove them with a skimming spoon or ladle and set them aside. Add the rest of the asparagus and blanch for about 30 seconds, then drain.

Add the blanched stalk pieces to the onion and garlic and sauté about 6 minutes more.

Add the cream to the vegetables, bring back to a boil, and simmer until the asparagus is completely tender and the liquid is thick, about 15 minutes.

Stir the remaining butter into the soup. Transfer the soup to a processor, in batches if necessary, and process until smooth. Press the soup through a fine-mesh sieve to remove the asparagus fibers. Return it to the pan, gently reheat, and season to taste with salt and pepper. Ladle into heated soup bowls and garnish with the asparagus tips and, if you prefer, strips of roasted red and yellow bell peppers.

MUSHROOM SOUP

•

FOR 6 SERVINGS

½ cup vegetable oil
2 pounds fresh mushrooms, coarsely
    chopped
4 tablespoons (½ stick) unsalted
    butter
1 small Maui, Walla Walla, Vidalia,
    or sweet red onion, chopped
3 medium-size cloves garlic, chopped
8 cups heavy cream
¼ cup dry sherry
Salt and freshly ground white pepper
1½ teaspoons chopped fresh chives

THIS IS THE WAY MUSHROOM SOUP OUGHT TO BE MADE. THE KEY IS THE intensification, quickly reducing the vegetable down to an essence of mushroom flavor and texture.

In a large skillet, heat the oil over medium heat. Add the mushrooms and sauté them, stirring frequently, until their juices have evaporated and they have cooked down to a thick paste, about 7 to 10 minutes.

Raise the heat, add the butter, onion, and garlic and sauté until the vegetables are lightly browned, about 10 minutes.

Add the cream to the skillet and bring it to a boil, then simmer until it reduces to a thick, creamy consistency, 10 to 15 minutes.

Transfer the soup to a processor, in batches if necessary, and process until smooth. Press it through a fine-mesh sieve, then return it to the pan, stir in the sherry, and heat the soup through, seasoning to taste with salt and pepper. Ladle into heated soup bowls and garnish with chives.

DEFINITIVE CORN
CHOWDER WITH
JALAPEÑO PEPPERS

MUSHROOM SOUP

CREAM OF ASPARAGUS
SOUP

LOBSTER BISQUE

MANILA CLAM
CHOWDER

BRAZILIAN MUSSEL
CHOWDER

LOBSTER BISQUE

■

FOR 6 SERVINGS

4 tablespoons (½ stick) unsalted
    butter
1 medium-size Maui, Walla Walla,
    Vidalia, or sweet red onion,
    chopped
2 medium-size shallots, chopped
2 medium-size cloves garlic, chopped
2 lobsters, 1½ pounds each, cooked
    in boiling water for 3 minutes,
    claws shelled, each tail shelled
    and cut into 5 medallions, all
    shells and heads reserved
2 cups dry white wine
2 cups water
8 cups heavy cream
Salt and freshly ground white pepper
2 tablespoons julienne of fresh basil
    or chopped fresh chives

THIS BISQUE AND THE ONE THAT FOLLOWS ARE SIMPLE, PURE, CREAMY essences of shellfish. It's excellent made with either Maine or West Coast lobsters.

In a large skillet, melt half the butter over medium heat. Add the onion, shallots, and garlic and sauté 10 minutes, then add the lobster shells and heads and sauté about 5 minutes more, stirring frequently.

Add the wine and water, bring to a boil, then simmer briskly for about 20 minutes. With a heavy wooden spoon, carefully but firmly pound the lobster shells and heads to break them up and extract their juices.

Pour the soup through a fine-mesh sieve to remove the shell fragments and vegetables. Rinse out the skillet and return the soup to it. Add the cream, bring back to a boil, and simmer briskly until the soup has reduced to a thick, creamy consistency, about 15 minutes. During the last 2 to 3 minutes, add the reserved lobster meat to warm through. Stir in the remaining butter and season to taste with salt and pepper.

Ladle the bisque into heated soup plates, dividing the lobster meat evenly. Garnish with a sprinkling of basil or chives.

Brazilian Mussel Chowder

■

FOR 6 SERVINGS

2 tablespoons butter

1 medium-size Maui, Walla Walla,
  Vidalia, or sweet red onion,
  chopped

2 medium-size carrots, 1 chopped, 1
  peeled and cut into ¼-inch dice

4 fresh white mushrooms, chopped

1 bunch parsley stems

Salt

1 cup dry white wine

42 small to medium-size mussels,
  scrubbed and bearded

1 medium-size boiling potato, peeled
  and cut into ¼-inch dice

1 medium-size zucchini, cut into ¼-
  inch dice

1 medium-size yellow squash, cut
  into ¼-inch dice

8 cups heavy cream

½ cup shredded coconut

½ jalapeño pepper, roasted (see page
  27), peeled, seeded, and finely
  chopped

Freshly ground white pepper

3 tablespoons sour cream, optional

2 tablespoons chopped fresh chives or
  cilantro

THIS OUTRAGEOUS SOUP BEGAN WITH THE IDEA OF DOING A VARIATION
on a standard New England clam chowder. I think mussels are fabulous, with their bright orange color, plump flesh, and sweet flavor. Coconut cream seemed a perfect complement to them—even though I don't usually like coconuts and I'm not even sure they grow in Brazil. I've added a touch of jalapeño to suggest the seductive heat of tropical nights.

Many fishmongers today sell well-cleaned mussels. But if yours are muddy or sandy, soak them in a lot of water and lift them out, repeating until the water stays clear.

In a large pot, melt the butter over low heat. Add the onion, chopped carrot, mushrooms, and parsley, then sprinkle lightly with salt and sauté, stirring occasionally, until the vegetables are soft but not yet browned, about 10 minutes.

Add the wine and raise the heat. When the wine boils, add the mussels and cover the pot. Steam, shaking the pot frequently, until all the mussels have opened, 3 to 5 minutes.

Line a sieve with a double thickness of cheesecloth and set it in a large bowl. Pour the contents of the pot into the sieve. Rinse out the pot and return the strained cooking liquid to it. Bring it back to a boil and boil it briskly until it has reduced by three quarters, 15 to 20 minutes.

Meanwhile, remove the mussels from the opened shells. Discard any unopened mussels along with the shells and cooked vegetables.

Bring a large pan of lightly salted water to a boil. Add the diced carrot and potato and cook until just done, about 2 minutes; then add the diced zucchini and yellow squash and cook about 1 minute more.

Add the cream and the coconut to the reduced cooking liquid and simmer briskly until the liquid is thick and has reduced by a third, about 15 minutes. Pour the liquid through a fine sieve to strain out the coconut.

Add the reserved mussels, vegetables, and the jalapeño and simmer briefly to heat them through. Season to taste with salt and pepper, then ladle into heated soup plates and top with a dollop of sour cream, if you like, and some chives or cilantro.

CONSOMMÉ WITH SCALLOPS, CHIVES, AND SHIITAKE MUSHROOMS

■

FOR 6 SERVINGS

1½ quarts chicken stock (see page 22)
4 large egg whites
1 medium-size Maui, Walla Walla, Vidalia, or sweet red onion, finely chopped
1 medium-size carrot, finely chopped
1 medium-size zucchini, finely chopped
2 tablespoons Madeira
Salt and freshly ground white pepper
2 tablespoons unsalted butter
¼ pound fresh shiitake mushrooms, stemmed and sliced in quarters
6 fresh sea scallops
1 tablespoon clarified butter (see page 23)
2 bunches fresh chives, trimmed

THIS SOUP HAS TWO INSPIRATIONS. THE FIRST IS CONSOMME—CLARIFIED broth, which is a classic French culinary exercise. The second is a simple, classic soup I used to eat at a great little Chinese restaurant in Paris—chicken broth garnished with crisp, fresh vegetables.

I got the idea of putting together a French consommé with Chinese-style garnishes. The funny thing is, in recent years Asian cooking has had such a big influence on cooking in this country and in France, that this soup no longer seems Chinese at all.

In a medium-size saucepan, bring the stock to a boil. In a mixing bowl, beat the egg whites just until they are smooth but still clear. Stir in the onion, carrot, and zucchini.

Reduce the heat to keep the stock at a gentle simmer. To clarify the stock, slowly pour and gently stir in the egg white and vegetable mixture. Let the stock continue simmering gently for about 20 minutes.

Line a sieve with a double layer of cheesecloth. Pour the stock through the sieve to remove the egg white mixture. The stock should be perfectly clear. If not, line the sieve with more cheesecloth and strain it again. Rinse out the saucepan and return the consommé to it.

Preheat the grill or broiler until very hot.

Add the Madeira to the consommé, season to taste with salt and white pepper, cover the saucepan, and put it over moderate heat to heat the soup through.

Meanwhile, in a medium-size skillet, melt the 2 tablespoons of butter over moderate to high heat until it foams. Add the shiitake mushrooms and sauté until golden and slightly crisp, 3 to 5 minutes.

Brush the scallops with the clarified butter and season them with salt and pepper. Grill them until seared, about 1½ minutes per side.

Ladle the soup into heated shallow soup plates. Place a scallop in the middle of each, scatter shiitake mushrooms around the sides, and place a few chives diagonally across the center.

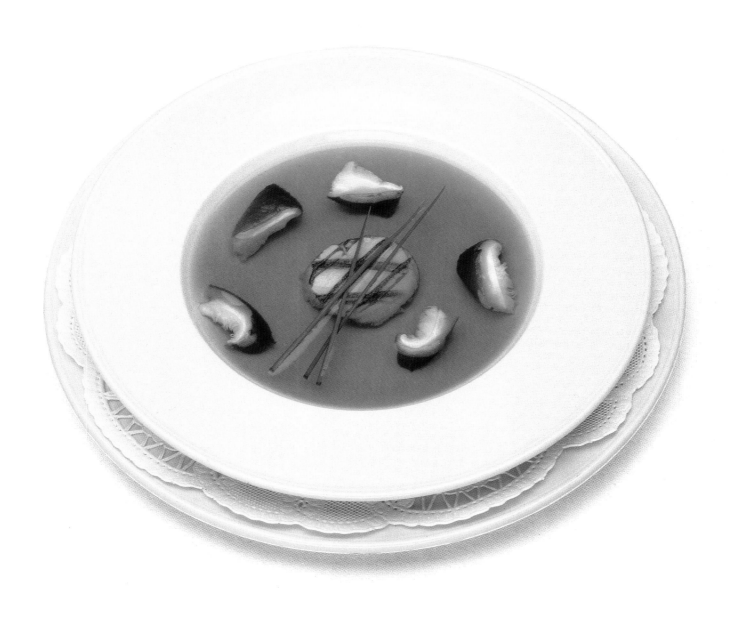

MANILA CLAM CHOWDER

■

FOR 6 SERVINGS

2 tablespoons unsalted butter

1 medium-size Maui, Walla Walla,
    Vidalia, or sweet red onion,
    chopped

2 medium-size carrots, 1 chopped, 1
    peeled and cut into ¼-inch dice

4 fresh white mushrooms, chopped

1 bunch parsley stems

Salt

1 cup dry white wine

2 pounds Manila clams, scrubbed
    and rinsed

3 strips, each ¼ inch thick, smoked
    slab bacon, as lean as possible

1 medium-size boiling potato, peeled
    and cut into ¼-inch dice

1 medium-size zucchini, cut into ¼-
    inch dice

8 cups heavy cream

Freshly ground white pepper

1½ teaspoons chopped fresh chives

IN DABOB BAY ON THE OREGON COAST, THEY FARM WONDERFUL MANILA clams. To me, these clams are the perfect combination of the Ipswich and the littleneck—having the tenderness and sweetness of the former without the sandiness or the soft shell, and the plump shape of the latter.

I use them in a classic New England chowder that I've refined with French technique, eliminating the flour thickening and using a reduction of wine, clam juices, and cream. You can substitute whole shelled littlenecks, cherrystones, or quahogs cut into strips. You can also make this chowder with lobster, scallops, mussels, or crayfish.

In a large pot, melt the butter over low heat. Add the onion, chopped carrot, mushrooms, and parsley, then sprinkle lightly with salt and sauté, stirring occasionally, until the vegetables are soft but not yet browned, about 10 minutes.

Add the wine and raise the heat. When the wine boils, add the clams and cover the pot. Steam, shaking the pot frequently, until all the clams have opened, 3 to 5 minutes.

Line a sieve with a double thickness of cheesecloth and set it over a large bowl. Pour the contents of the pot into the sieve. Rinse out the pot and return the strained cooking liquid to it. Bring it back to a boil and boil it briskly until it has reduced by three quarters, 15 to 20 minutes.

Meanwhile, remove the clam meat from the opened clams. Discard any unopened clams along with the shells and cooked vegetables.

On a preheated grill or in a skillet over medium heat, cook the bacon until crisp, about 2 minutes per side. Drain on paper towels. Cut the bacon crosswise into thin julienne strips and set them aside.

Bring a large pan of lightly salted water to a boil. Add the diced carrot and potato and cook until just done, about 2 minutes; then add the diced zucchini and cook for about 1 minute more.

Add the cream to the reduced cooking liquid and simmer briskly until the liquid is thick and has reduced by a third, about 15 minutes.

Add the reserved clam meat, vegetables, and bacon; simmer briefly to heat them through. Season to taste with salt and pepper, then ladle into heated soup plates and garnish with chives.

CRAYFISH BISQUE

■

FOR 6 SERVINGS

4 tablespoons (½ stick) unsalted
    butter
1 medium-size Maui, Walla Walla,
    Vidalia, or sweet red onion,
    chopped
1 medium-size carrot, chopped
1 bunch parsley stems
Salt
2 cups dry white wine
1 pinch dried thyme
3 bay leaves
1 tablespoon whole black peppercorns
2 pounds live crayfish
6 cups heavy cream
Freshly ground white pepper
2 tablespoons julienne of fresh basil

WE MAKE THIS SOUP WITH EITHER NEW ORLEANS OR SACRAMENTO RIVER crayfish—whichever is better quality at the time.

In a large saucepan, melt half the butter over low heat. Add the onion, carrot, and parsley, sprinkle lightly with salt, and sauté, stirring occasionally, until the vegetables are soft but not yet browned, about 10 minutes.

Add the wine, thyme, bay leaves, and peppercorns and raise the heat. When the wine boils, add the crayfish and cover the pot. Steam, shaking the pot frequently, until the crayfish are cooked, about 5 minutes.

Pour the soup through a sieve, reserving the liquid. When the crayfish are cool enough to handle, pull their heads and tails apart, reserving the head parts. Peel the tails, reserving the shells and setting the meat aside.

Rinse out the pan and add the cream, the reserved cooking liquid, and the crayfish heads and shells. Bring it to a boil and simmer briskly until the liquid has reduced by about a third, about 15 minutes.

Pour the bisque through a sturdy, fine-mesh sieve set over a bowl. With a heavy wooden spoon, pound the heads and shells in the sieve to break them up and extract all their juices. Discard the heads and shells.

Return the bisque to the pan and reheat, stirring in the remaining butter and adjusting the seasoning to taste with salt and pepper. Ladle the soup into heated soup plates and garnish with the crayfish tails and the basil.

Untitled by
Jasper Johns

CHAPTER FIVE
PASTA

FRESH ANGEL HAIR PASTA

.

FOR 6 SERVINGS

2 cups all-purpose flour
Pinch of salt
4 large egg yolks

PASTA TO ME IS A CANVAS ON WHICH A GREAT CHEF MAY PAINT. I LIKE to serve a small amount of light, delicate pasta that has many ingredients on top of it—the painting. When coupled with either of my Chardonnay cream sauces (recipes on pages 30–31), this angel hair pasta, with its fine texture and its thin strands, makes the perfect canvas.

In a mixing bowl or on a smooth work surface, combine the flour and salt and make a well in the center.

Put the egg yolks in the well. With your fingertips or a fork, break the yolks and gradually incorporate the flour into them, working from the center outward, to form a smooth, firm but still pliable dough. (If you like, you could also combine the ingredients in a food processor with the metal blade.) Gather the dough into a ball, then flatten it to a thickness of about ½ inch.

Set the rollers of a hand-cranked pasta machine at their widest setting. Lightly dust the dough with additional flour on both sides and crank it through the machine. Fold both ends of the dough toward each other, overlapping them. Rotate the dough 90 degrees, dust with flour again, and crank it through once more. Continue until the dough is smooth and firm.

Decrease the roller width by one setting and pass the dough through again. Continue, rolling the dough thinner and thinner, until the rollers are only about ⅛ inch apart (usually the next-to-narrowest setting).

Pass the sheet of dough through an angel hair pasta cutter, cutting them into thin strands. Lightly toss the angel hair with a little flour to keep the strands separate.

To cook the pasta, bring 8 quarts of lightly salted water to a boil in a large pot. Add 3 tablespoons of olive oil. Put the angel hair pasta in a sieve and lower it into the water, stirring with tongs or a spoon to keep the strands separate. Boil until al dente, cooked but still slightly chewy—no more than 2 minutes for freshly made pasta. Drain and toss with sauce as instructed in the recipe.

PASTA WITH GRILLED SHRIMP OR SCALLOPS, CAVIAR, AND CHARDONNAY CREAM SAUCE

■

FOR 6 SERVINGS

2 cups Chardonnay Cream Sauce I
 (see pages 30–31)
3 tablespoons extra-virgin olive oil
18 jumbo prawns or shrimp, shelled,
 shells reserved, or 18 large sea
 scallops, trimmed
2 tablespoons clarified butter (see
 page 23)
Salt and freshly ground white pepper
1 recipe Fresh Angel Hair Pasta
 (recipe precedes)
2 tablespoons julienne of fresh basil
¼ cup salmon roe caviar or American
 golden (whitefish) caviar
2 tablespoons chopped fresh chives

WE MAKE THIS PASTA—A SIGNATURE ITEM AT THE RESTAURANT—WITH Alaska spot prawns, Texas gulf shrimp, or Santa Barbara shrimp, using the largest jumbo shrimp we can find; as a variation, we'll use large sea scallops.

With fresh shrimp in their shells, you might also get a bonus of the shrimp's own dark red roe, tucked beneath the tail. Pull it off with your fingers and gently pick away any membranes, then serve this shrimp caviar in place of the salmon roe.

Prepare the sauce (if you're using shrimp, include their shells). Keep the sauce warm.

Preheat the grill or broiler.

In a large pot, bring 8 quarts of lightly salted water to a boil; add the olive oil.

At the same time, brush the shrimp or scallops with the butter and season lightly with salt and pepper. Grill them about 1½ minutes per side. Just before you turn the seafood over, add the pasta to the boiling water and cook until al dente, no more than 2 minutes; drain well.

Toss the pasta with the sauce and basil and mound it in the middle of each of 6 heated large serving plates. Place 3 shrimp or scallops on top of each serving. Garnish with salmon roe caviar for shrimp, golden caviar for scallops. Add a sprinkling of chopped chives.

WINE SUGGESTION

WITH THE SWEETNESS OF THE GRILLED SHRIMP OR SCALLOPS AND THE RICHNESS OF THE SAUCE, THIS IS AN ABSOLUTE SHOWPIECE FOR ANY CHARDONNAY FROM ANYWHERE IN THE WORLD— UNITED STATES, FRANCE, ITALY, OR AUSTRALIA.

PASTA WITH OYSTERS, CLAMS, AND MUSSELS IN CHARDONNAY CREAM SAUCE

■

FOR 6 SERVINGS

2 cups Chardonnay Cream Sauce I
    (see pages 30–31)
18 large mussels, shells scrubbed and
    debearded
18 large Manila clams, shells
    scrubbed
18 large California Belon oysters,
    shelled
3 tablespoons extra-virgin olive oil
1 recipe Fresh Angel Hair Pasta (see
    page 90)
¼ cup salmon caviar
2 tablespoons minced fresh chives

_____

WINE SUGGESTION

A LIGHTER, CRISPER CHARDONNAY SUCH
AS A SMITH-MADRONE, IRON HORSE, OR
DOMAINE MICHEL WILL SHOW OFF THE
FLAVORS OF THE SHELLFISH. YOU COULD
ALSO POUR A GOOD, FLINTY CALIFORNIA
BLANC DE BLANCS CHAMPAGNE SUCH AS
SCHRAMSBERG, SCHARFFENBERGER, OR
IRON HORSE.

THIS IS A GREAT PASTA FOR SHELLFISH LOVERS. I STEAM OPEN THE MUSsels and clams in the wine used to make the Chardonnay Cream Sauce, which gives the dish an even greater flavor. If you can't find Manila clams, substitute littlenecks or cherrystones; and if California Belon oysters aren't available in your area, any good, fresh oyster will do.

Prepare the sauce, steaming open the mussels and clams in the wine and then removing them with a slotted spoon before continuing with the sauce recipe. Be sure to strain the wine through cheesecloth to remove any sand from the shellfish.

Shell the mussels and clams.

In a large pot, bring 8 quarts of lightly salted water to a boil; add the olive oil. Add the pasta and cook until al dente, no more than 2 minutes; drain well.

While the pasta is cooking, put the mussels, clams, and oysters in the sauce to warm through for about 1 minute.

Ladle the sauce, without the shellfish, over the pasta and toss well. Mound the pasta in the middle of each of 6 heated large shallow serving plates. Place 3 each of the mussels, clams, and oysters on top of each serving and garnish with caviar and chopped chives.

PASTA WITH OYSTERS,
CLAMS, AND MUSSELS
IN CHARDONNAY
CREAM SAUCE

PASTA WITH GRILLED
SCALLOPS AND CAVIAR
IN CHARDONNAY
CREAM SAUCE

PASTA WITH GRILLED
SHRIMP AND CAVIAR IN
CHARDONNAY CREAM
SAUCE

Pasta with Shrimp, Vegetables, and Olive Oil

■

FOR 6 SERVINGS

1 cup plus 3 tablespoons dark green
    extra-virgin olive oil
18 Santa Barbara shrimp (1½ to 2
    pounds total), shelled, tailed,
    and deveined
3 tablespoons clarified butter (see
    page 23)
Salt and freshly ground white pepper
1 recipe Fresh Angel Hair Pasta (see
    page 90)
1 medium-size carrot, peeled and cut
    into 2 × ⅛-inch matchsticks
1 medium-size golden squash, cut
    into 2 × ⅛-inch matchsticks
1 medium-size zucchini, cut into
    2 × ⅛-inch matchsticks
¼ pound small snow peas, stemmed
    and stringed
½ cup Tomato Concasse (see page
    42)
1½ tablespoons fresh lemon juice
1½ tablespoons julienne of fresh basil
1½ tablespoons chopped fresh chives

WINE SUGGESTION

A FUMÉ BLANC, SUCH AS PHILIP TOGNI
OR IRON HORSE; A VIN GRIS SUCH AS
BONNY DOON OR EDNA VALLEY; OR A
FRENCH WHITE FROM THE LOIRE, SUCH AS
SANCERRE OR POUILLY-FUMÉ.

SOMETIMES PEOPLE AT THE RESTAURANT ASK FOR A SEAFOOD PASTA WITH-
out the Chardonnay Cream Sauce. A dark green extra-virgin olive oil
like the kind you get from the Lago del Garda region of Italy makes
a good, clean-tasting sauce for this pasta with shrimp and fresh vegetables.

I developed this dish with Santa Barbara shrimp, but you could
use Alaska spot prawns, Texas gulf prawns, or whatever jumbo fresh
shrimp or prawns you can find. Also feel free to substitute or add
other good-quality fresh vegetables in season.

I also do a version of this recipe without the shrimp—simply
spring vegetables and olive oil—which I call "Pritikin-style," since
the original Pritikin Center is on the beach at Santa Monica, virtually
across the Pacific Coast Highway from the restaurant. Though there
are still egg yolks in the pasta, and the olive oil could hardly be called
low in calories, it's pretty healthy stuff.

Preheat the grill or broiler until very hot.
    In a large pot, bring 8 quarts of lightly salted water to a boil;
add the 3 tablespoons olive oil. In another, medium-size pot, bring
lightly salted water to a boil

Brush the shrimp with the butter and season with salt and pepper.
Grill or broil them for about 1½ minutes per side; halfway through
the cooking on each side, rotate the shrimp 90 degrees to give them
crosshatched grill marks.

At the same time you put the shrimp on the grill, start cooking
the pasta and vegetables. Add the pasta to the large pot of boiling
water and cook until al dente, no more than 2 minutes. Drain well.

As soon as the pasta is cooking, put the carrot matchsticks into
the smaller pot of boiling water. After 30 seconds, add the squash,
zucchini, and snow peas, and boil 30 seconds more. Drain well.

Toss the pasta in a bowl with the cup of olive oil, the blanched
vegetables, the tomatoes, lemon juice, and salt and pepper to taste.
Mound the pasta in the middle of each of 6 heated large serving
plates, arranging the vegetables attractively. Place the shrimp on top
of the pasta and garnish with basil and chives.

PASTA WITH CRAYFISH, SALMON CAVIAR, AND CHARDONNAY CREAM SAUCE

•

FOR 6 SERVINGS

2 cups Chardonnay Cream Sauce I
    (see pages 30–31)
2 cups dry white wine
2 cups water
6 pounds live crayfish
18 small asparagus spears, trimmed
3 tablespoons extra-virgin olive oil
1 recipe Fresh Angel Hair Pasta (see
    page 90)
2 tablespoons julienne of fresh basil
1 each red and yellow bell pepper,
    halved, stemmed, and seeded,
    then roasted (see page 27),
    peeled, and cut into thin strips
2 tablespoons chopped fresh chives
6 tablespoons salmon roe caviar

ANOTHER SIMPLE YET ELEGANT COMBINATION OF SHELLFISH, CAVIAR, and pasta.

Prepare the sauce and keep it warm.

Bring the wine and water to a boil in a large pot. Add the crayfish and steam them for about 4 minutes. Strain them out. Handling them with a kitchen towel to protect your hands from the heat, twist off and discard the crayfish heads. Holding each tail in the towel, squeeze it to crack its shell; then peel off the shell and put the meat aside in a covered bowl, keeping it warm.

In a medium-size saucepan, bring lightly salted water to a boil. Add the asparagus and blanch for about 2 minutes, then drain well.

In a large pot, bring 8 quarts of lightly salted water to a boil; add the olive oil. Add the pasta to the boiling water and cook until al dente, no more than 2 minutes; drain well.

Toss the pasta with the sauce and basil. Mound the pasta in the middle of each of 6 heated large serving plates. Arrange the crayfish meat around the edge of the pasta. Place 3 asparagus spears on top of each serving, radiating from the center like the spokes of a wheel; place pepper strips on either side of each asparagus spear. Scatter the chives on top and garnish with a tablespoon of salmon caviar in the center.

WINE SUGGESTION
YOUR FAVORITE CHARDONNAY,
WHATEVER ITS STYLE AND WHEREVER IT
COMES FROM, WILL BE SHOWN OFF WELL
BY THIS DISH.

PASTA WITH THREE AMERICAN OR PERSIAN CAVIARS AND CHARDONNAY CREAM SAUCE

•

FOR 6 SERVINGS

2 cups Chardonnay Cream Sauce I
  (see pages 30–31)
3 tablespoons extra-virgin olive oil
1 recipe Angel Hair Pasta (see page
  90)
1½ tablespoons chopped fresh chives
1½ tablespoons julienne of fresh basil
6 tablespoons each of salmon roe
  caviar, American golden
  (whitefish) caviar, and American
  sturgeon caviar; or 6 tablespoons
  each of beluga caviar, osetra
  caviar, and sevruga caviar

WINE SUGGESTION
ANY GOOD AMERICAN CHARDONNAY,
WHATEVER ITS QUALITIES, WILL BE
TERRIFIC WITH THE AMERICAN CAVIARS.
FOR PERSIAN CAVIARS, SERVE A GREAT
FRENCH WHITE BURGUNDY—A PULIGNY-
MONTRACHET, CHASSAGNE-
MONTRACHET, CORTOGNE-
CHARLEMAGNE, OR MUSIGNY BLANC.

PASTA WITH THREE
AMERICAN CAVIARS IN
CHARDONNAY CREAM
SAUCE

AS CAVIARS BEGAN TO BE DEVELOPED IN AMERICA, WE DECIDED TO SHOW-case them on top of one of our pastas, to really show how spectacular they are. We use orange-pink salmon roe caviar, American golden (whitefish) caviar, and black American sturgeon caviar. It's a beautiful combination of colors as well as of tastes and textures.

If you really want to go big time, though, pass on the American caviars and serve the best beluga, osetra, and sevruga you can buy on the pasta. Gorbachev may get mad at me, but I happen to prefer Persian caviar, which has a cleaner, more briny flavor than Russian. If you like, you can use vodka in place of the wine in the sauce, or substitute melted butter for the sauce and serve the pasta with iced Stolichnaya vodka.

Prepare the sauce and keep it warm.

In a large pot, bring 8 quarts of lightly salted water to a boil; add the olive oil. Add the pasta to the boiling water and cook until al dente, no more than 2 minutes; drain well.

Toss the pasta with the sauce and half of the chives and basil. Mound the pasta in the middle of each of 6 heated large serving plates. Spoon a dollop of each caviar equidistant around the pasta on each plate. Garnish with the remaining herbs.

PASTA WITH THREE
PERSIAN CAVIARS IN
CHARDONNAY CREAM
SAUCE

PASTA WITH GRILLED
LOBSTER AND BELUGA
CAVIAR

PASTA WITH GRILLED LOBSTER AND BELUGA CAVIAR

■

FOR 6 SERVINGS

2 cups Chardonnay Cream Sauce I
    (see pages 30–31)
2 lobsters, 1½ pounds each, blanched
    for 5 minutes and shelled, shells
    reserved, claws left whole, tails
    cut into ¾-inch medallions
3 tablespoons extra-virgin olive oil
1 recipe Fresh Angel Hair Pasta (see
    page 90)
2 tablespoons clarified butter (see
    page 23)
Salt and freshly ground white pepper
2 tablespoons julienne of fresh basil
¼ cup beluga caviar

THIS IS THE MOST LUXURIOUS OF MY PASTAS, COMBINING THE BOTTOM line in shellfish with the bottom line in caviar. If you like, you may substitute black American sturgeon caviar.

Prepare the sauce, including the lobster shells. Keep it warm.
    Preheat the grill or broiler.
    In a large pot, bring 8 quarts of lightly salted water to a boil; add the olive oil. Add the pasta to the boiling water and cook until al dente, no more than 2 minutes; drain well.
    At the same time, brush the lobster medallions and claws with the butter and season lightly with salt and pepper. Grill them about 30 seconds per side.
    Toss the pasta with the sauce and mound it in the middle of each of 6 heated large, shallow serving plates. Place 3 pieces of lobster—2 medallions and a claw, or 3 medallions—on top of each serving, and garnish with basil and a dollop of caviar.

WINE SUGGESTION
THIS IS EXCELLENT WITH MATURE
CHARDONNAYS WITH A LOT OF OAK AND
BUTTER, SUCH AS MOUNT EDEN,
CHALONE, OR ACACIA. YOU CAN ALSO
SERVE A WHITE BURGUNDY WITH SIMILAR
QUALITIES—A PULIGNY-MONTRACHET OR
A BIG MEURSAULT.

PASTA WITH SWEETBREADS AND WILD MUSHROOMS

■

FOR 6 SERVINGS

½ cup walnut oil
12 medium-size fresh chanterelle
    mushrooms (about 1 pound
    total), each sliced into 3 pieces
2½ cups dry white wine
¼ cup chicken stock (see page 22)
4 cups heavy cream
2 cups water
1¼ pounds veal sweetbreads
3 tablespoons extra-virgin olive oil
Salt and freshly ground white pepper
¼ cup all-purpose flour
½ tablespoon unsalted butter
1 recipe Fresh Angel Hair Pasta (see
    page 90)
1½ tablespoons julienne of fresh basil
1½ tablespoons chopped fresh chives

WINE SUGGESTION
TO MATCH THE RICHNESS OF THE SAUCE
AND TOPPINGS, POUR A WELL-AGED,
FULL-BODIED, BUTTERY CALIFORNIA
CHARDONNAY SUCH AS GRGICH HILLS,
JORDAN, OR ACACIA.

WHILE MEATS WOULD BE OVERPOWERING ON MY ANGEL HAIR PASTA, crisply sautéed sweetbreads, along with sautéed wild mushrooms, make a wonderfully rich, satisfying topping with a great combination of textures and tastes.

Heat ¼ cup of the walnut oil in a skillet over high heat until the oil is almost smoking. Add the chanterelles. Let them set and brown, without stirring, for 30 seconds. Then turn them and let them set on the other side for 30 seconds more. Remove the mushrooms from the skillet and set them aside.

Pour off the oil from the skillet. Add ½ cup of wine and the chicken stock and simmer briskly for 2 minutes, stirring and scraping to dissolve the glaze in the skillet. Then add the cream and boil until it has reduced by half, 12 to 15 minutes.

While the cream is reducing, bring the remaining wine and the 2 cups of water to a boil in a saucepan. Add the sweetbreads and blanch them for 3 minutes. Then drain them and carefully use a small sharp knife and your fingertips to remove their membranes and trim and clean them. Cut the sweetbreads into 6 slices about ½ inch thick and set them aside.

In a large pot, bring 8 quarts of lightly salted water to a boil; add the olive oil.

A few minutes before the cream has finished reducing, season the sweetbreads with salt and pepper. Sprinkle the flour on a plate and lightly dredge the sweetbreads in it on both sides. Heat the remaining walnut oil with the butter in another skillet over high heat until the oil is almost smoking and the butter begins to brown. Add the sweetbreads and sauté them for 1½ minutes per side, until golden.

As soon as you start cooking the sweetbreads, put the pasta in the boiling water and cook until al dente, no more then 2 minutes. Drain well.

Add the reserved mushrooms to the cream sauce to heat through briefly and toss the pasta with the sauce and mushrooms, half of the basil and chives, and salt and pepper to taste. Mound the pasta in the middle of each of 6 large serving plates, arranging the mushrooms on top. Place the sweetbreads on top of the pasta and garnish with the remaining herbs.

PASTA WITH WHITE TRUFFLES, OLIVE OIL, PARMESAN, AND BASIL

•

FOR 6 SERVINGS

1 cup plus 3 tablespoons dark green
    extra-virgin olive oil
1 recipe Fresh Angel Hair Pasta (see
    page 90)
2 tablespoons julienne of fresh basil
Salt and freshly ground white pepper
¾ cup freshly grated Reggiano
    Parmesan cheese
2 ounces fresh white truffle

WINE SUGGESTION

THE BEST CHOICE WOULD BE A RED WINE
FROM THE PIEDMONT REGION OF ITALY,
WHERE THE TRUFFLES COME FROM—AN
OLDER BARBARESCO OR BAROLO, WHICH
HAS SOME OF THE NATURAL TRUFFLE
FLAVOR IN THE WINE. THE STRONG,
EARTHY FLAVORS IN THIS DISH WILL ALSO
MAKE A LESS-THAN-GREAT WHITE
BURGUNDY LOOK GOOD.

A STUDY IN PURE, SIMPLE, SPECTACULAR INGREDIENTS: SPICY, EARTHY, fresh white truffles; full-flavored and fruity, dark green Italian olive oil from the Lago del Garda area; rich and tangy Reggiano Parmesan cheese; and the accent of fresh basil. Don't compromise on your ingredients here, or the dish will be less than it can be.

In a large pot, bring 8 quarts of lightly salted water to a boil; add the 3 tablespoons olive oil. Add the pasta to the boiling water and cook until al dente, no more than 2 minutes; drain well.

Toss the pasta with the cup of olive oil, half the basil, and salt and pepper to taste. Mound the pasta in the middle of each of 6 heated large serving plates. Sprinkle the pasta with the Parmesan. With a truffle shaver or swivel-bladed vegetable peeler, shave the truffle over each serving. Garnish with the remaining basil.

PASTA WITH WHITE OR BLACK TRUFFLES AND CHARDONNAY CREAM SAUCE

■

FOR 6 SERVINGS

PASTA WITH WHITE
TRUFFLES

2 cups *Chardonnay Cream Sauce II*
   (see pages 30–31)
3 tablespoons *extra-virgin olive oil*
1 recipe *Fresh Angel Hair Pasta (see*
   page 90)
2 tablespoons *julienne of fresh basil*
2 ounces *fresh white or black truffle*

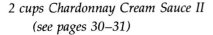

WINE SUGGESTION

POUR A FINE ITALIAN CHARDONNAY
FROM THE PIEDMONT—A GAJA OR CA DEL
BOSCO—TO COMPLEMENT THE FLAVORS
OF THE WHITE TRUFFLES AND THE SAUCE.
YOU COULD ALSO SERVE A GREAT
FRENCH WHITE BURGUNDY—A PULIGNY-
MONTRACHET, CHASSAGNE-
MONTRACHET, CORTON-CHARLEMAGNE,
OR MUSIGNY BLANC. FOR BLACK
TRUFFLES, ANY OLDER CALIFORNIA
CHARDONNAY WITH A LOT OF OAK AND
BUTTER TO IT—ACACIA, GRGICH HILLS,
OR CHALONE, FOR EXAMPLE—WILL DO
NICELY.

THE CHARDONNAY CREAM SAUCE FORMS A LUXURIOUS BACKGROUND FOR showing off the flavor of fresh white or black truffles—a classic treatment.

Prepare the sauce and keep it warm.
   In a large pot, bring 8 quarts of lightly salted water to a boil; add the olive oil. Add the pasta to the boiling water and cook until al dente, no more than 2 minutes; drain well.

Toss the pasta with the sauce and half of the basil. Mound the pasta in the middle of each of 6 heated large serving plates. With a truffle shaver or swivel-bladed vegetable peeler, shave the truffle over each serving. Garnish with the remaining basil.

PASTA WITH BLACK
TRUFFLES

PASTA WITH BABY SCALLOPS, GOAT CHEESE, AND BACON

•

FOR 6 SERVINGS

2 cups Chardonnay Cream Sauce I
    (see pages 30–31)
6 strips, each ¼ inch thick, smoked
    bacon, cut crosswise into thin
    julienne strips
18 small asparagus spears, trimmed
3 tablespoons extra-virgin olive oil
1 recipe Fresh Angel Hair Pasta (see
    page 90)
1 pound baby bay scallops
3 tablespoons clarified butter (see
    page 23)
Salt and freshly ground white pepper
½ pound fresh Montrachet or other
    fresh creamy goat cheese,
    crumbled
1 ½ tablespoons julienne of fresh
    basil
1 ½ tablespoons chopped fresh chives
1 each red and yellow bell pepper,
    halved, stemmed, and seeded,
    then roasted (see page 27), peeled
    and cut into thin strips

WINE SUGGESTION

SERVE A YOUNG, GREENER, CRISPER STYLE
OF CALIFORNIA CHARDONNAY, WITH A
LITTLE BIT OF BUTTER TO IT—SUCH AS
SONOMA-CUTRER, CLOS PEGASE,
TREFETHEN, OR ROBERT MONDAVI
RESERVE.

HERE'S A PERFECT EXAMPLE OF FRENCH ITALIAN AND AMERICAN INFLU-ences working together in one dish—a combination of rich, strong flavors that really work together without being overpowering. The French-style Montrachet goat cheese melts beautifully into the Chardonnay Cream Sauce, giving it a great, wonderfully rich quality. The roasted peppers and the basil—not to mention the pasta—supply the Italian element. And the combination of scallops and bacon reminds me of a classic New England-style chowder.

Prepare the sauce and keep it warm.

Meanwhile, put the bacon in a medium-size skillet and sauté it over medium heat until crisp. Drain off the fat and drain the bacon well on paper towels and put it aside.

Preheat the grill or broiler.

In a medium-size saucepan, bring lightly salted water to a boil. Add the asparagus and blanch for about 2 minutes, then drain well.

In a large pot, bring 8 quarts of lightly salted water to a boil; add the olive oil. Add the pasta to the boiling water and cook until al dente, no more than 2 minutes; drain well.

At the same time as the pasta is cooking, brush the scallops with the butter and season with salt and pepper, then grill or broil them for 30 to 45 seconds per side. Alternatively, you may sauté them in the butter in a skillet over high heat for the same amount of time.

While the pasta and scallops are cooking, stir the goat cheese into the sauce with a wire whisk, until the cheese melts. Toss the pasta with the sauce and half of the basil and chives. Mound the pasta in the middle of each of 6 heated large serving plates. Arrange the scallops around the edge of the pasta. Place 3 asparagus spears on top of each serving, radiating from the center like the spokes of a wheel; place pepper strips on either side of each asparagus spear. Scatter the bacon on top and garnish with the remaining herbs.

PASTA WITH SALMON, CAVIAR, AND CHARDONNAY CREAM SAUCE

■

FOR 6 SERVINGS

2 cups Chardonnay Cream Sauce I
    (see pages 30–31)
18 small asparagus spears, trimmed
3 tablespoons extra-virgin olive oil
1 recipe Fresh Angel Hair Pasta (see
    page 90)
1½ pounds fillet of salmon, cut into
    18 medallions, each about ½
    inch thick, or 18 (1-ounce) John
    Dory fillets
3 tablespoons clarified butter (see
    page 23)
Salt and freshly ground white pepper
2 tablespoons juliennne of fresh basil
1 each red and yellow bell pepper,
    halved, stemmed, and seeded,
    then roasted, peeled (see page
    27), and cut into thin strips
2 tablespoons chopped fresh chives
6 tablespoons American golden
    (whitefish) caviar or American
    sturgeon caviar

I USE VERY FEW FISH TO TOP MY PASTA, BECAUSE THEY SEEM UNWIELDY against the delicate canvas of the angel hair. But salmon—because of its beautiful color and its rich yet light flavor and texture—is a notable exception. Small medallions of salmon, accompanied by golden caviar—or an American sturgeon or Persian black caviar—make an absolutely gorgeous pasta dish.

You may also use John Dory; grilled, its fillets have an almost scallop-like taste that's perfect in this setting, accompanied by American sturgeon caviar.

Prepare the sauce and keep it warm.

Preheat the grill or broiler until very hot.

In a medium-size saucepan, bring lightly salted water to a boil. Add the asparagus and blanch for about 2 minutes, then drain well.

In a large pot, bring 8 quarts of lightly salted water to a boil; add the olive oil. Add the pasta to the boiling water and cook until al dente, no more than 2 minutes; drain well.

At the same time, brush the salmon medallions or John Dory fillets with the butter and season with salt and pepper. Grill or broil them for about 1 minute per side; halfway through the cooking on each side, rotate them 90 degrees to give them crosshatched grill marks.

Toss the pasta with the sauce and basil. Mound the pasta in the middle of each of 6 heated large serving plates. Place 3 asparagus spears on top of each serving, radiating from the center like the spokes of a wheel; place pepper strips on either side of each asparagus spear. Place 3 pieces of fish on top of each serving, in between the asparagus spears. Scatter the chives on top and garnish with a dollop of caviar in the center—golden for the salmon, American sturgeon for the John Dory.

WINE SUGGESTION

WITH THE SALMON, SERVE A
CHARDONNAY SUCH AS JORDAN OR
ACACIA; FOR JOHN DORY, SONOMA-
CUTTER, IRON HORSE, OR CHATEAU
MONTELENA, FOR EXAMPLE.

CHAPTER SIX
SALADS

WILD MUSHROOM SALAD WITH PANCETTA

∎

FOR 6 SERVINGS

3 bunches mâche, leaves separated
    and trimmed
2 bunches arugula, leaves separated
    and trimmed
2 heads baby limestone lettuce, leaves
    separated and trimmed
1 head baby radicchio, leaves
    separated and trimmed
¼ cup walnut oil
½ pound each fresh chanterelle,
    shiitake, and oyster mushrooms,
    trimmed and cut into ½-inch
    pieces
½ ounce pancetta, cut into thin
    julienne strips, optional
¼ cup pine nuts
2 large shallots, finely chopped
2 medium-size cloves garlic, finely
    chopped
¼ cup sherry wine vinegar
2 tablespoons each minced fresh basil,
    tarragon, thyme, and chives
Salt and freshly ground black pepper

WINE SUGGESTION

THIS IS WONDERFUL FOR A FINE
CALIFORNIA CHARDONNAY, WELL
BALANCED, WITH MEDIUM BODY AND A
MODERATE BUTTERINESS—TRY NEYERS,
ACACIA, OR CLOS DU VAL. OR SERVE A
BEAUJOLAIS TO COMPLEMENT THE
FLAVOR OF THE PANCETTA.

THIS COMBINATION OF THREE DIFFERENT KINDS OF WILD MUSHROOMS works, with each mushroom contributing a different taste, texture, and color—the vivid orange chanterelles, firm, rich, and slightly eggy in flavor; the pale oyster mushrooms, moist, succulent, and almost tasting of the sea; and the dark brown shiitakes, meaty and ducklike with their crisp-textured caps. You can make it with or without the Italian bacon, pancetta, which adds yet another dimension of flavor.

Browning the mushrooms quickly in searingly hot walnut oil brings out their aromatic, naturally sweet tastes; the fresh greens, which wilt on contact with the hot mixture, lighten up the whole salad. You can substitute a selection of whatever available salad greens are youngest, smallest, freshest, and most beautiful for those that are suggested in the recipe.

This is one of those combinations you have to eat the moment it hits the table to extract the maximum taste.

Toss all the greens together in a salad bowl.

In a large sauté pan, heat 3 tablespoons of the walnut oil over high heat until it just begins to smoke. Add the mushrooms and let them sear, without stirring, for about 30 seconds; then sauté them, stirring constantly, for about 2½ minutes more, until nicely browned. Add the mushrooms to the salad bowl.

To the same pan, still over high heat, add the remaining 1 table-spoon oil and sauté the pancetta for about 30 seconds; then add the pine nuts and sauté until golden, about 1 minute. Add the shallots and stir them quickly, then add the garlic and sauté about 30 seconds more. Add the vinegar and stir and scrape to deglaze the pan, then stir in the herbs, salt, and pepper.

Pour the hot dressing into the salad bowl and toss immediately to coat all the greens. Mound the mixture on salad plates and serve immediately.

POACHED EGG, BACON, WATERCRESS, AND ENDIVE SALAD

•

FOR 6 SERVINGS

1 cup white vinegar
14 or 15 large eggs, extra-fresh
6 heads baby Belgian endive, sliced
    crosswise ¼ inch thick
3 bunches watercress, stemmed
6 strips, each ¼ inch thick, smoked
    bacon, cut into ¼-inch pieces
¼ cup sherry wine vinegar
1 tablespoon Dijon mustard
1 cup peanut oil
1 to 2 teaspoons fresh lemon juice
Freshly ground black pepper
Salt, optional
Chopped fresh chives

WINE SUGGESTION
CHOOSE A YOUNG, LIGHT, FRUITY
FRENCH RED—A BEAUJOLAIS OR A YOUNG
CÔTES DU RHÔNE. OR SERVE A LIGHT
YOUNG CALIFORNIA ZINFANDEL—
PARTICULARLY THOSE OF JOSEPH PHELPS,
LOUIS MARTINI, OR FETZER.

I USED TO EAT A VERY CASUAL VERSION OF THIS SALAD IN PARIS BRASseries. I've smartened up the presentation here, but the philosophy is just the same. It's a great combination of textures and tastes—the crisp greens, the chewy bacon, and the smooth egg yolk; the sharpness of the watercress, the slight bitterness of the endive (use baby Belgian endive, which is not too bitter), and the richness of the eggs. You'll enjoy the salad most if, once it is in front of you, you cut up the eggs and mix it all together with your knife and fork, to get those contrasts in every bite.

In a wide, deep pan, bring 3 quarts of water to a boil. Add the white vinegar. Carefully break a few eggs into the briskly boiling water, holding the shell just over the surface. (A few might break, and others won't look good enough; you'll need 12 well-formed eggs for the 6 salads.) Poach the eggs just until the whites are solid, about 2 minutes; to test them, lift one out with a slotted spoon and touch the white with your fingertip to see if it's firm. With the slotted spoon, transfer the eggs to a large, deep pan filled with ice and water.

Cover each salad plate with the sliced endive. Place a cluster of watercress in the center of each plate.

Put the bacon in a medium-size skillet and sauté it over moderate heat until the bacon is browned but not yet crisp.

Drain the bacon on paper towels and reserve 3 tablespoons of the fat. Add the sherry wine vinegar to the skillet and stir and scrape with a wooden spoon over high heat to dissolve the glaze on the bottom and sides. Stir the mustard into the vinegar. Then slowly whisk in the oil and the reserved bacon fat, gradually adding more as the dressing thickens. Add fresh lemon juice, pepper to taste, and salt if necessary, depending on the saltiness of the bacon. Keep the dressing warm.

With a slotted spoon, carefully remove the eggs from the ice bath to a folded kitchen towel. With a small, sharp knife, carefully trim the whites to give the eggs a neat appearance. Fill a large bowl with very hot tap water and carefully slip in the eggs to heat through for about 1 minute.

Carefully remove the eggs from the hot water and drain them on the kitchen towel. Place 2 eggs side by side on top of the watercress on each salad. Scatter the bacon over each salad, drizzle with dressing, and scatter chives on top.

PAPAYA, AVOCADO, SHRIMP, AND WATERCRESS SALAD

■

FOR 6 SERVINGS

36 Belgian endive leaves

2 bunches watercress, stemmed

3 each ripe avocados and papayas,
    peeled, halved lengthwise, and
    seeded, each half sliced thinly
    crosswise with the slices left
    unseparated

30 medium-size shrimp (about 1
    ounce each), peeled and deveined

6 tablespoons clarified butter (see
    page 23)

Salt and freshly ground white pepper

1 cup Basic Vinaigrette (see page 34)

5 tablespoons chopped fresh chives

WINE SUGGESTION

HERE'S AN OCCASION FOR A GOOD VIN
GRIS OR "BLUSH" WINE TO SHOW OFF THE
FRUIT IN THE SALAD. BONNY DOON AND
EDNA VALLEY BOTH MAKE FINE VINS
GRIS.

THIS IS ONE OF MY FAVORITE LUNCH SALADS. I LIKE TO THINK OF IT AS perfectly Southern Californian in its combination of avocado, seafood, and tropical fruit. You can serve it as an appetizer or a main course.

On each salad plate, place 6 endive leaves, evenly spaced like spokes on a wheel. Place a clump of watercress at the center of each plate. Place an avocado half at the top, between two of the endive leaves, its wide end at the center of the plate; press down lightly to fan out its slices a bit. In the same way, place a papaya half at the bottom of the plate.

Preheat the grill or broiler. Brush the shrimp with the butter and season them lightly with salt and pepper. Grill or broil them lightly, about 1½ minutes per side.

Evenly arrange 5 grilled shrimp on each salad. Stir into the dressing 3 tablespoons of the chives. Spoon the dressing over the salads and sprinkle with the remaining chives.

PAPAYA, AVOCADO,
SHRIMP, AND
WATERCRESS SALAD

WILD MUSHROOM
SALAD WITH PANCETTA

POACHED EGG, BACON,
WATERCRESS, AND
ENDIVE SALAD

BUFFALO MOZZARELLA, TOMATO, AND CRAYFISH SALAD

•

FOR 6 SERVINGS

½ pound fresh buffalo mozzarella,
   halved and cut crosswise into
   eighteen ½-inch-thick slices
1 bunch fresh basil leaves, cut
   crosswise into thin julienne
½ cup extra-virgin olive oil
Salt and freshly ground white pepper
2 cups each dry white wine and
   water
6 pounds live crayfish
18 baby limestone lettuce leaves
18 baby oakleaf lettuce leaves
9 bunches baby mâche, leaves
   separated,
1 head baby radicchio, leaves
   separated
4 each medium-size yellow and red
   tomatoes (or all red tomatoes),
   stemmed, cored, and cut into
   thirds
2 tablespoons chopped fresh chives
¾ cup Balsamic Vinaigrette (see page
   34)

WINE SUGGESTION

THE FLINTY FLAVOR OF CALIFORNIA FUMÉ
BLANC WORKS. CHOOSE ONE WITH A
FLAVOR MIDWAY BETWEEN FUMÉ'S
CHARACTERISTIC GRASSY OR RIPE FIG
TASTES—CARMENET, VICHON, OR
CHIMNEY ROCK, FOR EXAMPLE.

FRESH SEASONAL CRAYFISH ARE A GREAT SALAD INGREDIENT THAT GOES wonderfully with fresh, moist buffalo mozzarella and good, vine-ripened tomatoes. The key to the salad's success is the freshness and moistness of all the ingredients: the crayfish tails just poached and chilled, the mozzarella newly made and packed in water, and the best tomatoes you can find. If my suggested greens aren't available, select an equivalent amount of the freshest young greens you can find.

Put the mozzarella slices in a bowl with the basil, olive oil, salt, and pepper. Cover and marinate at room temperature for 1 hour.

Bring the wine and water to a boil. Add the crayfish and boil them for 4 minutes. Drain them and refrigerate in a bowl until cool, about 1 hour.

Twist off and discard the crayfish heads. Holding each tail in a kitchen towel, squeeze to crack its shell, then peel off the shell and put the meat aside.

On each salad plate, arrange 3 baby limestone lettuce leaves in a spoke pattern, with 1 pointing upward and the other 2 down toward either side. Arrange the oakleaf leaves and mâche in between the first leaves to make a nicely patterned bed of lettuces; make a cup out of radicchio leaves in the center of each plate.

On each plate, equidistant around the outer edge of leaves, place 3 marinated mozzarella slices. Place the yellow and red tomato wedges equidistant around the leaves as well.

Fill the radicchio cups with the crayfish tails. Sprinkle the crayfish with the chives. Drizzle the vinaigrette all over each salad.

SALAD OF SHRIMP WITH BALSAMIC VINAIGRETTE

■

FOR 6 SERVINGS

18 baby limestone lettuce leaves
18 baby oakleaf lettuce leaves
9 bunches baby mâche, leaves
    separated
1 head baby radicchio, leaves
    separated
3 medium-size ripe avocados, halved,
    pitted, and peeled, halves cut
    crosswise into ¼-inch-thick slices
1 cup Maui Onion Confit (see page
    41)
1 cup Tomato Concasse (see page
    42), or ½ cup each red and
    yellow Tomato Concasse
1 tablespoon chopped fresh chives
18 medium-size shrimp (about 2
    pounds total), shelled, deveined,
    and tailed; or 18 medium sea
    scallops (about 2 pounds total);
    or 3 baby red snappers, filleted
    to yield 6 individual fillets
3 tablespoons clarified butter (see
    page 23)
Salt and freshly ground white pepper
¾ cup Balsamic Vinaigrette (see page
    34)

WINE SUGGESTION

THIS SALAD WORKS WELL WITH A
MEDIUM-BODIED CHARDONNAY OR FUMÉ
BLANC—TRY JORDAN, CHATEAU ST. JEAN,
OR JOSEPH PHELPS. OR YOU COULD SERVE
A SIMILAR FRENCH POUILLY-FUISSÉ.

A BED OF MIXED GREENS WITH TOMATO CONCASSE, MAUI ONIONS, AND sliced avocado: this is the canvas over which we arrange all of our fish salads. Grilled jumbo shrimp or scallops, or fillets of red snapper, work wonderfully in this context. If you like, you can also add haricots verts—French-style baby green beans—or baby asparagus, just cooked a few minutes in boiling water until al dente, then drained and refreshed under cold running water. If you can't find the greens I suggest, substitute an equivalent amount of the freshest young greens you can find.

Preheat the grill or broiler until very hot.
    For the shrimp or scallop salads, on each salad plate arrange 3 baby limestone lettuce leaves in a spoke pattern, with 1 pointing upward and 2 down toward either side. Arrange the other leaves, including the mâche and radicchio, in between the first leaves to make a nicely patterned bed of lettuces. For the snapper salad, arrange the green radiating from the center outward across the top two thirds of each salad plate, to make an amphitheater-like design.
    Nestle 3 fans of 3 or more avocado slices equidistant around the greens.
    Place a cluster of the Maui confit at the center of each bed of greens. Place heaping spoonfuls of the tomato concasse around the onion confit. Sprinkle the onions with chives.
    Brush the shrimp, scallops, or snapper fillets with the butter and sprinkle with salt and pepper. Grill or broil them until just done, about 1 minute per side, rotating them 90 degrees during the cooking on each side to give them a crisscross pattern.
    Place 3 shrimp or scallops equidistant around the edge of each salad, or place a snapper fillet at the bottom of each plate. Spoon the dressing over each salad.

AHI
CARPACCIO
SALAD

■

FOR 6 SERVINGS

1 (1½-pound) ahi fillet
6 medium-size bunches arugula,
    stemmed, leaves separated
Salt and freshly ground black pepper
6 tablespoons fruity green extra-
    virgin olive oil
6 ounces Parmesan cheese, freshly
    grated
1 ounce fresh black or white truffle
1 lemon, cut into 6 wedges

WINE SUGGESTION

SERVE WITH A SLIGHTLY YOUNG, FIRM-
BODIED CHARDONNAY WITH A FAIRLY
HIGH ACIDITY AND AN EDGE OF
BUTTERINESS—SONOMA-CUTRER, RIDGE,
OR MAYACAMAS WOULD BE GOOD. IT'S
ALSO APPROPRIATE, BECAUSE OF THE
WHITE TRUFFLES, TO SERVE A
CHARDONNAY FROM THE PIEDMONT
REGION OF ITALY, WHERE THE TRUFFLES
COME FROM—CA DEL BOSCO AND GAJA
ARE THE BEST. IT WOULD BE EXCELLENT
AS WELL WITH THE BEST OF CHAMPAGNES
—ROEDERER CRISTAL, DOM PERIGNON,
OR VINTAGE KRUG.

IN 1980, THERE SEEMED TO BE A RAGE IN L.A. SUSHI BARS FOR USING weird Hawaiian fish—wahoo, mahi mahi, and so on. It wasn't really my style, but one day a Japanese chef I knew gave me a thin slice of raw ahi—bluefin tuna—to sample.

It was fabulous, like a blood-rare piece of superb beef. Instantly, it became one of the two raw fish dishes I serve at Michael's, and I present it in a way very like the great raw beef appetizer known as carpaccio—thinly sliced, with spicy arugula leaves, fruity olive oil, a good sharp Parmesan cheese, and earthy black or white truffles. Since fresh white truffles are only available in late November and December, and black truffles in December and January, this is definitely a seasonal dish for me; canned truffles won't do.

If ahi is unavailable, use the best local tuna you can find. But it must be *absolutely* fresh—virtually "off the fin."

Chill the ahi in the refrigerator for 30 to 40 minutes, to firm it up for slicing.

With a sharp knife, cut the ahi across the grain into ⅛-inch-thick slices. Place the slices, sides touching, on large chilled serving plates, covering each plate from its center to within ¾ inch of the rim.

Arrange the arugula leaves around each plate, surrounding the ahi.

Season each serving with salt and pepper to taste. Drizzle with olive oil and sprinkle with Parmesan cheese.

With a truffle shaver or swivel-bladed vegetable peeler, shave the truffle over each serving.

Serve with lemon wedges.

BAKED GOAT CHEESE WITH RADICCHIO, BELGIAN ENDIVE, AND WALNUT VINAIGRETTE

■

FOR 6 SERVINGS

18 radicchio leaves
3 heads Belgian endive, cut crosswise
    into ¼-inch pieces
1½ cups Walnut Vinaigrette (recipe
    follows)
3 tablespoons walnut oil
3 (1½-ounce) crottins de chavignol
    aged goat cheeses, each cut
    horizontally in half
Salt and freshly ground black pepper
2 tablespoons chopped fresh chives
Toasted Walnut Bread (see page 35)

WINE SUGGESTION

RAW YOUNG WINES—BIG BODIED AND
WITH SOME BITE TO THEM FROM OAK OR
TANNIN—GO WELL WITH THE BRASHNESS
OF GOAT CHEESE. CHOOSE A CALIFORNIA
FUMÉ BLANC FROM MAYACAMAS,
MATANZAS CREEK, PHILIP TOGNI, OR
GRGICH HILLS. OR YOU COULD GO RED
WITH A CABERNET THAT'S STATISTICALLY
TOO YOUNG TO DRINK—FROM CLOS DU
VAL, STAG'S LEAP, OR CAYMUS.

I INVENTED THIS SALAD BY LOOKING IN THE FRIDGE AND FINDING SOME aged triple-cream goat cheese and salad greens. It reminds me of fall weekends in the forests of Brittany—the perfect warm salad for a chilly Sunday afternoon. The earthy walnuts are great with the goat cheese and bitter salad leaves.

Baking the cheese gives it a wonderfully rich, creamy quality. Be sure to choose a well-aged, creamy goat cheese that comes in the short cylindrical shape known as a *crottin de chavignol* (French slang for "horse dropping"!).

Preheat the broiler.
    Arrange 3 radicchio leaves on each plate, equally spaced like the spokes of a wheel, with 1 leaf pointing to 12 o'clock, 1 to 4 o'clock, and 1 to 8 o'clock. Place the sliced endive pieces at the center of each plate.

Prepare the vinaigrette and set it aside.

Put the walnut oil in a shallow baking dish. Put the goat cheese halves in the dish, cut sides up, and sprinkle with salt and pepper. Put the dish in the broiler, 3 to 4 inches from the heat, and broil until the tops of the cheeses are golden brown and bubbly, about 3 minutes.

With a spatula, transfer each goat cheese half to a salad, placing it on top of the endive. Spoon the dressing over the greens around the cheese and garnish with chives. Serve with walnut toast.

WALNUT VINAIGRETTE

.

FOR ABOUT 1½ CUPS

1 large egg yolk, at room
    temperature
2 heaping tablespoons whole-grain
    mustard
2 tablespoons sherry wine vinegar
½ cup walnut oil
Salt and freshly ground black pepper
3 tablespoons coarsely chopped
    walnuts

In a bowl, whisk together the egg yolk, mustard, and vinegar until smooth.

Whisking briskly and continuously, slowly pour in the walnut oil in a thin stream until it is thoroughly emulsified.

Season to taste with salt and pepper and add the walnuts.

SALADE CLASSIQUE

■

FOR 6 SERVINGS

30 red leaf lettuce leaves
30 large spinach leaves, stemmed
18 radicchio leaves
1¼ pounds French-style green beans
    (haricots verts), trimmed,
    parboiled for 3 to 10 minutes
    until al dente, then chilled in the
    refrigerator
12 medium-size fresh mushrooms,
    stemmed and cut into strips ¼
    inch wide and ¼ inch thick
¾ pound duck foie gras, cut into 2 ×
    ¼ × ¼-inch strips
Salt and freshly ground white pepper
6 lobster tails, poached, chilled, and
    cut into 5 medallions each
6 lobster claws, poached, chilled,
    shelled, and left whole
1 cup Basic Vinaigrette (see page 34)
6 tablespoons chopped fresh chives

WINE SUGGESTION

DIFFERENT WINES WILL GO WITH THIS
COMBINATION OF INGREDIENTS. YOU
COULD SERVE A VERY GOOD FRENCH
WHITE BURGUNDY—MEURSAULT,
PULIGNY-MONTRACHET, OR CHASSAGNE-
MONTRACHET. OR A WHITE RHÔNE—
CONDRIEU, HERMITAGE BLANC, OR
CHÂTEAUNEUF-DU-PAPE. OR YOU COULD
SERVE A LIGHTER, FRENCH-STYLE
CALIFORNIA CHARDONNAY—TREFETHEN,
CLOS PEGASE, OR ROBERT MONDAVI
RESERVE.

WHEN I FIRST CAME BACK TO THE U.S. FROM PARIS IN 1974, ALL THE exponents of nouvelle cuisine were serving experimental salads that turned the elements of classic cuisine on their heads. These wild combinations of crayfish, foie gras, truffle, and all kinds of other ingredients were given names like *salade folle* (crazy salad), *salade fantaisie, salade de luxe.*

I came up with my own simple version of a nouvelle-style salad. And since it was fairly simple and elegant, and it was by now my interpretation of a nouvelle standard, I called it Salade Classique.

If you like, you can add some shavings of black or white truffle, one on each lobster medallion and a few more on the claw.

Arrange 5 red leaf lettuce leaves in the center of each plate. Place 5 spinach leaves on top of the red leaf lettuce. Place 3 radicchio leaves in the center of each plate, forming a cup. Toss together the haricots verts and the mushrooms and set them aside.

Heat a dry large, heavy skillet until very hot. Season the foie gras with salt and pepper and sauté them very briefly, about 30 seconds per side.

Place 5 lobster medallions on each plate, around the radicchio cup. Place 5 pieces of foie gras on each plate, between the lobster medallions.

Gently toss the remaining foie gras with the haricots verts and mushrooms. Place the mixture inside the radicchio cups and place a lobster claw on top. Drizzle the salads with the vinaigrette and sprinkle with chives.

GRILLED QUAIL SALAD

6 baby quail, about 3 ounces each,
    split down backbones, spine and
    ribs removed, leg bones left in
1 recipe Basic Marinade (see page 23)
1 cup shucked fresh sweet corn
    (about 3 medium-size ears)
8 tablespoons (1 stick) unsalted
    butter
Salt and freshly ground white pepper
18 baby Belgian endive leaves
18 baby limestone lettuce leaves
18 baby oakleaf lettuce leaves
8 bunches baby mâche, leaves
    separated
1 head baby radicchio, leaves
    separated
1 cup Tomato Concasse (see page 42)
1 cup Maui Onion Confit (see page
    41)
1 cup hot cooked wild rice (see page
    41)
3 tablespoons Jalapeño-Cilantro-Lime
    Salsa (see page 33)

WINE SUGGESTION

SERVED WITH THE SALSA, THIS SALAD IS
SENSATIONAL WITH A YOUNGER
CALIFORNIA PINOT NOIR WITH GOOD
FRUITINESS AND SOFT TANNINS;
CHALONE AND ACACIA ARE GOOD
CHOICES. IF YOU GO WITH A CABERNET
CASSIS SAUCE, SHOW OFF A GOOD
YOUNG CABERNET WITH LOTS OF FRUIT
AND TANNIN TO IT, SUCH AS STAG'S LEAP,
CHATEAU MONTELENA, OR GRGICH HILLS.

THE KEY TO THIS SALAD IS TO MAKE SURE THAT THE QUAIL ARE GRILLED very quickly; for most of the cooking, the skin side should face the heat, and then they should be cooked very lightly on the other side. What you don't want to do is overcook them.

Instead of the salsa, you can also dress the salad with 1 cup of Cabernet Cassis Sauce (see page 30).

Again, if my suggested greens are not available, substitute your own combination of fresh young greens.

Three days before you plan to serve the salad, arrange the quail in a dish or bowl and cover them with the marinade. Cover the dish with plastic wrap and leave the quail to marinate in the refrigerator.

Preheat the grill or broiler until very hot.

Bring a pot of water to a boil, add the corn, and parboil for 3 minutes. Drain well. Melt the butter over medium heat in a skillet, add the corn, and sauté for 2 minutes; season with salt and pepper.

On each salad plate, arrange 3 baby Belgian endive leaves in a spoke pattern, with 1 pointing upward and the other 2 down toward either side. Arrange the other leaves, along with the mâche and radicchio, in between the first leaves to make a nicely patterned bed of lettuces. Spoon the tomato concasse along the center of each Belgian endive leaf.

Put spoonfuls of the Maui confit, wild rice, and corn in the center of each bed of leaves.

Wipe the marinade off the quail and season on both sides with salt and pepper. Cross their legs and grill them, skin sides toward the heat, for about 2 minutes, then turn and grill them for about 30 seconds to cook them medium-rare.

Place a quail in the center of each salad and sprinkle the salsa on top.

SALADE CLASSIQUE

GRILLED QUAIL SALAD

GRILLED CHICKEN AND GOAT CHEESE SALAD WITH JALAPEÑO-CILANTRO-LIME SALSA

■

FOR 6 SERVINGS

ONE OF THE GREAT PLEASURES OF THIS DISH IS ITS SPONTANEITY. THE salad greens are dressed not only with the balsamic-vinegar-and-olive-oil vinaigrette, but also with the juices that drip from the sliced grilled chicken breasts and the salsa. While it may seem like a wild combination, they all work together; it's one of those moments—like when all the planets align. Substitute your own combination of fresh young salad greens if the ones I suggest aren't available.

6 chicken breast halves, boned, skin left on, and wing bones attached

1 log, about 12 ounces, fresh, creamy white California goat cheese, cut into ¼-inch medallions

Salt and freshly ground black pepper

3 each red and yellow bell peppers, stemmed, seeded, and cut into ¾- to 1-inch-wide strips

1 large or 2 medium-size Maui, Walla Walla, Vidalia, or sweet red onions peeled and cut into ⅜-inch slices

2 tablespoons extra-virgin olive oil

3 heads limestone lettuce, leaves separated, washed, dried, and torn

3 bunches mâche, leaves separated, washed, dried, and torn

2 bunches arugula, leaves separated, washed, dried, and torn

2 heads baby red leaf lettuce, leaves separated, washed, dried, and torn

1 head baby radicchio, leaves separated

1 cup Tomato Concasse (see page 42)

1 cup Balsamic Vinaigrette (see page 34)

1 cup Jalapeño-Cilantro-Lime Salsa (see page 33)

1 bunch fresh chives, finely chopped

(see page 42)

(see page 34)

(see page 33)

WINE SUGGESTION

THIS IS A DISH FOR YOUNG WINES; IT BRINGS OUT THEIR FRUIT. TRY A SAUVIGNON OR FUMÉ BLANC WITH LOTS OF OAK AND FRUIT, SUCH AS GRGICH HILLS OR CHATEAU ST. JEAN. CHARDONNAYS WOULD BE PERFECTLY OKAY. THE DISH WOULD KILL MOST EUROPEAN WINES, EXCEPT FOR RED BURGUNDIES; A YOUNG PINOT NOIR, COOLED DOWN, WOULD BE FINE.

Preheat the grill or broiler.

With your finger, gently make a pocket between the skin and meat of each chicken breast, inserting your finger along the long side of each breast and leaving the skin attached along the other edges. Insert the medallions of goat cheese, overlapping slightly, inside the pockets to stuff the chicken breasts. Sprinkle the breasts with salt and pepper.

Brush the pepper strips and onion slices with the olive oil and season them with salt and pepper. Set them aside.

Grill the chicken breasts, skin side up first, until nicely browned, 3 to 5 minutes. Then turn them over and grill for 5 to 7 minutes more.

About 1 minute before the chicken is done, place the peppers and onion slices on the grill; grill them about 30 seconds per side, until heated through and lightly charred.

Arrange all the salad leaves on 6 large serving plates.

Cut each grilled breast crosswise into 4 or 5 slices and place in the center of a bed of greens. Garnish each plate with 3 spoonfuls of tomato concasse and the grilled peppers and onions. Dress the vegetables with the vinaigrette. Spoon the salsa over the chicken. Sprinkle each serving with chopped chives.

GRILLED SQUAB SALAD WITH CURLY ENDIVE, SPINACH, AND RASPBERRY VINEGAR SAUCE

■

FOR 6 SALADS

3 squabs, partially boned (leg and
   wing bones left in), and halved
1 recipe Basic Marinade (see page 23)
2 cups raspberry vinegar
3 medium-size shallots, finely
   chopped
2 cups chicken stock (see page 22)
1 cup heavy cream
Salt and freshly ground white pepper
30 perfect spinach leaves, washed and
   stemmed
3 cups curly endive leaves, torn into
   bite-sized pieces
¼ cup broken walnut pieces
30 fresh raspberries

WINE SUGGESTION

THIS SALAD WILL TAKE THE BEST YOUNG
CALIFORNIA PINOT NOIR AND, WITH THE
RASPBERRY SAUCE MATCHING THE
RASPBERRY FLAVOR IN THE WINE, SHOW
IT OFF UNBELIEVABLY WELL. CHALONE,
MOUNT EDEN, AND ACACIA ARE ALL FINE
CHOICES. IT WOULD ALSO BE GOOD WITH
AN EXCELLENT YOUNG GRAND CRU
BEAUJOLAIS OR A BEAUJOLAIS NOUVEAU.

PEOPLE COULDN'T BELIEVE IT WHEN I INTRODUCED THIS SALAD IN 1979: grilled poultry on salads was revolutionary. The idea came from the duck salads I'd eaten in France, but I think the squab we get in the United States now is truly spectacular for this dish.

If you like, have your butcher bone the squabs for you, leaving the bones in the legs and wings. Save the bones to add to the stock you use to make the sauce. And use only the pale yellow-green center leaves of the curly endive; they're less bitter than the dark green outer leaves.

The night before you plan to serve the salad, or up to 2 days before, arrange the squabs in a dish or bowl and cover them with the marinade. Cover the dish with plastic wrap and leave the squabs to marinate in the refrigerator.

For the sauce, put the vinegar and shallots in a medium-size saucepan over moderate heat and boil until the vinegar has almost evaporated but the shallots are still moist. Add the stock and reduce by about three quarters, about 15 minutes. Add the cream, bring it to a boil, and season to taste with salt and pepper. Remove from the heat and keep the sauce warm.

While the sauce is reducing, preheat the grill or broiler until very hot.

Prepare the salad plates. On each plate, place 5 spinach leaves in a star shape, their points touching the inner rim of the plate. Put ½ cup of curly endive leaves in the center of each star and sprinkle walnuts on top.

Wipe the marinade off the squabs and season with salt and pepper. Cook them with their skin sides facing the heat for about 2½ minutes; halfway through the cooking, rotate them 90 degrees to give them crosshatched grill marks. Then turn them over and cook 2½ minutes more, until medium-rare.

Carve each squab breast into 5 or 6 thin slices and drape them over the curly endive. Place a wing on one side of the endive and a leg on the other. Place 5 raspberries on each plate, in between the points of the spinach leaves. Spoon the sauce over the breast slices and the endive.

TENDERLOIN
OF LAMB
SALAD WITH
CASSIS SAUCE

•

FOR 6 SERVINGS

THIS IS A LIGHT SALAD ALTERNATIVE TO THE MAIN-COURSE GRILLED Saddle of Lamb with Black Currants (recipe on page 167). It originated because, when we bought the whole saddles of lamb for the main course, we had little tenderloins left over; served with the same sauce on a bed of greens (substitute your own combination if the ones I suggest aren't available), they made a great salad.

6 boned lamb tenderloins, 3 to 4
  ounces each
Salt and freshly ground white pepper
¼ cup red currant jelly, melted
1 cup shucked fresh sweet corn
  (about 3 medium-size ears)
¼ pound (1 stick) unsalted butter
18 each baby limestone and oakleaf
  lettuce leaves
9 bunches baby mâche, leaves
  separated
1 head baby radicchio, leaves
  separated
1 cup Tomato Concasse (see page 42)
1 cup hot cooked wild rice (see page
  41)
2 medium-size Maui, Walla Walla,
  Vidalia, or sweet red onions, cut
  crosswise into ¼-inch-thick slices
4 tablespoons clarified butter (see
  page 23)
¾ cup Cassis Sauce (see page 30)
2 tablespoons julienne of fresh basil

Preheat the grill or broiler until very hot. Season the lamb with salt and pepper, brush it with the red currant jelly, and leave it to marinate at room temperature.

Bring a pot of water to a boil, add the corn, and parboil it for 3 minutes. Drain well. Melt the butter over medium heat in a skillet, add the corn, and sauté for 2 minutes; season with salt and pepper.

On each salad plate, arrange the salad leaves radiating from the center outward across the top two thirds of each salad plate to make an amphitheater-like design, framing the bottom third of the plate with radicchio leaves. On each plate, place 2 heaping tablespoons of tomato concasse among the leaves; place a scoop of wild rice at the center of the radicchio, with spoonfuls of corn on either side.

Grill the lamb, about 3 minutes per side for medium-rare rare, rotating the fillets 90 degrees halfway through the cooking on each side to give them crosshatched grill marks.

At the same time, brush the onions with the butter, season them with salt and pepper, and grill them for about 1½ minutes per side.

Carve the lamb into ¼-inch slices and arrange them across the bottom third of each plate, hiding the bottoms of the radicchio leaves. Scatter the grilled onions over the center of each salad, spoon the sauce over the lamb, and garnish the lamb with the basil.

WINE SUGGESTION

SERVE A CABERNET IF YOU USE CABERNET SAUVIGNON IN THE SAUCE, A PINOT NOIR IF YOU USE PINOT NOIR. FOR CABERNETS, CHOOSE NIEBAUM-COPPOLA "RUBICON," MATANZAS CREEK, RIDGE, OR LAUREL GLEN; FOR PINOT NOIRS, CALERA AND MAYACAMAS.

SWEETBREAD AND WILD MUSHROOM SALAD

■

FOR 6 SERVINGS

2 cups each dry white wine and
    water
1¼ pounds veal sweetbreads
18 baby limestone lettuce leaves
18 baby oakleaf lettuce leaves
9 bunches baby mâche, leaves
    separated
1 head baby radicchio, leaves
    separated
1 cup Maui Onion Confit (see page
    41)
1 cup hot cooked wild rice (see page
    41)
Salt and freshly ground white pepper
¼ cup all-purpose flour
½ cup walnut oil
½ tablespoon unsalted butter
12 medium-size fresh chanterelle
    mushrooms (about 1 pound
    total), each sliced lengthwise into
    3 pieces
3 medium-size shallots, finely
    chopped
½ teaspoon finely chopped fresh
    thyme leaves
½ teaspoon julienne of fresh basil
¾ cup Balsamic Vinaigrette (see page
    34)
2 tablespoons chopped fresh chives

THE SUCCESS OF THIS SALAD DEPENDS ON THE COOKING OF THE SWEET-breads: they should be very crispy on the outside and nice and succulent on the inside. Follow the cooking directions carefully. Again, substitute your own combination of fresh young salad greens if the ones I have suggested aren't available.

In a medium-size saucepan, bring the white wine and water to a boil. Adjust the heat to a simmer, add the sweetbreads, and blanch them for 3 minutes. Drain them and, with a small, sharp knife and your fingertips, remove their membrances and trim them. Divide the sweetbreads into 6 equal portions about ½ inch thick.

On each salad plate, arrange 3 baby limestone lettuce leaves in a spoke pattern, with 1 pointing upward and the other 2 down toward either side. Arrange the other leaves, along with the mâche and radicchio, in between the first leaves to make a nicely patterned bed of lettuces.

Put 2 heaping tablespoons each of the Maui confit and the wild rice in the center of each bed of leaves.

Season the sweetbreads with salt and pepper. Sprinkle the flour on a plate and lightly dredge the sweetbreads in it on both sides.

Put ¼ cup of the walnut oil in each of 2 separate skillets, add butter to one of them, and heat both skillets over high heat until the oil begins to smoke and the butter to brown.

Simultaneously, put the sweetbreads in the skillet with the butter, and the chanterelles in the other skillet. Sauté the sweetbreads for 1½ minutes per side, until golden; then place them on top of the onions and rice in the center of each salad.

At the same time, let the chanterelles set and brown, without stirring, for 30 seconds; add the shallots, then turn the chanterelles and let them set on the other side for 30 seconds more. Add the thyme and basil and season to taste with salt and pepper. Distribute the chanterelles around the sweetbreads on each salad. Spoon the vinaigrette over the lettuces. Pour the pan juices over the sweetbreads and mushrooms and garnish with chives.

GRILLED SQUAB SALAD
WITH CURLY ENDIVE,
SPINACH, AND
RASPBERRY VINEGAR
SAUCE

TENDERLOIN OF LAMB
SALAD WITH CASSIS
SAUCE

CURLY ENDIVE AND BACON SALAD

■

FOR 6 SERVINGS

5 medium-size heads curly endive,
    dark outer leaves removed, pale
    inner leaves separated
6 strips, each ¼ inch thick, smoked
    bacon, cut into ¼-inch pieces
2 tablespoons Dijon mustard
¼ cup sherry wine vinegar
1 cup peanut oil
Salt and freshly ground white pepper
2 tablespoons chopped fresh chives

THIS VERY SIMPLE SALAD PLAYS A TRADITIONAL ROLE BETWEEN COURSES but is nevertheless very rich in taste, through the combination of the hot mustard and the bacon. It's a French classic that preceded the popular hot spinach salads you find all over the place today.

Mound the curly endive leaves on 6 salad plates.
    Put the bacon in a medium-size skillet and sauté it over high heat until the bacon is crisp, 3 to 5 minutes.

Drain the bacon on paper towels, reserving about ¾ cup of the fat in the skillet. Add the mustard to the skillet and stir briskly with a wire whisk over medium heat until just smooth. Remove the skillet from the heat and whisk in the vinegar, then the oil. Season to taste with salt, if necessary, and pepper.

Scatter the bacon pieces over the endive and pour the hot dressing over each salad. Top with chopped chives.

MIXED GREENS WITH BALSAMIC VINAIGRETTE

■

FOR 6 SERVINGS

*18 leaves each baby limestone lettuce,
baby radicchio, baby oakleaf
lettuce, and baby arugula*
*9 bunches baby mâche, leaves
separated*
*1 head curly endive, dark outer
leaves removed, pale inner leaves
separated*
*¾ cup Tomato Concasse (see page
42), optional*
*¾ cup Balsamic Vinaigrette (see page
34)*
2 tablespoons chopped fresh chives

WITH THE VAST INCREASE IN THE AVAILABILITY OF ALL KINDS OF BABY lettuces, I began to use them as an alternative to the classic mixed green salad. Although I list below the classic leaves that we prefer to use, the mixture is constantly changing to take advantage of the best produce.

Baby lettuces are available today in many supermarkets and produce shops. Use the freshest, smallest, best-quality baby greens you can find, whatever kind they may be. You will want about a cup of baby greens per person.

On each plate, arrange the salad leaves like the spokes of a wheel, starting with the limestone, then the radicchio, oakleaf, arugula, and mâche. Top the center of each salad with a cluster of curly endive leaves. If you like, place 3 spoonfuls of tomato concasse equidistant around the endive.

Spoon the dressing over the salads and sprinkle with chives.

Sinjerli Variation III
by Frank Stella

CHAPTER SEVEN
SEAFOOD

GRILLED WHITEFISH WITH BEURRE ROSE AND MAUI ONION CONFIT

∎

FOR 6 SERVINGS

1½ cups Beurre Rose (see page 29)
6 whitefish fillets, 6 ounces each
3 tablespoons clarified butter (see page 23)
Salt and freshly ground white pepper
¾ cup Maui Onion Confit (see page 41)
2 tablespoons chopped fresh chives

WINE SUGGESTION
WHILE SOME PEOPLE MAY ARGUE THAT THE RED WINE IN THE SAUCE WOULD LET YOU POUR A RED WINE, DOING SO WOULD MASK THE DELICACY OF THE WHITEFISH. SERVE A LIGHT, EVENLY BALANCED CHARDONNAY SUCH AS JOSEPH PHELPS OR ROBERT MONDAVI RESERVE.

THIS DISH IS MY HOMAGE TO THE LATE JEAN BERTRANOU, FOUNDER OF L'Ermitage in Los Angeles; I first tasted it at his restaurant right before I opened Michael's.

At the time, whitefish was very popular. The problem was, most fish that was called whitefish wasn't the real stuff. You need extremely clean, clear deep waters, cold year round—the kind of conditions you find in Lake Superior, where the best whitefish comes from. The fish is moist and pure in flavor, not at all fishy; it's so good you can eat it without anything, just a little salt and pepper and a touch of butter to keep it from sticking to the grill. Interestingly, the Beurre Rose, whose color and rich taste contrast with the fish, is a great sauce for it.

Nowadays, it's easier to find good, real whitefish, flown in from Michigan. Find the best fish purveyor in your area and ask for the best Lake Superior whitefish—the freshest, not frozen. If you can't locate whitefish, this recipe also tastes great with red snapper.

Preheat the grill or broiler until very hot. Meanwhile, prepare the beurre rose and keep it warm.

Brush the whitefish fillets with the butter and sprinkle them with salt and pepper. Grill or broil them until they are just cooked through but still moist, about 1½ minutes per side; halfway through the cooking on each side, rotate the fillets 90 degrees to give them crosshatched grill marks.

Place the fillets on heated serving plates. Place a spoonful of Maui Onion Confit on top, then spoon the sauce on top of the fish and sprinkle the sauce with chives.

GRILLED POMPANO WITH GINGER-LIME BEURRE BLANC

■

FOR 6 SERVINGS

1½ cups Beurre Blanc (see page 29)
3 whole pompano, 1 pound each,
    filleted and skinned to yield 6
    fillets
3 tablespoons clarified butter (see
    page 23)
Salt and freshly ground white pepper
3 tablespoons fresh lime juice
1½ teaspoons freshly grated ginger
2 tablespoons julienne of basil

WINE SUGGESTION
SERVE A FRESH YOUNG CHARDONNAY
WITH GOOD ACIDITY AND A FIRM BUT
LIGHT BALANCE OF BUTTER AND OAK,
SUCH AS CHIMNEY ROCK, CHATEAU
MONTELENA, OR EYRIE VINEYARD IN
OREGON.

FLORIDA POMPANO IS A VERY ELEGANT FISH WITH A DELICATE YET DIS-
tinctive flavor that is perfectly complemented by ginger and lime. It's
a seasonal fish, available only in winter; buy the smallest ones you
can find. The sauce is also good with whitefish, snapper, or sea bass,
and it's also excellent with lobster.

Preheat the grill or broiler until very hot. Meanwhile, prepare the
beurre blanc and keep it warm.

Brush the pompano fillets with the butter and sprinkle with salt
and pepper. Grill or broil them for about 1½ minutes per side; halfway
through the cooking on each side, rotate the fillets 90 degrees to give
them crosshatched grill marks.

While the pompano is grilling, stir the lime juice and ginger into
the beurre blanc.

When the pompano is done, place the fillets on heated serving
plates. Spoon the sauce alongside each fillet. Garnish with the basil.

GRILLED SALMON WITH BEURRE BLANC AND SALMON CAVIAR

■

FOR 6 SERVINGS

1½ cups Beurre Blanc (see page 29)
6 salmon fillets, 6 ounces each,
  skinned, small bones pulled out
  with tweezers
3 tablespoons clarified butter (see
  page 23)
Salt and freshly ground white pepper
¼ cup salmon caviar
2 tablespoons chopped fresh chives

WINE SUGGESTION
SERVE WITH A WELL-AGED CLASSIC
CALIFORNIA CHARDONNAY SUCH AS
ACACIA, CHATEAU MONTELENA, OR
SONOMA-CUTRER; OR WITH A GOOD
WHITE BURGUNDY—PULIGNY-
MONTRACHET, CHASSAGNE-
MONTRACHET, OR MEURSAULT.

ALMOST EVERY FINE RESTAURANT IN THE WORLD POACHES OR SAUTÉS its salmon. I prefer to grill it to seal in the salmon's elegant natural flavor. I serve the salmon with Beurre Blanc, a classic sauce whose richness complements the fish's own rich taste and texture, but it tastes equally good with Beurre Rose (see page 29).

Preheat the grill or broiler until very hot. Meanwhile, prepare the Beurre Blanc and keep it warm.

Brush the salmon fillets with the butter and season with salt and pepper. Grill or broil them until they are medium-rare, just beginning to cook in the center, 4 to 5 minutes per side; halfway through the cooking on each side, rotate the fillets 90 degrees to give them cross-hatched grill marks.

Place the fillet on heated serving plates. Spoon the Beurre Blanc around the salmon. Place 2 teaspoons of salmon caviar on top of each fillet and sprinkle the sauce with chives.

GRILLED SALMON WITH
BEURRE BLANC AND
SALMON CAVIAR

GRILLED WHITEFISH
WITH BEURRE ROSE AND
MAUI ONION CONFIT

GRILLED POMPANO
WITH GINGER-LIME
BEURRE BLANC

GRILLED SNAPPER WITH GINGER-LIME-CILANTRO BEURRE BLANC

∎

FOR 6 SERVINGS

1½ cups Beurre Blanc (see page 29)

3 whole red snappers, 1 pound each, scaled, skins left on, filleted to yield 2 whole fillets each

3 tablespoons clarified butter (see page 23)

Salt and freshly ground white pepper

3 tablespoons fresh lime juice

2 tablespoons finely chopped fresh cilantro leaves

1½ teaspoons freshly grated ginger

2 limes, segmented

1 tablespoon whole fresh cilantro leaves

GRILLED SNAPPER, WITH ITS CRISPY SKIN, GOES VERY WELL WITH THIS Oriental-style sauce.

Preheat the grill or broiler until very hot. Meanwhile, prepare the beurre blanc and keep it warm.

Brush the snapper fillets with the butter and sprinkle with salt and pepper. Grill or broil them, starting with the skin sides facing the heat, for about 1½ minutes per side; halfway through the cooking on each side, rotate the fillets 90 degrees to give them crosshatched grill marks.

While the snapper is grilling, stir the lime juice, chopped cilantro, and ginger into the Beurre Blanc.

When the snapper is done, place the fillets on heated serving plates. Spoon the sauce alongside each fillet. Garnish with the lime segments and cilantro leaves.

WINE SUGGESTION

THE ORIENTAL FLAVORS CALL FOR A MEDIUM-BODIED, SLIGHTLY OAKY CHARDONNAY—CHAPPELLET, TREFETHEN, OR CLOS DU VAL, FOR EXAMPLE.

GRILLED SNAPPER WITH VINAIGRETTE

•

FOR 6 SERVINGS

3 whole red snappers, 1 pound each,
    scaled, skins left on, filleted to
    yield 2 whole fillets each
3 tablespoons clarified butter (see
    page 23)
Salt and freshly ground white pepper
¾ cup Tomato Concasse (see page
    42)
1½ cups Sherry Wine Vinaigrette
    (recipe follows)
2 lemons, segmented
2 tablespoons julienne of fresh basil

BABY RED SNAPPERS, EITHER FROM FLORIDA OR NEW ZEALAND, ARE SPEC-tacularly good fish. If you buy the baby ones, about 1 pound each, and have them filleted, they're just the right size for a very elegant, simple presentation. The vinaigrette gives the fish a very Mediterranean flavor.

Preheat the grill or broiler until very hot.

Brush the snapper fillets with the butter and sprinkle with salt and pepper. Grill or broil them, starting with the skin sides facing the heat, for about 1½ minutes per side; halfway through the cooking on each side, rotate the fillets 90 degrees to give them crosshatched grill marks.

While the snapper is grilling, place the tomato concasse in a bowl and stir in the vinaigrette and salt and pepper to taste. Toss well.

When the snapper is done, place the fillets on heated serving plates. Spoon the sauce alongside each fillet. Garnish with the lemon segments and basil.

WINE SUGGESTION

THE LIGHTNESS OF THE SNAPPER AND THE SHARPNESS OF THE SAUCE GO WELL WITH A GOOD, MEDIUM-BODIED CALIFORNIA FUMÉ BLANC THAT'S A BIT TOO YOUNG TO DRINK ORDINARILY. TRY THOSE FROM CARMENET, VICHON, CHIMNEY ROCK, OR CHATEAU ST. JEAN.

GRILLED SNAPPER WITH
VINAIGRETTE

GRILLED SNAPPER WITH
GINGER-LIME-CILANTRO
BEURRE BLANC

SHERRY WINE VINAIGRETTE

•

FOR 1½ CUPS

⅓ cup sherry wine vinegar

1 cup extra-virgin olive oil or walnut
   oil

1 medium-size clove garlic, double-
   blanched (see page 28)

¾ teaspoon finely chopped fresh
   shallot

Fresh lemon juice

Salt and freshly ground white pepper

Put the vinegar in a mixing bowl and, whisking continuously, gradually pour in the oil. Stir in the garlic clove, shallot, and lemon juice to taste and set the bowl aside for about 10 minutes.

Strain out the garlic and shallots from the dressing. Stir in salt and pepper to taste.

GRILLED SWORDFISH WITH CHANTERELLES, CHARDONNAY CREAM SAUCE, AND TARRAGON

•

FOR 6 SERVINGS

1½ cups Chardonnay Cream Sauce I
   (see pages 30–31)
2 tablespoons unsalted butter
3 dozen medium-size fresh chanterelle
   mushrooms
6 swordfish fillet steaks, 6 ounces
   each
3 tablespoons clarified butter (see
   page 23)
Salt and freshly ground white pepper
2 tablespoons whole fresh tarragon
   leaves

WINE SUGGESTION

THE EARTHINESS OF THE MUSHROOMS
GOES WELL WITH THE EARTHINESS OF
CLASSIC FRENCH WHITE BURGUNDIES
SUCH AS PULIGNY-MONTRACHET,
CHASSAGNE-MONTRACHET, OR
MEURSAULT. YOU COULD ALSO SERVE A
BIG, WELL-BALANCED, CLASSIC
CALIFORNIA CHARDONNAY, WHETHER
YOUNG OR WELL AGED—SUCH AS
CHALONE, MOUNT EDEN, OR
MAYACAMAS.

Prepare the Chardonnay cream sauce and keep it warm.
   Preheat the grill or broiler until very hot.
   In a medium-size saucepan, melt the butter over moderate heat and sauté the chanterelles until tender. Set them aside.
   Brush the swordfish with the clarified butter and season with salt and pepper. Grill or broil them until medium-rare and just beginning to cook in the center, 4 to 5 minutes per side; halfway through the cooking on each side, rotate the fillets 90 degrees to give them cross-hatched grill marks.
   When the swordfish is almost done, add the chanterelles to the sauce to warm through. Adjust the seasoning of the sauce to taste.
   Place the swordfish fillets on heated serving plates. Spoon the sauce and the chanterelles alongside each fillet. Scatter tarragon leaves over the mushrooms and sauce, and serve immediately.

GRILLED SWORDFISH
WITH TOMATO-BASIL
VINAIGRETTE

GRILLED SWORDFISH
WITH POMMERY
MUSTARD CREAM SAUCE

GRILLED SWORDFISH WITH TOMATO-BASIL VINAIGRETTE

∎

FOR 6 SERVINGS

6 swordfish fillet steaks, 6 ounces
    each
3 tablespoons clarified butter (see
    page 23)
Salt and freshly ground white pepper
½ cup each red and yellow Tomato
    Concasse (see page 42)
1½ cups Balsamic Vinaigrette (see
    page 34)
2 tablespoons julienne of fresh basil

WINE SUGGESTION

THIS IS AN IDEAL DISH FOR A VERY
YOUNG, BIG CHARDONNAY, ONE YOU
MIGHT WANT TO TRY OUT BEFORE YOU
COMMIT TO BUYING A CASE; THE
COMBINATION OF THE MEATY SWORDFISH
AND THE SHARP SAUCE WILL GIVE YOU
AN IDEA OF WHAT THE WINE WILL BE LIKE
ONCE IT HAS HAD TIME TO DEVELOP. TRY
MATANZAS CREEK, MERRY VINTNERS, OR
SONOMA-CUTRER.

SWORDFISH IS A GREAT, MEATY FISH THAT GRILLS UP PERFECTLY. AT THE restaurant, I like to serve it with one of three very different sauces—the fresh tomato and basil combination here, the Pommery mustard cream, or Chardonnay cream with chanterelle mushrooms and fresh tarragon that follow.

Preheat the grill or broiler until very hot.

Brush the swordfish with the butter and sprinkle with salt and pepper. Grill or broil them until medium-rare and just beginning to cook in the center, 4 to 5 minutes per side; halfway through the cooking on each side, rotate the fillets 90 degrees to give them cross-hatched grill marks.

While the swordfish is grilling, place the red and yellow tomato concasses in separate bowls. Add half of the vinaigrette and basil to each bowl, along with salt and pepper to taste. Toss well.

When the swordfish is done, place the fillets on heated serving plates. Spoon the yellow and red tomato mixtures alongside each fillet and serve immediately.

GRILLED SWORDFISH WITH POMMERY MUSTARD CREAM SAUCE

·

FOR 6 SERVINGS

2 cups heavy cream
6 swordfish fillet steaks, 6 ounces
    each
3 tablespoons clarified butter (see
    page 23)
Salt and freshly ground white pepper
2 tablespoons Pommery mustard
2 tablespoons julienne of fresh basil

WINE SUGGESTION

THE MELLOWNESS OF THE SAUCE HERE
WILL COMPLEMENT A BIG, OLDER
CHARDONNAY. TRY GRGICH HILLS,
CHATEAU MONTELENA, STONY HILL, OR
WOLTNER.

In a medium-size saucepan, bring the cream to a boil. Reduce the heat and simmer briskly until it reduces by about half, about 15 minutes.

Meanwhile, preheat the grill or broiler until very hot.

Brush the swordfish with the butter and sprinkle with salt and pepper. Grill or broil them until medium-rare and just beginning to cook in the center, 4 to 5 minutes per side; halfway through the cooking on each side, rotate the fillets 90 degrees to give them cross-hatched grill marks.

When the cream is reduced and the swordfish is almost done, stir the mustard into the cream. Season the sauce to taste with salt and pepper.

Place the swordfish fillets on heated serving plates. Spoon the mustard cream sauce around each fillet, scatter basil over the sauce, and serve immediately.

GRILLED SCALLOPS WITH WATERCRESS-LIME BEURRE BLANC

•

FOR 6 SERVINGS

2¼ cups Beurre Blanc (see page 29)

2 bunches watercress, leaves finely
    chopped, stems discarded

3 limes, juiced

30 large sea scallops

6 tablespoons clarified butter (see
    page 23)

Salt and freshly ground white pepper

18 fresh raspberries

Vegetable Mosaics (see pages 44–45)

WINE SUGGESTION

WHILE YOU MIGHT ORDINARILY SERVE A
FUMÉ BLANC WITH SCALLOPS, THE
RICHNESS OF THE SAUCE CALLS FOR A
LIGHT-BODIED CHARDONNAY, FAIRLY
ACIDIC WITH JUST A LITTLE BUTTERINESS
TO IT—SUCH AS SMITH-MADRONE, IRON
HORSE, OR DOMAINE MICHEL. THESE
CHARACTERISTICS ALSO APPLY TO
CLASSIC FRENCH CHABLIS.

FRESH SCALLOPS ARE ONE OF MY FAVORITE CHARBROILED ITEMS, AND they're great when combined with a Beurre Blanc full of chopped dark green watercress and heavily accented with lime juice. I use only giant sea scallops, about an inch across and ¾ inch thick—they're plumper and sweeter.

I add three raspberries to each plate before serving, a funny old holdover from the days of nouvelle cuisine. They give an extra contrast of color, and the fruit plays off the sweetness of the scallops.

Preheat the grill or broiler.

Prepare the beurre blanc and, as soon as it is finished, stir in the chopped watercress leaves and lime juice. Keep the sauce warm.

Brush the scallops with the butter and season with salt and pepper. Grill them about 1 minute per side, until firm but still moist and slightly pink inside; halfway through the cooking on each side, rotate the scallops 90 degrees to give them crosshatched grill marks.

Spoon the sauce across the bottom half of heated serving plates prepared with vegetable mosaic garnishes. Place 5 scallops, slightly overlapping, on top of the sauce on each plate. Place 3 raspberries around the inner rim of each plate near the scallops.

LOBSTER WITH TOMATO BASIL BEURRE BLANC

•

FOR 6 SERVINGS

1½ cups Beurre Blanc (see page 29)

6 live lobsters, 1½ pounds each

3 tablespoons clarified butter (see page 23)

Salt and freshly ground white pepper

¾ cup Tomato Concasse (see page 42)

2 tablespoons julienne of fresh basil

WHEN I FIRST DECIDED TO SERVE LOBSTER AT THE RESTAURANT, I WANTED a simple, elegant way to present it without leaving shells all over the table. We developed this recipe, taking the meat completely out of the lobster and reforming it on the plate. Beurre Blanc combined with Tomato Concasse had the proper balance of acidity, sweetness, and richness to complement the lobster.

WINE SUGGESTION:

THE COMBINATION OF SHARPNESS AND RICHNESS IN THE SAUCE CALLS FOR A BIG, YOUNG, OAKY CHARDONNAY SUCH AS GRGICH HILLS, CHALONE, ACACIA, OR MATANZAS CREEK.

Preheat the grill or broiler until very hot. Meanwhile, prepare the beurre blanc and keep it warm.

Put about 8 inches of water in a very large pot big enough to hold all the lobsters at once. Bring the water to a full boil. Add all the lobsters and boil them for 2 to 3 minutes.

Carefully remove the lobsters from the pot. Put each lobster on its back, legs up, and with a heavy, sharp knife, split it in half lengthwise. Hit each claw with a heavy mallet to crack it slightly. Remove the claw meat and the two halves of tail meat from each lobster.

Brush the lobster tails and claws with the butter and sprinkle them with salt and pepper. Grill or broil them until they are just cooked through but still moist, about 1 minute per side; halfway through the cooking on each side, rotate the pieces of lobster 90 degrees to give them crosshatched grill marks.

While the lobster is grilling, stir the tomato concasse into the beurre blanc; season to taste.

Arrange the lobster tails and claws on each serving plate. Ladle the sauce over them and garnish with the basil.

LOBSTER CLAMBAKE-STYLE

■

FOR 6 SERVINGS

6 live lobsters, 1½ pounds each
5 dozen Manila or littleneck clams
1 pound (4 sticks) unsalted butter,
    clarified (see page 23)
3 tablespoons chopped fresh chives or
    basil
4 limes, cut into wedges

WINE SUGGESTION

THE LOBSTER CALLS FOR A CLASSIC, BIG,
OAKY, BUTTERY, WELL-AGED CALIFORNIA
CHARDONNAY—GRGICH HILLS,
CHALONE, ACACIA, OR MATANZAS
CREEK.

IT'S ALWAYS GREAT TO HAVE A BOILED LOBSTER AND FRESH STEAMED clams like you get at a New England clambake. This approach makes it possible to have them without spending a whole day preparing a clambake at the beach.

My wife and I serve this a lot at our house, and people just go completely crazy when they have to figure out how to eat a lobster that's just sitting whole on their plates. Begin by using your fork to pull the lobster tail out of the shell; you eat that with your knife and fork, dipping it in the butter. Then you break the claws off, take a lobster cracker, and crack them open; eat the meat inside them. Once that's done, you break apart the three little knuckles attached to each claw and use your little fork to pull the meat out of them. Next, you eat the coral—the tomalley or the liver of the lobster—inside the main shell, next to where the tail meat was; if you have a little bread, you spread it on that like you would a jam. If you really get into it, you separate the shell from the carcass and search for little bits of meat, like you would on a Dungeness crab. Finally, you break each little leg off the lobster and, inserting the broken end into your mouth, you work it between your teeth to squeeze out all the thin little slivers of meat and their juices. That's it!

Put about 8 inches of water in a very large pot big enough to hold all the lobsters at once. At the same time, put 2 inches of water in another large pot big enough to hold all the clams at once. Bring the water to a full boil in both pots.

Drop the lobsters into the pot with the 8 inches of water, leaving it uncovered. Put the clams into the other pot, reduce the heat to a simmer, and cover the pot. Boil the lobsters and steam the clams for 5 minutes.

Carefully remove the lobsters and clams from their pots. Put each lobster on its back, legs up, and with a heavy, sharp knife, split it in half lengthwise. Hit each claw with a heavy mallet to crack it slightly. Discard any unopened clams.

Place a small ramekin at the top center of each large serving plate. Fill the ramekins with clarified butter and chives or basil. Put a lobster half on each side of the plate, with the claws crossing above the ramekin. Pile the clams below the ramekin. Garnish the plate with lime wedges to squeeze over the seafood. Give each guest a small fork with which to remove lobster and clam meat from the shells and dip into the herb butter.

LOBSTER WITH BLACK TRUFFLES AND CHARDONNAY CREAM SAUCE

■

FOR 6 SERVINGS

1½ cups Chardonnay Cream Sauce I
(see pages 30–31)
6 live lobsters, 1½ pounds each
3 tablespoons clarified butter (see
page 23)
Salt and freshly ground white pepper
3 ounces fresh black truffle, cut into
1 × ⅛-inch matchsticks

WINE SUGGESTION
LOBSTER AND TRUFFLES TOGETHER
DEMAND THE VERY BEST, WELL-AGED
WHITE BURGUNDIES—PULIGNY-
MONTRACHET, CHASSAGNE-
MONTRACHET, OR MEURSAULT—OR THE
SAME IN CALIFORNIA CHARDONNAYS—
GRGICH HILLS, CHALONE, ACACIA, OR
MATANZAS CREEK.

CHARDONNAY CREAM SAUCE IS A TRADITIONAL FRENCH ACCOMPANI-ment to shelled lobster; black truffles and lobster classically go together. The ingredients make a gorgeous combination of colors—Art Deco and Oriental at the same time.

Prepare the sauce and keep it warm.

Preheat the grill or broiler until very hot. Meanwhile, put about 8 inches of water in a very large pot big enough to hold all the lobsters at once. Bring the water to a full boil. Add all the lobsters and boil them for 2 to 3 minutes.

Carefully remove the lobsters from the pot. Put each lobster on its back, legs up, and with a heavy, sharp knife, split it in half lengthwise. Hit each claw with a heavy mallet to crack it slightly. Remove the claw meat and the two halves of tail meat from each lobster.

Brush the lobster tails and claws with the butter and sprinkle them with salt and pepper. Grill or broil them until they are just cooked through but still moist, about 1 minute per side; halfway through the cooking on each side, rotate the pieces of lobster 90 degrees to give them crosshatched grill marks.

Arrange the lobster tails and claws on each heated serving plate. Ladle the sauce over them and garnish with black truffle.

Gateway by Helen
Frankenthaler

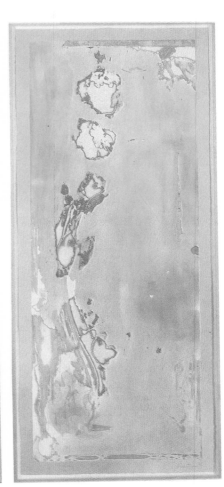

CHAPTER EIGHT
POULTRY

GRILLED CHICKEN WITH TARRAGON BUTTER AND POMMES FRITES

■

FOR 6 SERVINGS

3 medium-size chickens, about 2½
    pounds each, halved and boned
    to give 6 legs attached to 6
    boneless thighs, and 6 boneless
    breast halves attached to the
    wing bones, cutlet-style
Salt and freshly ground white pepper
Pommes Frites (see page 46)
6 tablespoons (¾ stick) unsalted
    butter
2 tablespoons coarsely chopped fresh
    tarragon leaves
2 bunches watercress, stemmed

WINE SUGGESTION

SIMPLE AND CASUAL AS THIS DISH IS, YOU
CAN REALLY SERVE ANY CALIFORNIA
CHARDONNAY, BUT A CLASSIC-STYLE ONE
—BIG, BUTTERY, AND OAKY—IS THE BEST.
TRY EDNA VALLEY, ACACIA, OR CHALONE.

IN THE BISTROS OF PARIS, THIS IS WHAT THEY MEAN BY FAST FOOD.
There, the chicken is preroasted, then crisped off in the oven at the
last minute before serving. I make the dish even faster in my own
way, by grilling it.

If you like, have the butcher prepare the chickens for you so you
have the pieces ready to throw on the grill.

Preheat the grill or broiler until very hot.

Sprinkle the chickens lightly with salt and pepper. Place
them on the grill or broiler with the skin side facing the heat and
cook them about 8 minutes per side for the thigh-leg pieces, until
cooked through but still moist and slightly pink at the bone; cook the
breasts 4 to 5 minutes on their skin sides, then flip them and cook 1
to 2 minutes more, until cooked through but still moist. Halfway
through the cooking on the skin sides for all the chicken, rotate them
90 degrees to give them crosshatched grill marks.

While the chicken is cooking, fry the pommes frites.

A minute or two before the chicken is done, melt the butter in a
small saucepan over moderate heat. Add the tarragon leaves and
season lightly with salt and pepper.

Arrange a clump of watercress in the center of each heated plate.
Place a big mound of potatoes at the top of the plate. Place a chicken
thigh-and-leg portion and a breast at the bottom of each plate and
spoon some of the tarragon butter over the chicken.

SAUTÉED CHICKEN BREASTS WITH FOIE GRAS AND MORELS

•

FOR 6 SERVINGS

18 medium-size dried morel caps
1½ cups water, at room temperature
3 medium-size shallots, finely
    chopped
2½ cups chicken stock (see page 22)
½ cup heavy cream
¼ cup Madeira
6 chicken breasts, 6 to 8 ounces each,
    wing bones attached
¾ pound fresh duck foie gras,
    trimmed and cut into 6 equal
    slices
3 tablespoons extra-virgin olive oil
Salt and freshly ground white pepper

WINE SUGGESTION

SERVE A REALLY BIG, HEAVY CABERNET
SAUVIGNON, SUCH AS BV PRIVATE
RESERVE, CHAPPELLET, OR CHATEAU
MONTELENA. YOU CAN EVEN SERVE ONE
THAT MIGHT ORDINARILY BE JUDGED TOO
BIG, TOO HEAVY, OR TOO TANNIC; THE
RICH COMBINATION OF FLAVORS IN THE
DISH WILL ROUND IT OFF. IF YOU LIKE,
YOU COULD ALSO POUR A BIG, OAKY,
BUTTERY, CLASSIC CHARDONNAY, SUCH
AS A CHALONE, ACACIA, OR BURGESS.

THIS DISH WAS INSPIRED BY THE FIRST MEAL I EVER HAD AT THE FAMOUS Lasserre in Paris, in 1974, where I ate their *mesclin de mère Irma*—a combination of chicken, foie gras, and morel mushrooms. It was such a perfect dish that when I opened Michael's, I set out to create my own version—using a boned chicken breast instead of a leg or wing.

Morels are among the few things that, dried and reconstituted, taste almost better than they did fresh; their flavor is intensified.

In a measuring cup or bowl, soak the morels in the water for about 30 minutes. Lift out the mushrooms and set them aside. Carefully pour the soaking water into a medium-size saucepan; stop pouring before any of the sediment leaves the cup or bowl.

Add the shallots to the saucepan and boil over moderate heat until the liquid has almost evaporated but the shallots are still moist, 8 to 10 minutes. Add the stock and continue boiling until it has reduced by about half, 5 to 7 minutes more. Stir in the cream and Madeira, bring the sauce back to the boil, then keep it warm.

While the sauce is reducing, preheat the oven to 400°F. Insert your finger between the skin and meat on each chicken breast and move it back and forth to make a pocket for the foie gras, taking care not to detach the skin completely. Carefully insert the foie gras between the skin and meat. In a large ovenproof sauté pan, heat the olive oil over high heat, until almost smoking. Season the chicken breasts with salt and pepper and sauté them, skin sides down, until their skin is golden. Carefully turn over the chicken breasts and put the skillet in the oven; cook the chicken until done, 5 to 6 minutes more.

Just before the chicken is done, stir the morels into the sauce to heat through and season the sauce to taste. Place the chicken breast on heated serving plates and spoon the sauce and morels around each breast.

GRILLED CHICKEN WITH
TARRAGON BUTTER
WITH POMMES FRITES

SAUTÉED CHICKEN
BREASTS WITH FOIE
GRAS AND MORELS

GRILLED CHICKEN BREASTS WITH BLACK AND WHITE TRUFFLES AND CHARDONNAY CREAM SAUCE

▪

FOR 6 SERVINGS

1½ cups Chardonnay Cream Sauce II
   (see pages 30–31)
6 chicken breasts, 6 to 8 ounces each,
   wing bones attached
Salt and freshly ground white pepper
3 ounces fresh black truffle, cut into
   1 × ⅛-inch matchsticks
2 ounces fresh white truffle

WINE SUGGESTION

SERVE A BIG CALIFORNIA CHARDONNAY—
CHALONE, ACACIA, OR MAYACAMAS—OR
ONE OF THE BEST WHITE BURGUNDIES,
SUCH AS PULIGNY-MONTRACHET,
MEURSAULT, OR CHASAGNE-
MONTRACHET. YOU COULD ALSO SERVE A
GOOD, DEEP-FLAVORED CALIFORNIA
PINOT NOIR OR A RED BURGUNDY, WHICH
HAVE SIMILAR TASTES TO CHARDONNAY
AND TO BLACK TRUFFLE—A MOUNT EDEN
OR CHALONE FOR THE FORMER, AND FOR
THE LATTER A DOMAINE DE LA ROMANÉE-
CONTI, COMTES DE VOGUE, OR DOMAINE
DUJAC.

LATE FALL IS THE TIME TO MAKE THIS CLASSIC COMBINATION, A BEAU-
tiful composition of black on white. You can also make it with one
or the other truffle alone.

Prepare the sauce and keep it warm.

Preheat the grill or broiler until very hot.

Season the chicken breasts with salt and pepper and cook them
with the skin side facing the heat until crisp and brown, 4 to 5 minutes;
halfway through the cooking, rotate the breasts 90 degrees to give
them crosshatched grill marks. Then flip them and cook 1 to 2 minutes
more, until cooked through but still moist.

With a sharp knife, cut each breast crosswise at a 45-degree angle
into pieces about ½ inch thick. Arrange the pieces on heated serving
plates. Spoon the sauce over the chicken and scatter the black truffle
on top. With a truffle shaver or a swivel-bladed vegetable peeler,
thinly shave the white truffle over each serving.

GRILLED QUAIL WITH LIME-THYME BUTTER

■

FOR 6 SERVINGS

12 baby quail, about 4 ounces each,
    boned except for leg and wing
    bones
1 recipe Basic Marinade (see page 23)
3 tablespoons clarified butter (see
    page 23)
Salt and freshly ground white pepper
½ pound (2 sticks) unsalted butter,
    cut into ½-inch cubes
1 lime, halved and seeded
1 tablespoon fresh thyme leaves

WINE SUGGESTION

YOU CAN SERVE THIS DISH WITH EITHER A
WHITE OR A RED WINE THAT IS FRESH
AND WELL BALANCED; IT'S PARTICULARLY
GOOD WITH CLASSIC WINES THAT WOULD
ORDINARILY BE JUDGED TOO YOUNG TO
DRINK WITH MOST DISHES. TRY A BIG,
FIRM, BUT NOT TOO OAKY CHARDONNAY,
SUCH AS THOSE FROM CHATEAU
MONTELENA, CHIMNEY ROCK, OR
MATANZAS CREEK. OR A BIG FUMÉ BLANC
SUCH AS GRGICH HILLS, CHIMNEY ROCK,
OR MATANZAS CREEK. FOR A RED WINE,
TRY ONE OF THE CLASSIC CABERNET
SAUVIGNONS SUCH AS NIEBAUM-
COPPOLA "RUBICON," STAG'S LEAP, OR
GRGICH HILLS.

WE SERVE ACTON VALLEY QUAIL AT MICHAEL'S, FARM-RAISED NORTH OF Los Angeles from French stock originally brought here by the late, great Jean Bertranou of L'Ermitage. You'll find the best quail at Oriental markets. Go for the smallest birds you can find, no more than about 4 ounces each; if it looks like a Cornish hen, you've got the wrong thing.

The key to grilled quail, which is so thin once it has been boned out except for the legs and the wings, is to cook it quickly on the skin side and just finish it briefly on the other side. If you're broiling instead of grilling, don't put the broiler pan in the broiler during preheating; place the quail skin up on the cold pan, and cook them as near to the heat as possible.

The fresh thyme in this recipe goes well with the slightly wild flavor of the quail, and the lime provides the perfect contrasting accent. This particular recipe goes great with Shoestring Potatoes (see page 43).

The night before you plan to serve the quail, or up to 2 days before, arrange the quail in a dish or bowl and cover them with the marinade. Cover the dish with plastic wrap and leave the quail to marinate in the refrigerator.

Preheat the grill or broiler until very hot. Wipe the marinade from the quail and brush with the clarified butter, then season them with salt and pepper. Cook the quail with the skin side facing the heat until crisp and brown, 4 to 5 minutes, until medium-rare, still pink around the bones; halfway through the cooking, rotate the quail 90 degrees to give them crosshatched grill marks. Then flip them and cook about 10 seconds more, just to color them slightly; be very careful not to overcook them.

In a small saucepan, melt the cubes of butter over medium heat; squeeze in the juice of the lime, stir in the thyme leaves, and season to taste with salt and pepper.

Place 2 quail side by side on each heated serving plate and spoon the sauce over them.

GRILLED QUAIL WITH MAUI ONION CONFIT AND BLACK CURRANTS

■

FOR 6 SERVINGS

12 baby quail, about 4 ounces each,
    boned except for leg and wing
    bones
1 recipe Basic Marinade (see page 23)
1½ cups Maui Onion Confit (see
    page 41)
1½ cups Cassis Sauce (see page 30)
¾ cup fresh or frozen black currants
3 tablespoons clarified butter (see
    page 23)
Salt and freshly ground white pepper
1 tablespoon fresh thyme leaves
2 bunches watercress, stems
    discarded

WINE SUGGESTION
POUR THE SAME VARIETY OF RED WINE
THAT YOU USE IN THE SAUCE. IF IT'S A
CABERNET SAUVIGNON, CHOOSE A
MEDIUM-BODIED CABERNET WITH SOME
BLACK CURRANT FLAVOR TO IT, SUCH AS
JOSEPH PHELPS, CAYMUS, OR LAUREL
GLEN. IF YOU USE A PINOT NOIR, SELECT
ONE OF THE BIGGER-BODIED, DEEPER-
COLORED ONES WITH MORE TANNIN,
SUCH AS CALERA, CHALONE, OR
MAYACAMAS.

THIS IS ONE OF MY FAVORITES, COMBINING THE EARTHINESS OF THE QUAIL with the sweetness of the Maui onions and black currants. With the red wine in the sauce, it's a great way to prepare quail, and you can serve them with a red wine.

Funnily enough, you don't need fresh black currants for this dish; frozen ones are fabulous, and they're now available, imported from New Zealand, in some supermarkets.

See the notes in the preceding recipe introduction on buying and cooking quail.

The night before you plan to serve the quail, or up to 2 days before, arrange the quail in a dish or bowl and cover them with the marinade. Cover the dish with plastic wrap and leave the quail to marinate in the refrigerator.

Before grilling the quails, prepare the Maui confit and the sauce and keep them warm. Add the black currants to the sauce to heat through.

Preheat the grill or broiler until very hot. Wipe the marinade from the quail and brush with the clarified butter, then season them with salt and pepper. Cook the quail, with the skin side facing the heat, until crisp and brown, 4 to 5 minutes, until medium-rare, still pink around the bones; halfway through the cooking, rotate the quail 90 degrees to give them crosshatched grill marks. Then flip them and cook about 10 seconds more, just to color them slightly; be very careful not to overcook them.

Spoon the sauce along the bottom edge of each heated serving plate, and sprinkle it with the thyme; place the Maui confit at its center. Place 2 quail side by side on each serving plate, on top of the sauce and just touching the confit. Garnish with watercress.

GRILLED QUAIL WITH WHITE TRUFFLES

■

FOR 6 SERVINGS

12 baby quail, about 4 ounces each, boned except for leg and wing bones
1 recipe Basic Marinade (see page 23)
3 tablespoons clarified butter (see page 23)
Salt and freshly ground white pepper
½ pound (2 sticks) unsalted butter, cut into ½-inch cubes
2 ounces fresh white truffle

WINE SUGGESTION
YOU OWE IT TO YOURSELF TO SERVE THE BEST WHITE BURGUNDY YOU CAN GET, LIKE A CHEVALIER-MONTRACHET, BÂTARD-MONTRACHET, OR CORTON-CHARLEMAGNE. OR SERVE ONE OF THE BEST BIG, OAKY CHARDONNAYS—MOUNT EDEN, STONY HILL, CHALONE, OR MAYACAMAS. OR GO WITH AN ITALIAN CHARDONNAY, FROM THE SAME REGION AS THE WHITE TRUFFLES—A GAJA OR CA DEL BOSCO.

SERVING QUAIL WITH WHITE TRUFFLES ISN'T JUST EARTHY PLUS EARTHY —it's earthy squared. This dish is just great. Serve it with Shoestring Potatoes (see page 43).

See the notes on buying and cooking quail on page 10.

The night before you plan to serve the quail, or up to 2 days before, arrange the quail in a dish or bowl and cover them with the marinade. Cover the dish with plastic wrap and leave the quail to marinate in the refrigerator.

Preheat the grill or broiler until very hot.

Wipe the marinade from the quail and brush with the clarified butter, then season them with salt and pepper. Cook the quail, with the skin side facing the heat, until crisp and brown, 4 to 5 minutes, until medium-rare, still pink at the bone; halfway through the cooking, rotate the quail 90 degrees to give them crosshatched grill marks. Then flip them and cook about 10 seconds more, just to color them slightly; be very careful not to overcook them.

In a small saucepan, melt the cubes of butter over medium heat and season to taste with salt and pepper.

Place 2 quail side by side on each heated serving plate and spoon the butter over them. With a truffle shaver or a swivel-bladed vegetable peeler, thinly shave the white truffle over the butter on each serving.

GRILLED QUAIL WITH
WHITE TRUFFLE

GRILLED QUAIL WITH
MAUI ONION CONFIT
AND BLACK CURRANTS

GRILLED QUAIL WITH
LIME-THYME BUTTER

GRILLED DUCK BREAST WITH GRAND MARNIER AND ORANGE

■

FOR 6 SERVINGS

5 medium-size oranges, 2 juiced
    (about 1 cup) and 3 peeled and
    segmented
½ cup granulated sugar
½ cup Cabernet vinegar or other red
    wine vinegar
¼ cup small pieces orange zest
2½ cups duck stock (see page 22)
¼ cup Grand Marnier
6 duck breasts, 6 to 8 ounces each
Salt and freshly ground white pepper

WINE SUGGESTION

THIS RECIPE IS A NATURAL FOR SHOWING
OFF ANY OF THE GOOD, BIG CALIFORNIA
RED VARIETAL WINES. IF YOU'RE GOING
WITH A CABERNET, CHOOSE ONE WITH
GOOD FLAVOR BUT WITH MORE ACIDITY
AND NOT THE OVERRIPE BLACK CURRANT
QUALITY SOME HAVE; MAYACAMAS,
ROBERT MONDAVI RESERVE, CHRISTIAN
MOUEIX "DOMINUS," AND CLOS DU VAL
ARE GOOD SELECTIONS. OR CHOOSE A
ZINFANDEL WITH SOME FIRMNESS AND
ACIDITY TO IT, BUT NOT ONE THAT TENDS
TO TASTE OVERRIPE LIKE A PORT; RIDGE
"YORK CREEK" OR MAYACAMAS WOULD
BE GOOD. OR SELECT ANY GOOD PINOT
NOIR OR PETITE SIRAH, IF YOU LIKE.

ALTHOUGH SOME PEOPLE MAKE FUN OF *CANARD À L'ORANGE*, IT IS STILL, today, one of the great combinations if it's perfectly done, with the sauce not too sweet. The combination of the vinegar with the orange gives it an Oriental flavor that is actually part of the classic treatment, though many cooks now leave it out. I've given the recipe my own modern simplification, with grilled duck breast.

Put the orange juice, sugar, vinegar, and orange zest in a medium-size saucepan and boil over moderate heat until the liquid has almost completely evaporated and a thick, almost caramelized syrup remains, 10 to 12 minutes. Add the stock and continue boiling until it has reduced by about half, 5 to 7 minutes more. Strain out and discard the zest, stir in the Grand Marnier, season the sauce to taste, and keep warm.

While the sauce is reducing, preheat the grill or broiler until very hot.

Season the duck breasts with salt and pepper and cook them with the skin side facing the heat until crisp and brown, about 3 minutes; halfway through the cooking, rotate them 90 degrees to give them crosshatched grill marks. Then flip them and cook about 3 minutes more, until medium-rare, still pink in the center.

With a sharp knife, cut each breast at a 45-degree angle into slices about ¼ inch thick. Arrange each breast on a heated serving plate. Spoon the sauce over it and garnish with orange segments.

GRILLED DUCK BREAST WITH BLACK CURRANTS

■

FOR 6 SERVINGS

2 cups Cabernet Sauvignon or other
    good red wine
½ cup fresh or frozen black currants
2 tablespoons cassis syrup
2½ cups duck stock (see page 22)
6 duck breasts (6 to 8 ounces) each
Salt and freshly ground white pepper

_____

WINE SUGGESTION
THIS WILL SHOW OFF EVERYTHING THAT'S
GREAT ABOUT CALIFORNIA CABERNET
SAUVIGNON—THE COMPLEXITY OF
FLAVOR, BIG BODY, AND BLACK CURRANT
UNDERTONES. SERVE A WELL-AGED OR
EVEN A YOUNG VINTAGE OF JOSEPH
PHELPS "INSIGNIA," MONDAVI-
ROTHSCHILD "OPUS ONE," MOUNT EDEN,
DIAMOND CREEK, OR CAYMUS.

ANOTHER INSTANCE OF A SWEET, FRUITY SAUCE WITH RICH, MEATY grilled duck breast. Be sure to buy a high-quality cassis syrup, available in most wine and liquor shops or gourmet markets; black currant liqueurs are not acceptable substitutes.

Place the wine, half the black currants, and the cassis syrup in a medium-size saucepan and boil over moderate heat until the wine has reduced to about ¼ cup, 8 to 10 minutes. Add the stock and continue boiling until it has reduced by about half, 5 to 7 minutes more. Strain out and discard the black currants, season the sauce to taste, and keep warm.

While the sauce is reducing, preheat the grill or broiler until very hot.

Season the duck breasts with salt and pepper and cook them, with the skin side facing the heat, until crisp and brown, about 3 minutes; halfway through the cooking, rotate them 90 degrees to give them crosshatched grill marks. Then flip them and cook about 3 minutes more, until medium-rare, still pink in the center.

With a sharp knife, cut each breast at a 45-degree angle into slices about ¼ inch thick. Arrange each breast on a heated serving plate. Spoon the sauce over it and scatter the remaining black currants on top.

GRILLED DUCK BREAST WITH FIGS AND PORT

•

FOR 6 SERVINGS

2 cups port
6 medium-size ripe figs
2½ cups duck stock (see page 22)
6 duck breasts, 6 to 8 ounces each
Salt and freshly ground white pepper
1 scallion, white part only, thinly
    sliced

WINE SUGGESTION

THE RICH FLAVORS IN THIS DISH CALL
FOR A BIG, HEAVY, TANNIC CALIFORNIA
PETITE SIRAH OR ZINFANDEL, WHETHER
YOUNG OR OLD. AMONG PETITE SIRAHS,
RIDGE, JOSEPH PHELPS, AND BONNY
DOON ARE GOOD CHOICES; GO FOR A
ZINFANDEL FROM RIDGE, STORYBOOK,
GRGICH HILLS, OR CHATEAU
MONTELENA.

GRILLED DUCK BREAST
WITH GRAND MARNIER
AND ORANGE

GRILLED DUCK BREAST
WITH BLACK CURRANTS

GRILLED DUCK BREAST
WITH FIGS AND PORT

RICH, MEATY DUCK BREAST WITH INTENSE, SWEET PORT AND RIPE FIGS IS
a classic combination. I've modernized the recipe by grilling the duck,
and given it a slight Oriental twist with a garnish of scallions.

Put the port and 3 figs, cut into several chunks each, in a medium-
size saucepan and boil over moderate heat until the port has
reduced to about ¼ cup, 8 to 10 minutes. Add the stock and continue
boiling until it has reduced by about half, 5 to 7 minutes more. Strain
out and discard the figs, season the sauce to taste, and keep warm.

While the sauce is reducing, preheat the grill or broiler until very
hot. Season the duck breasts with salt and pepper and cook them,
with the skin side facing the heat, until crisp and brown, about 3
minutes; halfway through the cooking, rotate them 90 degrees to give
them crosshatched grill marks. Then flip them and cook about 3 minutes more, until medium-rare, still pink in the center.

With a sharp knife, cut each breast at a 45-degree angle into slices
about ¼ inch thick. Cut each of the remaining figs into thin wedges.
Arrange each breast on a heated serving plate. Spoon the sauce over
it and intersperse fig wedges between the slices. Garnish with scallion.

GRILLED SQUAB WITH
FOIE GRAS AND
RASPBERRIES

GRILLED TENDERLOIN
OF RABBIT WITH
POMMERY MUSTARD
CREAM SAUCE

GRILLED SQUAB WITH FOIE GRAS AND RASPBERRIES

■

FOR 6 SERVINGS

6 baby squab, about 8 ounces each,
  partially boned except for leg and
  wing bones
1 recipe Basic Marinade (see page 23)
2 cups raspberry vinegar
3 medium-size shallots, finely
  chopped
2 cups chicken or squab stock (see
  page 22)
1 cup heavy cream
Salt and freshly ground white pepper
¾ pound duck foie gras, trimmed
  and cut into 6 equal slices
18 fresh raspberries

WINE SUGGESTION

A GREAT DISH FOR A BRASH YOUNG
CALIFORNIA PINOT NOIR, A LIGHTER
VINTAGE FROM A GOOD VINEYARD; THE
YOUNG WINES HAVE MORE OF THEIR
INHERENT RASPBERRY FLAVOR. TRY ONE
FROM THE CARNEROS AREA, WHERE THEY
TEND TO HAVE EVEN MORE RASPBERRY
TANG—CHATEAU BOUCHAINE, ACACIA,
OR SINSKEY; OR TRY EYRIE, FROM
OREGON. YOU COULD ALSO POUR A
SLIGHTLY TOO YOUNG FRENCH RED
BURGUNDY—SAY, A VOLNAY OR
POMMARD.

THIS IS ONE OF MY MORE SINFUL CREATIONS. THE RASPBERRY VINEGAR in the sauce is the perfect sweet-sour bridge between the charcoal-grilled squab and the seared, buttery foie gras.

When you shop for the squab, look for huge, plump breasts, good and meaty like a steak; that tells you they've been raised properly and will have the best flavor.

The night before you plan to serve the squab, or up to 2 days before, arrange the squab in a dish or bowl and cover them with the marinade. Cover the dish with plastic wrap and leave the squab to marinate in the refrigerator.

Preheat the grill or broiler until very hot.

For the sauce, put the vinegar and shallots in a medium-size saucepan over moderate heat and boil until the vinegar has almost evaporated but the shallots are still moist, 8 to 10 minutes. Add the stock and continue boiling until it has reduced by about three quarters to a good coating consistency, 8 to 10 minutes. Stir in the cream, bring the sauce back to the boil, and season to taste with salt and pepper. Keep the sauce warm.

Wipe the marinade from the squabs and season with salt and pepper. Cook them, with the skin side facing the heat, until crisp and brown, about 2½ minutes; halfway through the cooking, rotate the squab 90 degrees to give them crosshatched grill marks. Then flip them and cook about 2½ minutes more, until medium-rare, still pink at the bones and in the center of the meat.

While the squabs are cooking on the second side, heat a heavy skillet over high heat until very hot. About 1 minute before the squab are done, season the foie gras slices with salt and pepper and sauté about 30 seconds per side, until seared.

Place squabs on heated serving plates. Spoon the sauce over the squabs, place a slice of foie gras alongside each, and garnish each with 3 raspberries.

GRILLED TENDERLOIN OF RABBIT WITH POMMERY MUSTARD CREAM SAUCE

•

FOR 6 SERVINGS

6 bone-in rabbit tenderloins, 10 to 12
    ounces each; or 6 boned
    tenderloins, 6 to 8 ounces each
1 recipe Basic Marinade (see page 23)
2 cups Chardonnay
3 medium-size shallots, finely
    chopped
2½ cups heavy cream
¼ cup Pommery mustard
½ cup chicken stock (see page 22)
Salt and freshly ground white pepper
3 tablespoons julienne of fresh basil

WINE SUGGESTION

THIS CALLS FOR A BIG, BUTTERY
CHARDONNAY SUCH AS ACACIA, MOUNT
EDEN, OR EDNA VALLEY. IF YOU PREFER A
RED WINE, CHOOSE A WELL-BALANCED,
NOT TOO HEAVY OR RIPE PINOT NOIR—
LIKE CHALONE, CHATEAU BOUCHAINE,
OR ACACIA.

PEOPLE GET VERY FREAKED OUT ABOUT EATING RABBIT. BUT SERVING NICE charcoal-grilled tenderloins with a creamy mustard sauce is a great way to get them into it. Rabbit is tender, it does definitely taste more like poultry than meat, and like chicken it's a great canvas for a distinctive sauce like this one. Give it a shot.

The night before you plan to serve the rabbit, or up to 2 days before, arrange the tenderloins in a dish or bowl and cover them with the marinade. Cover the dish with plastic wrap and leave the rabbit to marinate in the refrigerator.

Preheat the grill or broiler until very hot.

For the sauce, put the Chardonnay and shallots in a medium-size saucepan over moderate heat and boil until the wine has almost evaporated but the shallots are still moist, 8 to 10 minutes. Add the cream and mustard and continue boiling until it has reduced by about half to a good coating consistency, 5 to 7 minutes. Stir in the stock, bring the sauce back to the boil, and season to taste with salt and pepper. Keep the sauce warm.

Wipe the marinade from the rabbit. If using bone-in tenderloins, with a boning knife or other small, sharp knife, fillet the tenderloins, discarding the bones and leaving a large and small fillet from each tenderloin. Season the tenderloins with salt and pepper and cook them about 2½ minutes per side, until medium-rare; halfway through the cooking, rotate them 90 degrees to give them crossshatched grill marks.

With a sharp knife, cut each tenderloin at a 45-degree angle into slices about ½ inch thick and arrange on a heated serving plate. Spoon the sauce over them and garnish with basil.

Green by Richard
Diebenkorn

CHAPTER NINE
MEATS

GRILLED TENDERLOIN OF PORK WITH APPLES AND CALVADOS

■

FOR 6 SERVINGS

6 pork tenderloin fillets, 6 ounces
   each
1 recipe Basic Marinade (see page 23)
4 tablespoons (½ stick) unsalted
   butter
2 medium-size Red Delicious apples
   or other good, firm, sweet
   apples, peeled, cored, and cut
   into ¼-inch wedges
1 cup Calvados
2 medium-size shallots, finely
   chopped
2 cups heavy cream
Salt and freshly ground white pepper
2 tablespoons chopped fresh chives

WINE SUGGESTION

GO WITH A GOOD-QUALITY
CHARDONNAY THAT HAS GOOD
FRUITINESS AND TASTES MORE OF CRISP
APPLES THAN OF BUTTER—CHATEAU ST.
JEAN, SONOMA-CUTRER, OR ROBERT
MONDAVI RESERVE, FOR EXAMPLE. YOU
COULD ALSO SERVE A DRY RIESLING OR
GEWÜRZTRAMINER—FROM HUGEL OR
TRIMBACH IN FRANCE, OR JOSEPH PHELPS
OR CLAIBORNE & CHURCHILL IN
CALIFORNIA.

THIS IS MY CALIFORNIA-STYLE MODERN SIMPLIFICATION OF THE CLASSIC Normandy sautéed or roast pork dish. If you like, you can add an additional garnish of a few strips of grilled bacon, cut into thin julienne strips.

Put the pork fillets in a glass or ceramic bowl and add the marinade. Cover the bowl and leave the pork to marinate at room temperature for 1 to 2 hours, or overnight in the refrigerator.

Preheat the grill or broiler until very hot.

Meanwhile, melt the butter in a medium-size skillet over high heat. When the butter foams, add the apples and sauté them, stirring constantly, until they are golden, 5 to 7 minutes.

Remove the skillet from the heat and add the Calvados and shallots. Carefully return the skillet to the heat, taking care not to slosh the Calvados, and boil until the liquid reduces to ¼ cup, about 15 minutes. Add the cream and continue cooking until the sauce is reduced to coating consistency, 5 to 7 minutes more. Season to taste and keep the sauce warm.

While the sauce is reducing, wipe the marinade from the pork fillets and lightly season them with salt and pepper. Grill them 5 to 7 minutes per side for medium; halfway through the cooking on each side, rotate the meat 90 degrees to give it crosshatched grill marks.

Slice each tenderloin at a 45-degree angle into pieces about ½ inch thick and place them, overlapping, on a heated serving plate. Spoon the sauce and apples around the meat and sprinkle the sauce with chives.

GRILLED TENDERLOIN OF PORK WITH SHERRY WINE VINEGAR SAUCE

•

FOR 6 SERVINGS

6 pork tenderloin fillets, about 6
 ounces each, trimmed,
 trimmings saved
1 recipe Basic Marinade (see page 23)
2 tablespoons unsalted butter
6 tablespoons sherry wine vinegar
2 medium-size shallots, finely
 chopped
½ cup veal, pork, or chicken stock
 (see page 22)
1½ cups heavy cream
Salt and freshly ground white pepper
2 tablespoons chopped fresh chives

WINE SUGGESTION
SINCE PORK IS ALMOST A WHITE MEAT,
AND THE SHERRY VINEGAR HAS A TASTE
OF OAK, SERVE A REALLY BIG, BUTTERY,
OAKY CALIFORNIA CHARDONNAY SUCH
AS STAG'S LEAP, CHALONE, OR EDNA
VALLEY. YOU COULD ALSO SERVE A
REALLY AGED FRENCH RED BURGUNDY
FROM BEAUNE, POMMARD, OR MOREY-
ST.-DENIS, SINCE THE SHERRY VINEGAR
WILL MASK ITS SOMEWHAT OXIDIZED
FLAVOR.

IN FRANCE, ROAST PORK AU JUS WITH FRIED POTATOES IS A RESTAURANT staple; I ate it all the time during my student days in Paris. But at the time I opened Michael's, no refined restaurant menu in America had pork on it.

That's a shame, because pork is a great-tasting meat. And this recipe was the first way I featured it on my own menu, counterbalancing the rich, slightly sweet meat with a sauce made sweet, sharp, and mellow by the addition of sherry vinegar.

Put the pork fillets in a glass or ceramic bowl and add the marinade. Cover the bowl and leave the pork to marinate at room temperature for 1 to 2 hours, or overnight in the refrigerator.

Preheat the grill or broiler until very hot.

Meanwhile, melt the butter in a medium-size skillet over moderate heat. Add the pork trimmings and sauté until well browned and the skillet is coated with a rich glaze.

Add the sherry wine vinegar to the skillet and stir and scrape to deglaze. Add the shallots and cook until the vinegar has almost completely evaporated, about 5 minutes. Add the stock and cook until reduced by half, 5 to 7 minutes more. Add the cream and continue cooking until the sauce is reduced to coating consistency, 5 to 7 minutes more.

While the sauce is reducing, wipe the marinade from the pork fillets and lightly season them with salt and pepper. Grill them 5 to 7 minutes per side for medium; halfway through the cooking on each side, rotate the meat 90 degrees to give it crosshatched grill marks.

Slice each tenderloin at a 45-degree angle into pieces about ½ inch thick and place them, overlapping, on a heated serving plate. Spoon the sauce around the meat and sprinkle the sauce with chives.

GRILLED TENDERLOIN
OF PORK WITH APPLES
AND CALVADOS

GRILLED TENDERLOIN
OF PORK WITH COGNAC
AND GREEN
PEPPERCORN SAUCE

GRILLED TENDERLOIN
OF PORK WITH SHERRY
WINE VINEGAR SAUCE

GRILLED TENDERLOIN OF PORK WITH COGNAC AND GREEN PEPPERCORN SAUCE

■

FOR 6 SERVINGS

6 pork tenderloin fillets, 6 ounces
   each
1 recipe Basic Marinade (see page 23)
1 cup Cognac
2 medium-size shallots, finely
   chopped
2 cups pork, veal, or chicken stock
   (see page 22)
¼ cup green peppercorns
Salt and freshly ground white pepper

WINE SUGGESTION

THIS IS A GOOD DISH FOR COMPARATIVE
WINE TASTINGS. YOU COULD GO WITH
WHITE RHÔNE WINES SUCH AS CONDRIEU,
HERMITAGE, OR CHÂTEAUNEUF-DU-PAPE,
YOUNG OR AGED, WHICH HAVE HIGH
ALCOHOL AND A PEPPERY SPICINESS
THAT COMPLEMENTS THE COGNAC AND
PEPPERCORNS. OR YOU COULD SERVE
WHATEVER CALIFORNIA CHARDONNAY
YOU LIKE THAT HAS SOME OAK AND
BUTTER TO LINK WITH THE OAKINESS OF
THE COGNAC AND THE RICHNESS OF THE
CREAM.

THIS SAUCE IS MORE COMMONLY SERVED WITH STEAK, BUT THE SMOKI-
ness of the Cognac and the zestiness of the peppercorns are great
with pork.

Put the pork fillets in a glass or ceramic bowl and add the marinade. Cover the bowl and leave the pork to marinate at room
temperature for 1 to 2 hours, or overnight in the refrigerator.

Preheat the grill or broiler until very hot.

Put the Cognac and shallots in a medium-size saucepan and boil
over medium heat until the Cognac reduces to ¼ cup, about 15 minutes. Add the stock and half the green peppercorns and continue
cooking until the sauce is reduced to coating consistency, 5 to 7 minutes more. Strain out and discard the peppercorns, season the sauce
to taste, and keep warm.

While the sauce is reducing, wipe the marinade from the pork
fillets and lightly season them with salt and pepper. Grill them 5 to
7 minutes per side for medium; halfway through the cooking on each
side, rotate the meat 90 degrees to give it crosshatched grill marks.

Slice each tenderloin at a 45-degree angle into pieces about ½ inch
thick and place them, overlapping, on a heated serving plate. Spoon
the sauce around the meat and garnish with the remaining green
peppercorns.

GRILLED SADDLE OF VEAL WITH CARAMELIZED LEMON ZESTS

■

FOR 6 SERVINGS

3 tablespoons unsalted butter

6 boneless saddles of veal, 6 ounces
    each, trimmed, trimmings saved

1 medium-size carrot, coarsely
    chopped

1 small Maui, Walla Walla, Vidalia,
    or sweet red onion, coarsely
    chopped

5 medium-size fresh white
    mushrooms, coarsely chopped

1 bunch parsley stems

2 cups Chardonnay or other dry
    white wine

2 cups veal stock (see page 22)

1 cup heavy cream

1 sprig fresh thyme

2½ lemons

¼ cup granulated sugar

¼ cup water

Salt and freshly ground white pepper

_____

WINE SUGGESTION

CHOOSE A CALIFORNIA CHARDONNAY
THAT'S MEDIUM-TO-FULL-BODIED, WITH
MODERATE OAK AND BUTTER—ACACIA,
ST. CLEMENT, OR STERLING. YOU COULD
ALSO SERVE A WHITE BURGUNDY SUCH AS
POUILLY-FUISSÉ OR MEURSAULT, OR A
WHITE RHÔNE WINE SUCH AS HERMITAGE
OR CHÂTEAUNEUF-DU-PAPE.

THIS IS MY VARIATION ON THE WORLD-FAMOUS VEAL SCALOPPINE. THE caramelized lemon complements the natural sweetness of the veal, which itself is intensified from the caramelization of juices that takes place when the meat is grilled.

In a large pot, melt the butter over medium heat. Add the veal trimmings, carrot, onion, mushrooms, and parsley stems. Reduce the heat to low, and cook, covered, stirring occasionally, for about 15 minutes.

Add the wine and boil over medium heat until it reduces to about ¼ cup, about 15 minutes. Then add the veal stock and continue boiling until it reduces by about half, 8 to 10 minutes more. Add the cream and thyme; squeeze in the juice from the lemon half, then add the lemon, too. Bring the sauce back to a boil, then strain it, adjust the seasoning to taste, and keep warm.

While the sauce is still reducing, carefully cut the zest from the 2 other lemons in fine strips with a zester or swivel-bladed vegetable peeler. Put the zest in a sauté pan and add the juice from the lemons, the sugar, and the water. Cook over high heat, stirring frequently, until the liquid has reduced to form a golden caramel syrup, 7 to 10 minutes. With tongs, remove the zest from the syrup and set aside.

Meanwhile, preheat the grill or broiler until very hot.

Season the veal with salt and pepper and grill about 3 minutes per side for medium; halfway through the cooking on each side, rotate the meat 90 degrees to give it crosshatched grill marks.

Carve each veal at a 45-degree angle into ¼-inch slices and arrange on a heated serving plate. Spoon the sauce around the veal and scatter the caramelized lemon zests on top.

GRILLED SADDLE OF VEAL WITH SWEETBREADS, FOIE GRAS, AND MORELS

■

FOR 6 SERVINGS

18 medium-size dried morel caps
1½ cups water, at room temperature
3 medium-size shallots, finely
    chopped
2½ cups veal stock (see page 22)
½ cup heavy cream
¼ cup Madeira
1 cup each dry white wine and water
12 ounces veal sweetbreads
Salt and freshly ground white pepper
¼ cup all-purpose flour
12 ounces boned saddle of veal, cut
    into 6 (2-ounce) pieces
¼ cup walnut oil
½ tablespoon unsalted butter
12 ounces duck foie gras, cut into 6
    (2-ounce) slices

WINE SUGGESTION

ANY CALIFORNIA CHARDONNAY WILL
WORK FINE, THOUGH THE BEST CONTRAST
TO THE DISH WOULD BE A BIGGER, FULL-
BODIED ONE WITHOUT EXCESSIVE OAK OR
BUTTER, SUCH AS CHATEAU MONTELENA,
SONOMA-CUTRER, OR DOMAINE MICHEL.
YOU COULD ALSO SERVE ONE OF THE
LIGHTER, MEDIUM-BODIED PINOT NOIRS,
SUCH AS SMITH MADRONE, ROBERT
MONDAVI RESERVE, OR STERLING
"WINERY LAKE."

THIS DISH WAS INSPIRED BY ONE I ATE AT CHEZ DUMONET IN PARIS.
There it was served as an hors d'oeuvre. I decided to make it into a
main course, though you could cut the portions in half and serve it
at the start of a meal.

In a measuring cup or bowl, soak the morels in the water for about
30 minutes. Lift out the mushrooms and set them aside. Carefully
pour the soaking water into a medium-size saucepan; stop pouring
before any of the sediment leaves the cup or bowl.

Add the shallots to the saucepan and boil over moderate heat
until the liquid has almost evaporated but the shallots are still moist,
8 to 10 minutes. Add the stock and continue boiling until it has
reduced by about half, 5 to 7 minutes more. Stir in the cream and
Madeira, bring the sauce back to the boil, then keep it warm.

While the sauce is reducing, preheat the grill or broiler until
very hot.

At the same time, bring the white wine and water to a boil in a
medium-size saucepan. Adjust the heat to a simmer, add the sweetbreads, and blanch them for 3 minutes. Drain them and, with a small
sharp knife and your fingertips, remove their membranes and trim
them. Divide the sweetbreads into 6 equal portions.

Season the sweetbreads with salt and pepper. Sprinkle the flour
on a plate and lightly dredge the sweetbreads in it on both sides.

Season the pieces of veal saddle with salt and pepper and grill
them about 3 minutes per side for medium-rare; halfway through the
cooking on each side, rotate the meat 90 degrees to give it crosshatched grill marks.

As soon as you put the veal saddles on the grill, put the walnut
oil and butter in a large skillet and heat it over high heat until the oil
begins to smoke and the butter to brown. Put the sweetbreads in the
skillet and sauté them for 1½ minutes per side, until golden.

After you turn the veal on the grill, heat a heavy skillet over high
heat until very hot. About 1 minute before the veal and sweetbreads
are done, season the foie gras slices with salt and pepper and sauté
them about 30 seconds per side, until seared.

As soon as you turn the foie gras, stir the morels into the sauce
to heat through and season the sauce to taste. Place the grilled veal
on heated serving plates with the sweetbreads and foie gras on either
side. Spoon the sauce and morels around them.

GRILLED SADDLE OF VEAL WITH WHITE TRUFFLES

■

FOR 6 SERVINGS

1½ cups Chardonnay Cream Sauce II
(see pages 30–31)
6 boneless saddles of veal, 6 ounces
each
Salt and freshly ground white pepper
2 ounces fresh white truffle

WINE SUGGESTION
SERVE A GREAT CALIFORNIA
CHARDONNAY, BIG AND OAKY WITH A
REAL COMPLEXITY OF FLAVOR, SUCH AS
MOUNT EDEN, MAYACAMAS, OR
CHALONE; OR A SIMILAR WHITE
BURGUNDY, SUCH AS CORTON
CHARLEMAGNE, PULIGNY-MONTRACHET,
OR CHASSAGNE-MONTRACHET. YOU
COULD ALSO POUR A GOOD, COMPLEX,
AND OAKY PINOT NOIR SUCH AS
CHALONE OR ACACIA, OR ANY GOOD RED
BURGUNDY OF A LIGHTER VINTAGE FROM,
SAY, VOLNAY, BEAUNE, OR CHAMBOLLE-
MUSIGNY.

THIS IS THE SIMPLE KIND OF DISH I LIKE TO EAT—JUST A GREAT PIECE
of grilled veal and fresh white truffles. It's a classic.

Prepare the sauce and keep it warm.
Preheat the grill or broiler until very hot.
Season the veal with salt and pepper and grill about 3 minutes
per side for medium; halfway through the cooking on each side, rotate
the meat 90 degrees to give it crosshatched grill marks.
Carve each veal saddle at a 45-degree angle into ¼-inch slices and
arrange on a heated serving plate. Spoon the sauce around the veal.
With a truffle shaver or a swivel-blade vegetable peeler, thinly shave
the white truffle over each serving.

GRILLED SADDLE OF
VEAL WITH
SWEETBREADS, FOIE
GRAS, AND MORELS

GRILLED SADDLE OF
VEAL WITH
CARAMELIZED LEMON
ZESTS

SAUTÉED SWEETBREADS WITH MORELS

■

FOR 6 SERVINGS

18 medium-size dried morel caps
1½ cups water, at room temperature
3 medium-size shallots, finely
 chopped
2½ cups veal stock (see page 22)
½ cup heavy cream
¼ cup Madeira
2 cups dry white wine
2 cups water
2½ pounds veal sweetbreads
Salt and freshly ground white pepper
½ cup all-purpose flour
½ cup walnut oil
1 tablespoon unsalted butter

WINE SUGGESTION

TO FOIL THE RICHNESS OF THE DISH, GO
WITH A GOOD, CRISP WHITE OR A
YOUNGISH RED FROM FRANCE. CHOOSE A
WHITE BORDEAUX SUCH AS HAUT-BRION
OR PAVILLON BLANC DE CHÂTEAU
MARGAUX; OR A GRAND CRU CHABLIS; OR
A WHITE RHÔNE SUCH AS CONDRIEU OR
HERMITAGE. OR SELECT A YOUNGISH RED
BORDEAUX FROM A GOOD CHATEAU
SUCH AS DUHART-MILON-ROTHSCHILD,
CHÂTEAU FIGEAC, OR CHÂTEAU
BEYCHEVELLE. YOU COULD ALSO SERVE A
GOOD ALSATIAN DRY RIESLING OR
GEWÜRZTRAMINER, SUCH AS THOSE FROM
HUGEL OR TRIMBACH, WITH A HINT OF
SPICE AND FRUIT THAT COMPLEMENTS
THE SWEETBREADS.

SAUTÉED IN HOT WALNUT OIL, JUST LONG ENOUGH TO CRISP THEM ON the outside but leave them moist and creamy within, sweetbreads are at their ultimate. With a rich, creamy Madeira and veal stock sauce and the intense flavor of morels, this is a perfect dish.

In a measuring cup or bowl, soak the morels in the water for about 30 minutes. Lift out the mushrooms and set them aside. Carefully pour the soaking water into a medium-size saucepan; stop pouring before any of the sediment leaves the cup or bowl.

Add the shallots to the saucepan and boil over moderate heat until the liquid has almost evaporated but the shallots are still moist, 8 to 10 minutes. Add the stock and continue boiling until it has reduced by about half, 5 to 7 minutes more. Stir in the cream and Madeira, bring the sauce back to the boil, then keep it warm.

While the sauce is reducing, bring the white wine and water to a boil in a second medium-size saucepan. Adjust the heat to a simmer, add the sweetbreads, and blanch them for 3 minutes. Drain them and, with a small, sharp knife and your fingertips, remove their membranes and trim them. Divide the sweetbreads into 6 equal portions.

Season the sweetbreads with salt and pepper. Sprinkle the flour on a plate and lightly dredge the sweetbreads in it on both sides.

Put the walnut oil and butter in a large skillet and heat it over high heat until the oil begins to smoke and the butter to brown. Put the sweetbreads in the skillet and sauté them for 1½ minutes per side, until golden.

Just before the sweetbreads are done, stir the morels into the sauce to heat through and season the sauce to taste. Place the sweetbreads on heated serving plates and spoon the sauce and morels around them.

GRILLED SADDLE OF LAMB WITH BLACK CURRANTS

∎

FOR 6 SERVINGS

1 whole saddle of lamb, about 10
    pounds, boned to give 2 loins
    (about 10 ounces each) and 2
    tenderloins (about 3 ounces each)
½ cup red currant jelly, melted
1½ cups Cabernet Cassis Sauce (see
    page 30)
¾ cup fresh or frozen black currants
1 tablespoon fresh tarragon leaves
1 teaspoon fresh thyme leaves

WINE SUGGESTION

DRINK THE SAME VARIETY THAT YOU USE
IN THE SAUCE; THE PAIRING WILL WORK
WITH ANY GOOD CABERNET, PINOT NOIR,
OR ZINFANDEL. IT'S ESPECIALLY GOOD
WITH BIG, YOUNG CABERNETS THAT STILL
HAVE QUITE A BIT OF TANNIN, SUCH AS
STAG'S LEAP, CAYMUS, OR RIDGE. IF YOU
USE PINOT NOIR, POUR ACACIA,
CHALONE, OR MOUNT EDEN. RIDGE,
GRGICH HILLS, AND CHATEAU
MONTELENA ARE GOOD CHOICES FOR
ZINFANDELS. IF YOU'D LIKE TO SERVE A
BURGUNDY—SUCH AS BONNES MARES,
MUSIGNY, OR NUITS-ST.-GEORGES—
SUBSTITUTE RED CURRANTS FOR THE
BLACK CURRANTS, TO CLOSER MATCH
THE WINE'S HIGHER ACIDITY.

THIS IS MY VERSION OF A RECIPE TAUGHT TO ME IN PARIS IN 1971 BY my old friend Mark Rudkin, an expatriate American art collector and lover of opera and great food and wine. Mark got this recipe from his mother, Martha, an amazing woman who founded the Pepperidge Farm baking company in the kitchen of the family's Connecticut home.

Mrs. Rudkin used a whole bone-in leg of lamb. Mark's variation was to use a butterflied leg, which makes a great party dish: the thicker parts of the meat cook rare, the thinner parts well, so there's something to suit the taste of every guest. I've made the dish a little more elegant for the restaurant, using the loin and tenderloin from a boned saddle of lamb. (Have your butcher bone the saddle for you, and save the bones for lamb stock.)

The black currant flavor of the cassis sauce is a wonderful complement to the lamb. The red currant jelly brushed over the meat before grilling gives it a rich, almost black caramelized coating, and it's one of the few things besides molasses barbecue sauce that I'll put on a piece of grilled meat. (An excellent side benefit of the resulting flavors is that any leftover meat makes a terrific picnic dish accompanied by a new Beaujolais, which has a unique raspberry–black currant flavor of its own.)

Serve the lamb with Galettes de Pommes de Terre (see page 46).

Brush the lamb liberally with the red currant jelly and leave it to marinate for about 30 minutes at room temperature.

Prepare the sauce and add the black currants to heat through. Keep the sauce warm.

Preheat the grill or broiler until very hot.

Grill the lamb, about 3 minutes per side for medium-rare on the tenderloins, 5 minutes per side on the loins; halfway through the cooking on each side, rotate the meat 90 degrees to give it cross-hatched grill marks.

Carve the lamb into ¼-inch slices and arrange on heated serving plates. Spoon the sauce with the black currants on top, and garnish with a sprinkling of fresh tarragon and thyme.

SAUTÉED SWEETBREADS
AND MORELS

GRILLED SADDLE OF
LAMB WITH BLACK
CURRANTS

GRILLED TENDERLOIN OF LAMB WITH BLACK TRUFFLE AND PARSLEY BUTTER

■

FOR 6 SERVINGS

6 lamb tenderloin fillets, 6 ounces
    each
Salt and freshly ground white pepper
½ pound (2 sticks) plus 2 tablespoons
    unsalted butter, cut into several
    chunks
3 tablespoons chopped fresh parsley
2 ounces fresh black truffle, cut into
    1 × ⅛-inch matchsticks

THE IDEA FOR THIS DISH CAME TO ME BY ACCIDENT ONE DAY, WHEN I was eating some plain grilled lamb and on the same plate were some new potatoes with parsley butter and shavings of fresh black truffle. I just happened to get a bite of the lamb with some of the butter, parsley, and truffle—and it was fabulous.

Preheat the grill or broiler until very hot.

Season the lamb tenderloins with salt and pepper. Grill or broil them close to the heat, about 3 minutes per side for medium-rare; halfway through the cooking on each side, rotate the tenderloins 90 degrees to give them crosshatched grill marks.

While the lamb is cooking, melt the butter in a medium-size saucepan over medium heat. As the lamb finishes cooking, stir in 2 tablespoons of the parsley and season to taste.

With a sharp knife, cut each tenderloin at a 45-degree angle into ¼-inch-thick slices and arrange on a heated serving plate. Spoon the parsley butter over it. Scatter the truffle over the lamb and sauce, then garnish with the remaining parsley.

GRILLED TENDERLOIN
OF LAMB WITH
BLACKBERRY-BLACK
CURRANT SAUCE

GRILLED TENDERLOIN
OF LAMB WITH DOUBLE-
BLANCHED GARLIC,
PINE NUTS, AND
POMMERY MUSTARD
CREAM SAUCE

GRILLED TENDERLOIN OF LAMB WITH BLACKBERRY–BLACK CURRANT SAUCE

■

FOR 6 SERVINGS

2 cups dry red wine

2 cups fresh blackberries, ½ cup
    reserved for garnish

4 large shallots, finely chopped

1½ cups lamb stock (see page 22)

2 to 3 tablespoons cassis syrup

Salt and freshly ground black pepper

6 lamb tenderloin fillets, 6 ounces
    each

½ cup red currant jelly, melted

6 tablespoons (¾ stick) unsalted
    butter

WINE SUGGESTION

THIS IS A NATURAL FOR A REALLY BIG,
LUSH, AND FRUITY CALIFORNIA
CABERNET, ZINFANDEL, OR PETITE SIRAH,
DEPENDING ON WHICH WINE YOU USE IN
THE SAUCE. CHOOSE A CABERNET SUCH
AS MONDAVI-ROTHSCHILD "OPUS ONE,"
PHELPS "INSIGNIA," OR NIEBAUM-
COPPOLA "RUBICON"; A ZINFANDEL SUCH
AS RIDGE "LYTTON SPRINGS," CHATEAU
MONTELENA, OR GRGICH HILLS; OR A
PETITE SYRAH SUCH AS JOSEPH PHELPS,
RIDGE "YORK CREEK," OR STAG'S LEAP.

THIS IS A SPIN-OFF OF MY GRILLED SADDLE OF LAMB WITH BLACK CUR-
rants. You could substitute any good, dark, fresh berry—including
boysenberries and ollalaberries—for the blackberries. Be sure to buy
a high-quality cassis syrup, available in most wine and liquor shops
or gourmet markets; black currant liqueurs are not acceptable substitutes.

In a small saucepan over moderately high heat, boil the wine with
the blackberries and shallots until the wine has reduced to about
¼ cup, 8 to 10 minutes. Add the lamb stock and 2 tablespoons of
cassis and continue boiling until the sauce is thick enough to coat a
spoon, 5 to 10 minutes more. Strain the sauce, crushing the berries
with a wooden spoon, and season to taste with salt and pepper; keep
it covered over very low heat.

While the sauce is reducing, brush the lamb liberally with the red
currant jelly and leave it to marinate.

Preheat the grill or broiler until very hot.

Grill the tenderloins, about 3 minutes per side for medium-rare;
halfway through the cooking on each side, rotate the meat 90 degrees
to give it crosshatched grill marks.

A tablespoon at a time, whisk the butter into the sauce. Taste the
sauce and, if necessary, add a little more cassis to make its flavor
distinctive but not dominant.

Carve the lamb into ¼-inch slices and arrange on heated serving
plates. Spoon the sauce on top and garnish with the remaining blackberries.

GRILLED TENDERLOIN OF LAMB WITH DOUBLE-BLANCHED GARLIC, PINE NUTS, AND POMMERY MUSTARD–CREAM SAUCE

•

FOR 6 SERVINGS

2 cups Chardonnay

3 medium-size shallots, finely
    chopped

2½ cups heavy cream

¼ cup whole-grain Pommery
    mustard

½ cup veal stock (see page 22)

Salt and freshly ground white pepper

2 medium-size cloves garlic, double-
    blanched (see page 28), and
    thinly sliced

6 tablespoons pine nuts

3 tablespoons walnut oil

6 lamb tenderloin fillets, 6 ounces
    each

3 tablespoons julienne of fresh basil

WINE SUGGESTION

DISH IN THE REALM OF WHITE WINES.

SERVE A CALIFORNIA CHARDONNAY,

SUCH AS ACACIA OR JOSEPH PHELPS, OR

A WHITE BURGUNDY SUCH AS PULIGNY-

MONTRACHET OR CHASSAGNE-

MONTRACHET.

YOU MIGHT NOT THINK THAT LAMB WOULD GO WELL WITH A CREAM sauce. But with the sweetness of the double-blanched garlic cloves—cooked twice in boiling water—along with the sautéed pine nuts, the sharp mustard, and the fresh basil, this dish comes together and works beautifully.

Put the Chardonnay and shallots in a medium-size saucepan over moderate heat and boil until the wine has almost evaporated but the shallots are still moist, 5 to 7 minutes. Add the cream and mustard and continue boiling until it has reduced by about half to a good coating consistency, 5 to 7 minutes. Stir in the stock, bring the sauce back to the boil, and season to taste with salt and pepper. Stir the double-blanched garlic into the sauce. Keep the sauce warm.

While the sauce is reducing, heat the walnut oil in a small skillet over high heat; when the oil is very hot, add the pine nuts and sauté, stirring continuously, until they are golden, about 30 seconds; then drain and reserve.

Meanwhile, heat the grill or broiler until very hot.

Season the lamb tenderloins with salt and pepper. Grill or broil them close to the heat, about 3 minutes per side for medium-rare; halfway through the cooking on each side, rotate the tenderloins 90 degrees to give them crosshatched grill marks.

With a sharp knife, cut each tenderloin at a 45-degree angle into ¼-inch-thick slices and arrange on a heated serving plate. Spoon the sauce and garlic over it. Scatter the pine nuts over the lamb and sauce, then garnish with basil.

Hotel Acatlan:
2 weeks later
by David Hockney

CHAPTER TEN
BRUNCH

SCRAMBLED EGGS WITH SMOKED SALMON AND CAVIAR

■

FOR 6 SERVINGS

18 large fresh eggs
6 tablespoons heavy cream
6 tablespoons clarified butter (see
    page 23)
12 slices Walnut Bread, each ¼ inch
    thick (see page 35)
6 tablespoons (¾ stick) unsalted
    butter, at room temperature
2 tablespoons chopped fresh chives
6 tablespoons Persian or American
    sturgeon caviar
12 long, thin slices (1 ounce each)
    Scottish smoked salmon

WINE SUGGESTION
SERVE WITH A GOOD CHAMPAGNE SUCH
AS ONE FROM TAITTINGER IN FRANCE OR
SCHRAMSBERG IN CALIFORNIA.

SALLY CLARKE, WHO HAS A GREAT RESTAURANT IN LONDON CALLED Clarke's, taught me the key to scrambled eggs. First, you mix the eggs with heavy cream to make them creamy, and you cook them in good butter. When you cook the eggs, you do not swirl them around like most people do. You should use a white plastic spatula to gather them continuously from the edge toward the center in big, moist ribbons; as new layers form, you keep gathering them in, and while the eggs are solid but still moist and creamy, you put them on the plate and serve them immediately. Accompanied by smoked salmon and great caviar, they make a very elegant brunch.

Another favorite elaboration on scrambled eggs is to add a bunch of coarsely chopped watercress leaves to the eggs as soon as they go into the pan. You get fabulous eggs, flecked with the dark green watercress.

For an even more luxurious scrambled egg dish, you can serve them with black or white truffles in season. Put the truffles—about 2 to 3 ounces for 6 servings—in a bowl with the unshelled eggs overnight; the eggs will absorb the truffles' aroma through their shells, becoming permeated with their flavor. Then, with a truffle shaver or vegetable peeler, shave the truffles into the beaten egg mixture and scramble the eggs as described below. Garnish the eggs with chives.

In a mixing bowl, use a wire whisk to beat the eggs and cream together until well blended and slightly frothy.

Heat the clarified butter in a large skillet over medium heat. Add the eggs and let them set for about 30 seconds. Then gather them continuously from the edge toward the center of the skillet in big, moist ribbons, until the eggs form soft, creamy curds, about 5 minutes.

While the eggs are cooking, toast the walnut bread in a toaster or under the broiler. Butter the toast and cut the slices diagonally into triangles.

Spoon the eggs along the center of heated large serving plates. Sprinkle them with chives and place a dollop of caviar at their center. Loosely roll up the slices of salmon and place a salmon roll on either side of each portion of eggs. Place 2 toast triangles next to each roll of salmon.

THE
CALIFORNIA
OMELET

·

FOR 6 SERVINGS

1 tablespoon unsalted butter

*1 medium-size Maui, Walla Walla,
    Vidalia, or sweet red onion,
    finely chopped*

*6 medium-size fresh white
    mushrooms, thinly sliced*

*3 (¼-inch-thick) slices smoked slab
    bacon, as lean as possible*

18 extra-large fresh eggs

Salt and freshly ground white pepper

*2 tablespoons clarified butter (see
    page 23)*

*1½ medium-size ripe avocados,
    thinly sliced lengthwise*

*½ cup Tomato Concasse (see page
    42), unseasoned*

*½ cup coarsely chopped watercress
    leaves*

6 tablespoons sour cream

*12 slices Walnut Bread, each ¼ inch
    thick (see page 35)*

*6 tablespoons (¾ stick) unsalted
    butter, at room temperature*

I DECIDED TO PUT EVERY CLICHÉ CALIFORNIA OMELET INGREDIENT TO-
gether into one omelet, and the combination is fabulous. Though they
aren't listed, you can even add some bean sprouts if you really want
to get carried away. Serve the omelets with fresh seasonal fruit salad.

In a small skillet or saucepan, heat the 1 tablespoon butter over
medium heat. Add the onion and mushrooms and sauté until the
onion is translucent, about 5 minutes.

On a preheated grill or in a skillet over medium heat, cook the
bacon until golden, about 2 minutes per side. Drain on paper towels.
Cut the bacon crosswise into thin julienne strips.

Preheat the broiler.

For each omelet, beat 3 eggs until lightly frothy and season to
taste with salt and pepper. Heat 1 teaspoon of clarified butter in a 7-
inch nonstick skillet over medium to high heat. Pour in the eggs and
cook them, gently stirring with a rubber spatula and gathering them
toward the center as they set. When the eggs are well set but still
moist, smooth their surface and set them under the broiler for about
30 seconds. Then arrange the fillings along the center third of the
eggs, perpendicular to the pan's handle: the onion-mushroom mixture, bacon, avocado slices, tomatoes, watercress leaves, and sour
cream.

While the eggs are cooking, toast the walnut bread in a toaster
or under the broiler. Butter the toast and cut the slices diagonally into
triangles.

Loosen the edges of the eggs with the spatula. Holding the pan
handle with your palm up, tilt the pan over a heated serving plate
and gently ease the omelet out from the side opposite the handle. As
it slides out, tuck the first third over the fillings, then tilt the pan and
use the spatula to tuck the last third of the omelet underneath, completely enfolding the fillings.

Serve each omelet with 2 triangles of walnut toast.

BLOOD ORANGE MIMOSAS

■

FOR 6 SERVINGS

2 cups fresh blood orange juice,
   chilled
1 bottle Blanc de Blanc champagne,
   chilled

IT'S A MORNING CLASSIC IN ITALIAN CAFÉS—A TRAY WITH A SHOT OF espresso and a shot of blood orange juice, freshly squeezed from Maltese blood oranges. Though these deep-red-fleshed oranges used to be a seasonal springtime thing, they're just now on the verge of being produced year round in this country. And their juice is fabulous in place of regular orange juice—in Stolichnaya screwdrivers or, as here, mixed with champagne to make a brunch mimosa.

Obviously, you can use regular orange juice if you can't find blood oranges.

Fill champagne flutes one third full with the juice. Top up each glass with champagne and serve immediately.

SCRAMBLED EGGS WITH
SMOKED SALMON AND
CAVIAR

PAPER-THIN BLUEBERRY
PANCAKES

BRIOCHE FRENCH TOAST

PAPER-THIN BLUEBERRY PANCAKES

·

FOR 6 SERVINGS

2 cups packed Bisquick

2⅔ cups milk

¼ pound (1 stick) unsalted butter, chilled

2 cups fresh or frozen blueberries (do not defrost if frozen)

¾ pound (3 sticks) salted butter, melted

1½ cups Vermont grade A maple syrup, heated

WHEN I WAS A KID, MY MOTHER USED BISQUICK ALL THE TIME TO MAKE great peach cobbler. I loved its flavor. When I lived in Brittany, I discovered their paper-thin crêpes, made from a thin, creamy batter. So when I set out to make blueberry pancakes, it seemed logical to cross Bisquick with French crêpes; this is the result.

These pancakes have that perfect, straightforward all-American flavor, but they're incredibly light, like crêpes, and really show off the taste of the blueberries, butter, and pure maple syrup. Don't make the mistake of serving the toppings on the side, like so many people do; pour the warm syrup and melted butter over each serving before you bring it to the table.

Serve with grilled breakfast sausages or bacon.

Put the Bisquick in a mixing bowl and make a well in the center. Pour in all the milk and stir with a wire whisk until just blended. Do not overwork the batter; lumps are okay. Let the batter rest for about 30 minutes at room temperature.

Preheat an electric griddle to 400°F or a regular stovetop griddle until very hot.

Pour the batter through a fine-mesh sieve to strain out any lumps. The batter should have the consistency of heavy cream.

With the end of the stick of unsalted butter, quickly grease the hot griddle for each batch of pancakes. Using a 2-ounce (¼-cup) ladle (or measuring with a measuring cup), pour the batter onto the griddle to form paper-thin, 5- to 6-inch-round pancakes; if the first one is too thick to spread thinly, stir a little more milk into the batter. Scatter 6 or so berries on top of each pancake, patting them into the batter with a large spatula.

When the edges of the pancakes are brown, about 1 minute, very carefully flip the pancakes with the spatula; tuck any stray berries back under the pancakes. Cook for about 30 seconds more, then carefully transfer the pancakes to a heated large serving plate, overlapping them. Repeat with the remaining batter and berries.

Pour about 2 ounces (¼ cup) each of melted butter and maple syrup over each serving of pancakes.

BRIOCHE FRENCH TOAST

•

FOR 6 SERVINGS

4 extra-large fresh eggs

1 cup milk

1 heaping teaspoon ground cinnamon

¼ teaspoon freshly grated nutmeg

¼ pound (1 stick) unsalted butter, chilled

18 slices Brioche, each ½ inch thick (see page 36)

1 tablespoon clarified butter (see page 23)

6 slices Virginia ham, 3½ to 4 ounces each

¾ pound (3 sticks) salted butter, melted

1½ cups Vermont grade A maple syrup, heated

OUR FRESH-BAKED BRIOCHE AT MICHAEL'S IS SO FABULOUS—FULL OF BUT-ter and eggs—that it just seemed logical to use it as the basis for French toast on the brunch menu.

Unlike most French toast recipes, you don't soak this bread in the batter; just a quick dunk is enough. Fried in butter, it gets wonderfully crisp on the outside and stays incredibly moist within.

In a mixing bowl, whisk together the eggs, milk, cinnamon, and nutmeg until well blended.

Preheat an electric griddle to 400°F or a regular stovetop griddle until very hot.

With the end of the stick of unsalted butter, quickly grease the hot griddle for each batch of French toast. Several slices at a time, quickly dredge the brioche in the egg mixture and place on the griddle. Fry them for 1½ to 2 minutes per side, until browned.

At the same time, heat the clarified butter in a medium-size skillet over high heat. Add the ham and sauté until browned, about 1 minute per side.

Place 3 slices of French toast on each heated serving plate. Pour about 2 ounces (¼ cup) each of melted butter and maple syrup over each serving. Serve with the ham.

SCOTTISH SMOKED SALMON, BAGEL, AND CREAM CHEESE WITH MAUI ONION, RED AND YELLOW TOMATOES, AND GIANT CAPERS

•

FOR 6 SERVINGS

6 poppy seed bagels

12 (1-ounce) long, thin slices
  Scottish smoked salmon, each
  loosely rolled up

1 each medium-size red and yellow
  tomatoes, cut into ¼-inch slices

1 medium-size Maui, Walla Walla,
  Vidalia, or sweet red onion,
  thinly sliced

12 baby limestone lettuce leaves

1 cup whipped cream cheese

6 tablespoons large capers

HERE'S MY ANSWER TO THE CALIFORNIA DELI BRUNCH. IF YOU BUY GREAT bagels, great salmon, great cream cheese, great Mauis, and tomatoes and capers, you can't beat it.

Split the bagels and toast their cut sides on a grill or under the broiler. Reassemble each bagel and cut it in half crosswise, making 4 quarters. Place each bagel on a large serving plate.

Place 2 rolls of salmon next to the bagel. Arrange red and yellow tomato slices and onion slices overlapping on each plate. In the remaining space, place 2 lettuce leaves; on one, place a scoop of cream cheese, and on the other a spoonful of capers.

WINE SUGGESTION

THE RICH, SWEET TASTE OF THE SALMON
MAKES THIS DISH GREAT TO SERVE WITH
A SPICY, FRUITY CALIFORNIA
CHARDONNAY SUCH AS JOSEPH PHELPS,
NEYERS, OR SINSKEY.

MICHAEL'S STEAK SANDWICH WITH POMMERY MUSTARD AND SALSA

·

FOR 6 SERVINGS

2½ pounds dry-aged New York strip
    steak
Salt and freshly ground white pepper
1 medium-size Maui, Walla Walla,
    Vidalia, or sweet red onion, cut
    into ¼-inch-thick slices
¾ cup clarified butter (see page 23)
2 sourdough baguettes, each 18
    inches long, or 6 sourdough
    rolls, each 6 inches long
6 tablespoons Jalapeño-Cilantro-Lime
    Salsa (see page 33)
6 tablespoons Pommery mustard
1½ cups Tomato Concasse (see page
    42)
2 bunches watercress leaves, coarsely
    chopped
1 recipe Mixed Greens with Balsamic
    Vinaigrette (see page 123)

WINE SUGGESTION

THE STEAK IS COMPLEMENTED BY A
BUTTERY CALIFORNIA CHARDONNAY
SUCH AS ACACIA, JOSEPH PHELPS, OR
MERRY VINTNERS. YOU COULD ALSO
SERVE A BIG FUMÉ BLANC—GRGICH HILLS,
CARMENET, OR CHIMNEY ROCK, FOR
EXAMPLE.

I NEVER SAW A STEAK SANDWICH I DIDN'T LIKE, BUT THIS IS THE BOTTOM line—the quintessential steak sandwich. A great, aged New York strip steak, bought from a good butcher, has the best flavor and texture for the sandwich, though you could substitute another good steak of your choice. The combination of the Pommery mustard and the salsa with the meat is sensational.

Preheat the grill or broiler until very hot.
　　Season the steak with salt and pepper. Grill 2½ to 3 minutes per side for medium-rare.

About 3 minutes before the steak is done, lightly brush the onion slices with clarified butter, sprinkle with salt and pepper, and grill them for about 1½ minutes per side.

Cut each sourdough baguette into 3 (6-inch) pieces and halve the bread lengthwise. Paint the split sides of the bread with the butter and toast on the grill as the steak finishes cooking.

After they're toasted, lightly paint the bottom half of the bread for each portion with the mustard and then the salsa, then spread the tomato concasse on top. Cut the steak diagonally into ¼-inch-thick slices and arrange them on top. Spread the watercress leaves and then the grilled onions on top of the steak. Place the other half of sourdough on top, cut each sandwich in half, and serve on a large plate with mixed green salad.

MICHAEL'S STEAK
SANDWICH WITH
POMMERY MUSTARD
AND SALSA

MOLASSES BARBECUED
PORK SANDWICH

MOLASSES BARBECUED PORK SANDWICH

■

FOR 6 SERVINGS

2½ pounds pork tenderloin

4 cups good tomato-molasses-based
    commercial barbecue sauce

¾ cup molasses

¼ cup strong black coffee

1 lime, juiced

1 small Maui, Walla Walla, Vidalia,
    or sweet red onion, finely
    chopped

2 medium-size cloves garlic, finely
    chopped

1 each small red and yellow bell
    pepper, stemmed, seeded, and
    finely chopped

1 medium-size jalapeño pepper,
    roasted (see page 27), stemmed,
    seeded, and finely chopped

Salt and freshly ground white pepper

1 medium-size Maui onion, cut into
    ¼-inch-thick slices

¾ cup clarified butter (see page 23)

2 (18-inch-long) sourdough
    baguettes, each 18 inches long,
    or 6 sourdough rolls, each 6
    inches long

2 bunches watercress leaves, coarsely
    chopped

6 tablespoons Jalapeño-Cilantro-Lime
    Salsa (see page 33)

1 recipe Mixed Greens with Balsamic
    Vinaigrette (see page 123)

THIS IS ONE OF MY FAVORITE HOME RECIPES, ADAPTED FROM ONE MY parents made, that I introduced into the brunch menu at Michael's. I start with a really good commercial tomato-molasses barbecue sauce—KC Masterpiece's Original Recipe is the kind we use at the restaurant—and then build on it with molasses, coffee, and other flavorings. I marinate the pork in it overnight—though you can get away with as little as 45 minutes of marinating and still get good results—and then baste the pork with the sauce as it grills. More of the sauce goes on the sandwiches themselves, along with Jalapeño-Cilantro-Lime Salsa, which provides a hot contrast to its sweetness.

Start marinating the pork the night before you plan to serve the sandwiches. In a bowl, stir together 3 cups of the barbecue sauce, the molasses, coffee, lime juice, chopped onion, garlic, peppers, and jalapeño. Place the tenderloin in the bowl, cover with plastic wrap, and leave to marinate in the refrigerator.

Before cooking the pork, preheat the grill or broiler until very hot.

Wipe the marinade from the pork, saving the marinade, and lightly season with salt and pepper. Grill the pork 5 to 7 minutes per side for medium-rare, basting frequently with marinade.

About 3 minutes before the pork is done, lightly brush the onion slices with some of the clarified butter, sprinkle with salt and pepper, and grill them for about 1½ minutes per side.

Cut each sourdough baguette into 3 (6-inch) pieces and halve the bread lengthwise. Paint the split sides of the bread with butter and toast on the grill as the pork finishes cooking.

After they're toasted, lightly paint the bottom half of the bread for each portion with some of the remaining barbecue sauce and spread the watercress leaves on top. Cut the pork diagonally into ¼-inch-thick slices and arrange them on top of the watercress; spoon the salsa over the pork. Arrange the grilled onions on top of the pork and spoon more sauce over the onions and pork. Place the other half of sourdough on top, cut each sandwich in half, and serve on a large plate with mixed green salad.

JALAPEÑO BLOODY BULLS

■

FOR 6 SERVINGS

1 to 3 fresh jalapeño peppers

1 large red bell pepper, quartered

1 large bunch fresh cilantro

1 (5-ounce) bottle Worcestershire sauce

1 tablespoon freshly ground black pepper

1 or 2 dashes Tabasco sauce

Salt

6 cups tomato juice

1½ cups Stolichnaya vodka

1½ cups canned beef consommé

6 celery stalks

3 limes, quartered

1 fresh jalapeño pepper, sliced crosswise, for garnish (optional)

THESE ARE GREAT WITH MY BLTS, AND THE STEAK AND BARBECUE PORK sandwiches. Mix up a double batch; drink them while you fix the sandwiches and go right on drinking them when you sit down to eat.

Use a good thick tomato juice. My brand of choice is Sacramento. I use only Stolichnaya vodka, which has the purest taste. Finishing off each glass with lots of fresh lime is a must.

The day before you plan to serve the drinks, quarter 1 or 2 jalapeños (depending on how hot you want them) and the bell pepper—seeds, stems, and all—into a large glass jar or pitcher along with the cilantro, Worcestershire sauce, pepper, Tabasco, and salt to taste. Add the tomato juice, cover the jar, and refrigerate for 24 hours.

Before serving, pour the juice through a sieve to remove the solids.

Fill six 12-ounce glasses with ice cubes. Pour 2 ounces of vodka and 2 ounces of consommé into each glass. Top off each glass with the tomato juice. Add a celery stalk to each glass and use it to stir up the drink slightly. Add 2 lime quarters to each glass, squeezing them as you put them in. If you like, slice another jalapeño and use to garnish the drinks.

*Conversation in the
Studio* by David
Hockney

CHAPTER ELEVEN
DESSERTS

FRESH FRUIT OR BERRY TART

■

FOR ONE 10-INCH TART

8 to 10 ripe apricots, 3 ripe freestone
    peaches, or 3 ripe pears, or 5
    cups fresh berries
3 large eggs
1 cup granulated sugar
5 tablespoons (1½ ounces) all-
    purpose flour
2 teaspoons vanilla extract
12 tablespoons (1½ sticks) unsalted
    butter
1 Pâte Sucrée pastry shell (see page
    40), chilled
½ cup Simple Syrup (see page 24)
¼ cup red currant jelly (if using
    berries) or apricot jelly (if using
    fruit)
Confectioner's sugar

WINE SUGGESTION

A GREAT DESSERT FOR SHOWING OFF A
GREAT, AGED FRENCH SAUTERNES, A
GERMAN TROCKENBEERENAUSLESE, OR A
CALIFORNIA LATE-HARVEST WINE SUCH
AS ONE FROM JOSEPH PHELPS OR
CHATEAU ST. JEAN.

I ORIGINALLY LEARNED TO MAKE FRESH FRUIT TARTS IN THE CLASSIC French manner—a pastry cream filling in a prebaked shell, topped with the fruit.

My own version has a browned butter custard filling baked inside the tart shell. If I'm using fresh berries, I pile them on top; other fruits, I bake into the custard.

Serve the tart with a dollop of whipped cream, if you like.

Preheat the oven to 350°F.

For the apricots or the peaches, bring a medium-size saucepan of water to a boil. Add the fruit and simmer about 30 seconds, then drain well and rinse under cold running water. With a small, sharp knife, nick the skins of the fruit and carefully peel off the skins. For apricots, halve and stone; for peaches, halve and stone, then cut them into thin wedges. For the pears, simply peel, halve, and core the fruit, then cut each half crosswise into thin slices, keeping the slices together.

In a mixing bowl, whisk together the eggs and sugar, then whisk in the flour and the vanilla until smooth.

In a medium-size saucepan over high heat, melt the butter and cook it, whisking continuously, until it browns to the color of hazelnuts, about 5 minutes. Whisk the butter into the egg mixture.

For a blueberry tart, distribute half the blueberries inside the shell. For an apricot tart, arrange the apricot halves cut sides down in the pastry shell. For the peach tart, place the slices of fruit in the shell in a neat spiral pattern. For the pear tart, fan out each sliced half in the shell from the center to the edge, like the spokes of a wheel. Pour the brown butter filling into the shell around the fruit, taking care to follow the fruit's contours and not to cover it completely. Bake the tart for about 1 hour, until the filling has set and the edges of the crust are golden. Let the tart cool to room temperature.

Put the Simple Syrup and jelly in a small saucepan and cook over high heat, stirring, until thick and bubbly. If making a berry tart, glaze the tart with half of the melted jelly, then neatly arrange the berries on top (or mound the remaining blueberries in the center) and brush them with the remaining jelly until lightly glazed. Otherwise, glaze the tart with all the melted jelly and dust the edges of the tart with confectioner's sugar.

LIME TART

.

FOR ONE 10-INCH TART

4 large eggs
4 large egg yolks
1⅓ cups granulated sugar
1½ cups freshly squeezed lime juice
½ pound (2 sticks) minus 1
    tablespoon unsalted butter, cut
    into ½-inch pieces
1 Pâte Sucrée pastry shell (see page
    40)
Confectioner's sugar
¼ cup finely chopped candied violets
3 paper-thin slices fresh lime

THIS IS A CROSS BETWEEN THE CLASSIC FRENCH LEMON TART AND THE American classic Key lime pie—a thin pastry shell filled with an intensely tart-sweet fresh lime curd. If you like, serve it with whipped cream or with Raspberry Sauce (see page 32).

Bring water to a boil in the bottom of a double boiler, then reduce the heat to a simmer.

Put the eggs, yolks, sugar, and lime juice into the top of the boiler and, away from the heat, whisk until smooth.

Add the butter pieces, set the boiler top over the simmering water, and cook, whisking thoroughly every 3 minutes or so, until the mixture thickens, about 25 minutes. Remove from the heat, pass the lime curd through a sieve, and let it come to room temperature; then chill it in the refrigerator for at least 1 hour.

As soon as the lime curd is done cooking, preheat the oven to 350°F.

Line the tart shell with parchment paper or a large flat coffee filter and fill it with pie weights or dried beans. Bake until evenly golden brown, about 30 minutes. Let it cool to room temperature.

Fill the baked shell with the lime curd, smoothing the top with a metal pastry spatula or a rubber spatula. Carefully sprinkle the edge of the crust with confectioner's sugar. Just inside the rim, sprinkle the candied violets in a thin line around the tart. Cut each lime slice in half and, giving each half a twist, place them around the tart inside the line of candied violets.

LIME TART

PEAR TART

APRICOT TART

PEACH TART

BLACKBERRY TART

BLUEBERRY TART

RASPBERRY TART

TARTE TATIN

·

FOR ONE 10-INCH TART

15 crisp medium-size Red Delicious
    apples
2 lemons, halved
¾ pound (3 sticks) unsalted butter,
    chilled, sticks cut lengthwise into
    ⅛-inch-thick slices
1⅔ cups granulated sugar
½ recipe Feuilletage (see pages
    38–39)
2 cups heavy cream, whipped to soft
    peaks

WINE SUGGESTION

THIS IS A WONDERFUL DESSERT FOR
SHOWING OFF THE FLAVOR OF A GREAT
AGED FRENCH SAUTERNES, A GERMAN
TROCKENBEERENAUSLESE, OR A
CALIFORNIA LATE-HARVEST WINE SUCH
AS ONE FROM JOSEPH PHELPS OR
CHATEAU ST. JEAN.

THIS IS THE CLASSIC FRENCH UPSIDE-DOWN TART OF CARAMELIZED AP-
ples. There's nothing different about my treatment—I just pay careful
attention to using the best Red Delicious apples and caramelizing
them properly, and using a good, buttery puff pastry.

Peel, core, and halve the apples and put them in a bowl. Squeeze
the lemon halves over them, adding them to the bowl with the
apples and tossing lightly to coat the apples with the juice.

Arrange the slices of butter in a concentric, overlapping pattern
to cover the bottom of a 3-inch-deep, 10-inch-wide, heavy nonstick
ovenproof skillet. Sprinkle the sugar evenly on top of the butter.

Working in a neat, compact, concentric pattern, place the apple
halves, round sides out, along the side of the skillet; continue placing
them this way in concentric circles, filling the skillet. Force the apples
in as the pan becomes full, but take care not to crack or crush them;
set any excess apples aside.

Put the skillet over medium to high heat and cook, shaking the
pan occasionally until the apples just begin to soften and are submerged in juice, 15 to 20 minutes. Keep an eye on the pan and adjust
the heat so that the juices don't boil over.

Place a skillet of similar size on top of the apples and, tightly
holding the handles of the skillets together, carefully pour off the
juices into a saucepan. Set aside the skillet with the apples. Boil the
juices in the saucepan over high heat until they are thick, syrupy,
and golden brown, 8 to 12 minutes.

Meanwhile, fit the remaining apple halves into any free spaces
in the skillet containing the cooked apples.

As soon as the juices are reduced to a thick, brown syrup, quickly
pour them back over the apples. Return the skillet to the stove and
continue cooking, over medium to low heat, for about 1 hour more,
until the apples and their juices are a dark caramel brown; shake the
skillet every 3 minutes or so in a circular motion to keep the apples
from sticking and burning.

Preheat the oven to 375°F.

Roll out the pastry to a circle about 12 inches across and ⅛ inch
thick; prick the dough all over with a fork. Carefully drape the pastry
over the apples, tucking the edges under and inside the skillet. Put
the skillet in the oven and bake until the dough is golden brown,
about 20 minutes.

Carefully remove the skillet from the oven and invert a serving plate over the pastry, holding it firmly in place. In one quick motion, carefully turn over the plate and skillet; then lift off the skillet to unmold the tart. With a rubber spatula, scrape any remaining caramel from the skillet onto the apples and smooth the apples, gently pressing them into place. Use a sharp knife to cut the tart into wedges and serve it warm, with whipped cream.

LINZERTORTE

•

FOR ONE 9-INCH TORTE

½ pound (2 sticks) unsalted butter, at room temperature

1 cup plus 1 tablespoon (5 ounces) all-purpose flour

1½ cups finely chopped unblanched almonds

½ cup granulated sugar

⅛ teaspoon ground cinnamon

⅛ teaspoon ground cloves

2 large egg yolks

½ cup raspberry jam

1½ cups fresh raspberries

½ large egg white, lightly beaten

1½ tablespoons confectioner's sugar

WINE SUGGESTION

SERVE WITH A FORTIFIED DESSERT WINE— A PORT, QUADY'S ELYSSIUM OR ESSENCIA, A SWEET MADEIRA, OR A SWEET SHERRY.

THIS IS ONE OF THE CLASSIC AUSTRIAN PASTRIES. I'VE ELABORATED ON the basic recipe by adding a layer of fresh raspberries along with the usual raspberry jam.

In an electric mixer on low speed, blend together the butter and flour, then beat in the almonds. Add the sugar, cinnamon, cloves, and egg yolks, and continue beating on low speed until just smoothly blended.

Press two thirds of the dough into the bottom of a 9-inch springform cake pan; it should fill the pan halfway up the sides. Spread the jam over the dough; then, crushing them with your hands, distribute the raspberries on top.

Roll out the remaining dough on waxed paper to a circle about 9 inches in diameter. With a knife or a pastry cutter, cut the dough into ¼-inch-wide strips. Refrigerate the dough for about 30 minutes.

Preheat the oven to 325°F.

Use a spatula to carefully transfer the strips, one at a time, to the top of the torte, arranging them in a latticework pattern and pressing gently to seal them to the edges of the crust.

Brush the pastry lattice with the egg white and bake the torte on the lower shelf of the oven for about 1¼ hours, until golden brown. Transfer the pan to a wire rack to cool, then dust the top of the torte with confectioner's sugar.

TARTE TATIN

LINZERTORTE

CRÈME BRÛLÉE TART

RICE TART

CRÈME BRÛLÉE TART

.

FOR ONE 8-INCH TART

3 cups heavy cream
7 large egg yolks
6 tablespoons granulated sugar
¼ recipe Pâte Sucrée (see page 40)
¾ cup firmly packed brown sugar

WHEN WE WERE DEVELOPING OUR MENU, WE SET OURSELVES THE GOAL of achieving a crème brûlée that was distinctly different from the little ramekins you get everywhere else. The idea we came up with was to prepare it in a flaky pastry crust. To this day, people are surprised by this version, and it's one of the most successful desserts in the restaurant.

In a heavy saucepan, bring the cream to a boil over moderate heat. At the same time, bring water to a boil in the bottom of a double boiler, then reduce the heat to a simmer. Combine the egg yolks and granulated sugar in the top of the boiler, set over the simmering water, and whisk together until very thick.

Whisking continuously, pour the hot cream into the yolks.

Reduce the heat to the lowest possible setting. Let the mixture cook for 30 minutes, whisking every 3 minutes or so.

Meanwhile, preheat the oven to 350°F.

Place a cake ring 8 inches in diameter and 2 inches high on a baking sheet lined with parchment paper. Roll out the pastry to a circle about 10 inches in diameter. Roll it up around the rolling pin and unroll it onto the cake ring. Press the pastry into the bottom and up the sides of the ring, raising and pinching the edges just barely over the rim. Place a large flat coffee filter inside and fill with pie weights or dried beans. Bake the pastry on the lowest oven rack until its edges are light golden brown, about 20 minutes. Remove the weights and filter. Slide a circle of heavy cardboard under the pastry and remove the ring.

Preheat the broiler.

Fill the pastry shell with the thick crème mixture. With a sifter, sift an even layer of brown sugar on top. Crimp a strip of foil over the edge of the pastry to protect it. Broil until the sugar has melted, 1 to 1½ minutes; watching carefully to prevent burning.

Refrigerate the crème brûlée until the filling has set, about 2 hours.

RICE TART

·

FOR ONE 8-INCH TART

2 cups milk

¼ cup plus 2 tablespoons granulated
    sugar

1 vanilla bean, split lengthwise

Grated zest of 2 oranges

½ cup (¼ pound) uncooked Arborio
    rice

¾ packet powdered gelatin

2 tablespoons Grand Marnier

4 large egg yolks

2 tablespoons unsalted butter

¼ recipe Pâte Sucrée (see page 40)

½ cup heavy cream, lightly whipped
    just until thickened

AFTER TASTING OUR CRÈME BRÛLÉE TART, ONE OF OUR CUSTOMERS SUG-
gested I develop a Rice Tart as a variation on that theme. This is the
result—a sophisticated presentation of a fairly homey recipe, sparked
with orange zest and Grand Marnier.

In a heavy ovenproof saucepan, combine the milk, ¼ cup sugar,
vanilla, and orange zest, and place over moderate heat.

In a separate pan, boil the rice in enough water to cover generously just until semicooked, about 5 minutes. Drain and rinse well
under cold running water.

When the milk mixture comes to a boil, add the rice. Cover the
pan and put it in the oven at 350°F to cook until the rice is tender,
about 30 minutes, adding more hot milk if necessary to keep the rice
from drying out. Remove from the oven.

Put the gelatin in a small bowl and add just enough ice water to
soften. In a small saucepan, heat the Grand Marnier and add it to
the softened gelatin.

Bring water to a boil in the bottom of a double boiler, then reduce
the heat to a simmer. Combine the egg yolks and butter in the top
of the boiler, set over the simmering water, and cook, stirring continuously, just until the yolks begin to thicken, about 5 minutes; do
not let them curdle. Stir the yolks into the rice mixture.

Stir the gelatin into the rice mixture, then set the pan in a bowl
of ice and water and let the mixture cool, stirring occasionally.

Meanwhile, preheat the oven to 400°F.

Place a cake ring 8 inches in diameter and 2 inches high on a
baking sheet lined with parchment paper. Roll out the pastry to a
circle about 10 inches in diameter. Roll it up around the rolling pin
and unroll it onto the cake ring. Press the pastry evenly into the
bottom and up the sides of the ring, raising and pinching the edges
just barely over the rim. Place a large flat coffee filter inside and fill
with pie weights or dried beans. Bake the pastry on the lowest oven
rack until its edges are light golden brown, about 20 minutes. Remove
the weights and filter. Slide a circle of heavy cardboard under the
pastry and remove the ring.

Preheat the broiler.

Stir the whipped cream into the rice mixture, then pour into the
pastry shell. Sprinkle the 2 tablespoons sugar on top and broil just
until the sugar caramelizes, 1 to 1½ minutes.

GÂTEAUX NOIX

■

FOR ONE 8-INCH TORTE

½ recipe Pâte Sucrée (see page 40)
1 cup granulated sugar
1 cup cold water
1 cup less 2 tablespoons heavy cream
¼ pound (1 stick) butter, cut into ½-
    inch pieces
1 cup broken walnut pieces
1 large egg yolk lightly beaten with
    ¼ teaspoon heavy cream
¾ cup Ganache (see page 26)
3 ounces white chocolate, broken into
    pieces
½ cup Praline Powder (see page 26)

MORE LIKE A CANDY BAR THAN A PASTRY, THIS CLASSIC FRENCH WALNUT torte is the perfect combination of chocolate, caramel, and walnuts on a crisp pastry base.

Place a cake ring 8 inches in diameter and 2 inches high on a baking sheet lined with parchment paper. Divide the pastry into 2 balls. On a floured work surface, roll out one of the balls to a circle about 10 inches in diameter. Roll it up around the rolling pin and unroll it onto the cake ring. Press the dough evenly into the bottom and up the sides of the ring, extending just above the rim. Roll out the other ball of dough to a diameter slightly greater than 8 inches; place another ring on top of it and cut loosely around the outer edge of the ring to make a lid slightly bigger than the torte. Transfer the lid to the baking sheet, next to the shell, and place them in the refrigerator.

In a heavy saucepan, bring the sugar and water to a boil over high heat. Continue boiling until the syrup turns a light golden color, about 10 minutes. Pour the cream in and place the whisk in the pan but do not stir. Add the butter and walnuts and cook over high heat until the mixture reduces to a thick but still liquid tan-colored caramel, about 7 minutes, stirring every 30 seconds or so to prevent the nuts from scorching. Pour the mixture into a metal bowl and let it cool to room temperature, about 2 hours.

Preheat the oven to 375°F.

Remove the baking sheet with the pastry from the refrigerator. Brush the egg yolk–cream mixture over the edges of the torte shell. Evenly spoon the caramelized walnuts into the shell, taking care not to tear the pastry. Place the pastry lid on top of the filling and press down all around the edges to seal the lid to the shell.

Bake the torte until the crust is golden brown, 35 to 40 minutes. Remove it from the oven and let it cool to room temperature.

Place a circular cardboard cake base on top of the torte. Slip the metal removable bottom of a tart shell, or a large spatula, under the torte and flip it over onto the cardboard. With a small, sharp knife, loosen the ring; lift it off and carefully scrape away any rough edges of pastry from the torte.

Stir the ganache over a double boiler until it is smooth and spreadable. In the top of a double boiler over simmering water, melt the white chocolate, stirring with a whisk so it melts smoothly.

WINE SUGGESTION

THE ABUNDANCE OF WALNUTS IN THIS DESSERT MAKES IT EXCELLENT WITH YOUR FAVORITE DESSERT WINE OR A GLASS OF PORT.

With a metal spatula, evenly spread the ganache over the top and side of the torte. Spoon the white chocolate into a pastry bag fitted with a writing tip; starting at the center of the torte, pipe circles of white chocolate, gradually growing out toward the edge. To create a rippled pattern, run the tip of a small, sharp knife through the ganache and white circles in 8 equidistant spokes from the center of the tart outward, wiping the tip after each stroke; then, in between each spoke, run the knife tip from the outer edge to the center to complete the pattern. Finally, with a spoon or your fingers, press the praline powder into the side of the torte.

OPERA CAKE

.

FOR ONE 10-INCH CAKE

12 large eggs
1¾ cups granulated sugar
⅓ cup glucose syrup
1 cup plus 2 tablespoons
    unsweetened cocoa powder
1½ cups plus 3 tablespoons (½
    pound) pastry flour
3 cups Buttercream (see page 24)
½ cup coffee extract
½ pound bittersweet melting
    chocolate, such as Valrhona
    Caraque or Tobler Tobamera or
    Lindt, broken into pieces
½ cup Kahlua liqueur
½ cup Simple Syrup (see page 24)
1 cup Ganache (see page 26)
3 ounces white chocolate, broken into
    pieces
1½ cups Crème Anglaise (see page
    25)

THE FLAVORS OF CHOCOLATE, COFFEE, CARAMEL, AND VANILLA ARE ALL wonderfully combined in this classic, rich French sheet cake. We serve it cut into small squares, in a pool of Crème Anglaise.

Preheat the oven to 325°F. Butter and flour two 20 × 10-inch sheet cake pans and line them with parchment paper. Butter and flour the paper.

Put the eggs, sugar, and glucose in a metal mixing bowl and, holding it over medium heat, whisk them together just until the mixture is warm to the touch, feeling carefully to the bottom of the mixture to make sure it is evenly warmed.

With an electric mixer on high speed, beat the mixture until it doubles in volume and the bottom of the mixing bowl is cool to the touch, about 8 minutes.

Sift together the cocoa and flour and, with a rubber spatula, quickly but thoroughly fold them into the egg mixture, taking care not to leave any pockets of flour.

Divide the batter evenly between the 2 prepared cake pans, smoothing it out evenly. Bake until the cakes begin to pull from the sides of the pans, about 8 minutes. Remove them from the oven and let them cool to room temperature for 1 hour.

Meanwhile, prepare the buttercream and divide it into 3 equal portions. Set aside one portion. Stir the coffee extract into another portion. For the third portion, melt the bittersweet chocolate in the top of a double boiler over simmering water, then stir it into the buttercream.

To remove the cakes from the pans, carefully slide a spatula around their sides and under the paper to loosen them. Place a fresh sheet of parchment paper on top of each cake and, holding it in place, carefully invert each cake onto a work surface. Carefully peel off the parchment paper and neatly trim off about ¼ inch around the edges of each cake. Cut each cake exactly in half, making 4 equal 10-inch squares in all from the 2 cakes.

Place a square of cake on a large flat serving platter or cake base. Stir together the Kahlua and simple syrup and sprinkle about ⅓ cup of it over this first layer generously but without actually soaking it. Evenly spread the chocolate buttercream on top, to within ¼ inch of the cake's edges. Carefully place another square of cake on top; sprinkle it with the Kahlua mixture and spread with the coffee buttercream. Then place a third square on top, sprinkle it, spread with the plain buttercream, and top with the final square of cake. Dampen the top layer with the Kahlua mixture and put the cake in the refrigerator to chill for 2 hours.

Meanwhile, prepare the ganache, or warm some already prepared ganache in the top of a double boiler over simmering water until it is soft and spreadable. Evenly spread the ganache over the top of the cake with a rubber spatula.

Melt the white chocolate in the top of a double boiler over simmering water. Roll a small piping cone out of waxed paper, or use a pastry bag fitted with a writing tip, and spoon the chocolate into it. Pipe a series of parallel lines, about 1 inch apart, across the ganache. To create a rippled design, run the tip of a small, sharp knife back and forth across the top of the cake perpendicular to the lines of white chocolate, wiping the tip after each stroke.

With a serrated bread knife, carefully trim the sides of the cake so that the layers of cake and filling are perfectly even. To serve, pour ¼ cup of crème anglaise into the center of each dessert plate. Cut a 2½-inch square of cake and place it on top.

BERRY PRALINE CAKE

·

FOR ONE 12-INCH CAKE

1 pound white chocolate, broken into
    pieces
10 tablespoons (1¼ sticks) unsalted
    butter, cut into pieces
6 large eggs, separated
½ cup plus 2½ tablespoons
    pulverized almonds (see page 28)
½ cup plus 2½ tablespoons
    granulated sugar
2 recipes Buttercream (see page 24)
8 cups fresh raspberries or
    blackberries
1 cup Praline Powder (see page 26)
1½ cups Crème Anglaise (see page
    25)

THIS IS THE ULTIMATE COMBINATION OF BERRIES, WHITE CHOCOLATE, and hazelnut praline. You can make it with raspberries, blackberries, or equal parts of both; or use strawberries, if you like. Serve with Crème Anglaise.

Using ¼ pound of the white chocolate, the butter, eggs, pulverized almonds, and sugar, prepare, bake, refrigerate, and cut the cake as directed for the Flourless Dark Chocolate Cake on pages 206–207.

Remove the buttercream from the refrigerator and beat it with an electric mixer until soft. Beat the praline powder into the buttercream.

Using the berries, and substituting the Praline Buttercream for White Chocolate Charlotte Mousse, assemble the cake as directed for the Raspberry–White Chocolate Charlotte Cake on pages 206–207. Make the band using the 1 pound remaining white chocolate. Serve with crème anglaise.

HEATH BAR

■

FOR ONE 9-INCH TORTE

¼ recipe Pâte Sucrée (see page 40)

3 cups Caramel Sauce (see page 32)

4 egg yolks

2½ cups heavy cream

1 cup Ganache (see page 26)

1 pound bittersweet melting
   chocolate, such as Valrhona
   Caraque, Tobler Tobamera,
   broken into pieces

1½ cups Pastry Cream (see page 25)

1½ packets powdered gelatin

1½ cups Buttercream (see page 24)

1¾ ounces white chocolate, broken
   into pieces

ONE OF THE SINGLE GREATEST DESSERTS WE SERVE, THE HEATH BAR developed from our desire to create the ultimate caramel dessert. We placed it in a pâte sucrée shell, then added a thin layer of bittersweet chocolate. The dessert grew more elaborate, and someone was inspired to start calling it by the name of the popular caramel-chocolate bar. Actually, I think of that as a misnomer; my own background is with the Sugar Daddy!

It's a fairly complicated dessert to make, but the results are stunningly good.

Preheat the oven to 350°F.

Place a cake ring 9 inches in diameter and 2 inches high on a baking sheet lined with parchment paper. Roll out the pastry to a thickness of ⅛ inch, roll it up around the rolling pin and unroll it onto the cake ring. Press the pastry evenly into the bottom and up the sides of the ring, trimming any excess. Place a large flat coffee filter inside and fill with pie weights or dried beans. Bake the pastry on the lowest oven rack until its edges are light golden brown, about 20 minutes. Remove the weights and filter.

In a saucepan, heat the caramel sauce until warm and liquid. In a bowl, whisk together the egg yolks and 1 cup of cream until smooth, then stir in 1 cup of the caramel sauce. Pour the mixture into the pastry shell, then return it to the oven and bake until the filling is browned, bubbling, and set, about 20 to 30 minutes more.

Let the shell cool to room temperature, then spoon about ½ cup more of caramel sauce in a thin layer over the surface of the filling. Refrigerate until the filling sets, about 30 minutes.

Meanwhile, warm the ganache in the top of a double boiler over simmering water. Spread ¼ cup of the ganache evenly inside the shell, and return it to the refrigerator to set for about 30 minutes more. Keep the remaining ganache warm.

Place a round cardboard cake support underneath the shell and remove the cake ring. Place the dark chocolate in a metal bowl and melt over simmering water in a saucepan or in a second double boiler. Cut a strip of waxed paper 2¼ inches wide and about 30 inches long and place it on top of a wider sheet of waxed paper on a cool work surface. With a metal spatula, spread the chocolate evenly over the waxed paper. Carefully lift the waxed paper strip, place it on a cool work surface, and let chocolate set for 1 to 2 minutes, until firm but still slightly wet, shiny, and flexible.

Lift the waxed paper strip up from the work surface and wrap it, chocolate side in, around the side of the pastry shell. Put the shell in the refrigerator for about 30 minutes, until the chocolate is hard. Keep the shell refrigerated.

Meanwhile, put the pastry cream and remaining caramel sauce in a saucepan and bring to a boil, stirring occasionally, over medium heat. While it is heating, put the gelatin in a bowl, add ice water to cover, and leave it to soften for about 3 minutes. Transfer the softened gelatin to another bowl and gradually whisk in the caramel mixture, dissolving the gelatin. Set the bowl inside a larger bowl of ice and, stirring every 30 seconds, chill thoroughly.

In the small bowl of an electric mixer, beat the buttercream until light and fluffy, then stir it into the caramel-gelatin mixture. In another mixing bowl, beat the remaining cream until soft peaks form; then blend it, too, into the caramel-gelatin mixture.

Remove the chocolate-wrapped pastry shell from the refrigerator and fill it to the top with the caramel mixture, smoothing it evenly. Return the shell to the refrigerator and let the filling chill and set for about 20 minutes.

Spread the remaining warm ganache evenly on top of the caramel filling. Then melt the white chocolate in the double boiler over simmering water. Use a pastry bag fitted with a writing tip to pipe a crisscross pattern of melted white chocolate on top of the ganache. Then lightly draw the tip of a small, sharp knife back and forth across the pattern—wiping it after each change of direction—to make a wavelike pattern. Before serving, carefully peel off the paper from the chocolate band surrounding the shell.

CINNAMON CAKE

·

MAKES ONE 9-INCH CAKE

MY DAD'S ALL-TIME FAVORITE CAKE WAS A DUNCAN HINES-STYLE SPICE cake. This is my modern version, with layers of cinnamon-flavored biscuit, a spiced buttercream, and a white chocolate band and flowers.

Don't be put off by how long the recipe is or how many steps there are. If you go at it stage by stage, it's pretty easy to do.

CINNAMON BISCUIT

1 cup plus 2 tablespoons
    confectioner's sugar
1¼ cup plus 3 tablespoons (2 ounces)
    all-purpose flour
5 large eggs
1½ tablespoons ground cinnamon
1½ teaspoons freshly grated nutmeg
5 tablespoons unsalted butter
6 large egg whites
¼ cup granulated sugar

CINNAMON BUTTERCREAM

½ cup granulated sugar
1½ cups cold water
8 large egg yolks
1½ teaspoons ground cinnamon
1½ teaspoons grated nutmeg
¾ pound (3 sticks) unsalted butter,
    softened, in pieces

CARAMELIZED APPLES

¼ cup Simple Syrup (see page 24)
2 tablespoons unsalted butter
3 Red Delicious apples, peeled and
    thinly sliced

ASSEMBLY

1 cup walnuts, coarsely chopped

WHITE CHOCOLATE BANDS AND FLOWERS

1 pound white chocolate, broken into
    pieces

FOR THE CINNAMON BISCUIT

Butter a 24 × 12-inch sheet cake pan. Cover it with parchment paper, then butter and flour the paper.

In the small bowl of an electric mixer, put the confectioner's sugar, flour, and 2 eggs. Mix at slow speed until combined, then turn up to high speed. After 1 minute, add the other 3 eggs, the cinnamon, and nutmeg. Continue beating for 3 minutes, then set the mixture aside.

Melt the butter in a saucepan and set it aside.

In another bowl, beat the egg whites to soft peaks. Add the granulated sugar and beat until just combined. Set aside.

Preheat the oven to 375°F.

With a rubber spatula, mix a small amount of the flour-and-egg mixture with the melted butter. Pour the butter mixture into the rest of the flour and egg whites and mix together quickly. With the spatula, fold a small amount of the egg white mixture into the flour-and-egg mixture. Then quickly but gently fold this mixture into the remaining whites.

Pour the batter into the prepared pan and bake until the biscuit is light brown and pulls away from the sides, about 12 minutes. Remove from the oven and let cool.

FOR THE CINNAMON BUTTERCREAM

In a saucepan, bring the sugar and water to a boil and continue boiling until the syrup reaches 300°F to 310°F on a candy thermometer, about 15 minutes.

Meanwhile, in the large bowl of the electric mixer, beat the egg yolks on high speed until creamy, about 10 minutes. As soon as the syrup is ready, slowly pour it into the yolks with the mixer running. When the mixture is cool, continue beating and add the cinnamon and nutmeg and, piece by piece, the butter. Continue beating until shiny and smooth.

FOR THE CARAMELIZED APPLES

In a large skillet, bring the simple syrup to a boil over medium heat. Add the butter and simmer until the mixture is thick and bubbly, about 30 seconds. Add the apple slices and sauté, stirring gently, until soft and golden, about 10 minutes.

FOR THE ASSEMBLY

Use a cake ring 9 inches wide and 3 inches high to cut out three circles from the biscuit. Place one biscuit layer on a 9-inch cardboard circle and place the metal ring around it to hold the layers in place.

Spread half of the apples evenly on top of the biscuit. Spread a ¼-inch layer of the buttercream on top, and sprinkle with half the walnuts. Place a second layer of biscuit on top and top with the remaining apples and all but about ¼ cup of the remaining buttercream. Sprinkle with the remaining walnuts. Place the last biscuit layer on top and spread with a thin layer of the remaining buttercream.

Place the cake in the refrigerator to chill for about 1½ hours.

FOR THE WHITE CHOCOLATE BAND AND FLOWERS

Melt the chocolate on the top of a double boiler over simmering water.

Pour three fourths of the chocolate on the back of a clean large baking sheet and use a metal pastry spatula to spread it thinly; keep the remaining chocolate warm and melted. Refrigerate the spread chocolate for about 2 minutes, until almost but not quite hard. Using a wide-bladed painting spatula, make flower petals: Place the blade edge at a 45-degree angle to the chocolate. Pressing down and using one corner of the edge as a pivot, rotate the blade in a 90-degree arc to create a broad curled petal. Set the petal aside on a tray and repeat to make about 10 petals. Put the petals in the refrigerator to chill.

Cut a strip of waxed paper 4 inches wide and about 30 inches long. Place it on a larger sheet of waxed paper on a cool work surface. Spread the remaining white chocolate evenly on top of the strip. Carefully lift the waxed paper strip, place it on a cool work surface, and let chocolate set for 1 to 2 minutes, until firm but still slightly wet, shiny, and flexible.

Meanwhile, remove the cake from the refrigerator. Soak a kitchen towel in hot water, wring it out, and wrap it around the cake ring to warm and loosen it. Lift off the ring.

Lift the waxed paper strip up from the work surface and wrap it, chocolate side in, around the cake. Put the cake in the refrigerator for about 30 minutes, until the chocolate is hard, then carefully peel off the paper.

Carefully place the white chocolate petals on top of the cake in a flower pattern, gently pushing their narrow ends into the buttercream.

CINNAMON CAKE

BERRY PRALINE CAKE

RASPBERRY–WHITE CHOCOLATE CHARLOTTE CAKE

■

FOR ONE 12-INCH CAKE

WHITE CHOCOLATE CHARLOTTE MOUSSE
¾ *pound white chocolate, broken into pieces*
6 *tablespoons Simple Syrup (see page 24)*
3 *large egg yolks*
2½ *cups heavy cream, whipped to soft peaks*

FLOURLESS DARK CHOCOLATE CAKE
¼ *pound bittersweet melting chocolate, such as Valrhona Caraque or Tobler Tobamera, broken into pieces*
10 *tablespoons (1¼ sticks) unsalted butter, cut into pieces*
6 *large eggs, separated*
½ *cup plus 2½ tablespoons pulverized almonds (see page 28)*
½ *cup plus 2½ tablespoons granulated sugar*

HERE IS ANOTHER VARIATION ON A CHOCOLATE MOUSSE CAKE—THIS one a flourless dark chocolate cake layered with white chocolate charlotte mousse and fresh raspberries. If you like, you can substitute blackberries or ollalaberries.

FOR THE WHITE CHOCOLATE CHARLOTTE MOUSSE
Melt a little less than a third of the white chocolate in the top of a double boiler over simmering water.

In a saucepan, bring the syrup to a boil.

Put the egg yolks in a metal mixing bowl and beat them lightly with a wire whisk. Add the syrup to the yolks and beat with a wire whisk just until the mixture forms ribbons when the whisk is lifted out. Then beat with an electric mixer at high speed until the mixture is cool and has tripled in volume, 5 to 7 minutes.

Reduce the beater speed to medium and beat in the melted chocolate until smoothly blended. Then, with a rubber spatula, fold in half the whipped cream. Cover and refrigerate for 1 hour. While the mixture is chilling, prepare the cake and begin its assembly right up to the point when you're ready to add the mousse filling to the first layer (see instructions below).

After the mixture has chilled for 1 hour and the cake construction has begun, melt the remaining white chocolate in the top of a double boiler over simmering water. Remove the chilled mixture from the refrigerator and whisk it briefly to soften. Whisk in the remaining whipped cream, then whisk in the melted chocolate a quarter at a time until smooth.

FOR THE FLOURLESS DARK CHOCOLATE CAKE
Prepare the cake while the white chocolate mixture is chilling. Preheat the oven to 375°F. Butter and flour an 18 × 12 × 1-inch sheet cake pan and line it with parchment paper.

Melt the ¼ pound bittersweet chocolate and butter in the top of a double boiler over simmering water.

In a bowl, whisk the egg yolks and almonds together. In the large bowl of an electric mixer, beat the egg whites until they form soft peaks, then beat in the sugar just to mix.

Whisk the chocolate-butter mixture into the egg yolk–almond mixture until blended. Whisk in a third of the egg whites, then pour the chocolate mixture into the bowl with the remaining egg whites and fold them together, using a rubber spatula.

ASSEMBLY

8 cups fresh raspberries

¾ pound bittersweet melting chocolate, such as Valrhona Caraque or Tobler Tobamera, broken into pieces

1½ cups Crème Anglaise (see page 25)

Pour the batter into the prepared cake pan. Bake until the cake pulls away slightly from the edges of the pan, 20 to 25 minutes.

Let the cake cool to room temperature, then chill it in the refrigerator for 1 hour.

Place another sheet of parchment paper on top of the chilled cake, slide a spatula underneath the bottom paper lining to loosen it, and, holding the pan and paper, flip the cake over onto a work surface. Lift off the pan and peel off the paper lining. With a sharp, serrated knife, trim the edges of the cake and then cut it crosswise into 3 equal (12 × 6-inch) pieces.

FOR THE ASSEMBLY

Place 1 layer of the cake on a rectangular cake cardboard. Place a row of perfect raspberries upright and as close together as possible around the edges of the cake. Then, steadying the outer row with your hand, fill the space inside with a layer of berries.

At this point, complete the mousse, melting and adding the white chocolate (see instructions above). Spoon a little less than half of the white chocolate mousse on top and, again steadying the outer berries with your hand, use a metal spatula to spread the mousse evenly over the berries right up to the edge and corners.

Repeat the process with another layer of cake, another layer of berries (save about 3 cups of the best-looking berries to decorate the cake at the end), and all but about ½ cup of the remaining mousse. Place the third layer of cake on top and spread the remaining mousse in a thin layer on top of the cake. Then chill the cake in the refrigerator for about 45 minutes.

Before wrapping the cake with chocolate, neatly trim its edges once more with a serrated knife. Melt the ¾ pound bittersweet chocolate in the top of a double boiler over simmering water. Cut a strip of waxed paper about 3½ inches wide and 36 inches long and place it on top of a wider sheet of waxed paper on a cool work surface. With a metal spatula, spread the melted chocolate evenly over the strip of waxed paper. Carefully lift the waxed paper strip, place it on a cool work surface, and let chocolate set for 1 to 2 minutes, until firm but still slightly wet, shiny, and flexible.

Remove the cake from the refrigerator. Lift the waxed paper strip up from the work surface and wrap it, chocolate side in, around the cake. Return the cake to the refrigerator until the chocolate band hardens completely, about 30 minutes.

Place the remaining raspberries in neat, tight rows on top of the cake inside the chocolate band, gently pressing them into the layer of mousse. Before serving, carefully peel off the paper from the chocolate band surrounding the shell. With a sharp knife, cut the cake into squares and serve with crème anglaise.

MILLEFEUILLE

RASPBERRY-WHITE
CHOCOLATE
CHARLOTTE CAKE

CHOCOLATE TRUFFLE
CAKE

MILLEFEUILLE

▪

FOR ONE 6 × 20-INCH
MILLEFEUILLE

1 recipe Feuilletage (see pages 38–39)
½ cup granulated sugar
1½ cups Pastry Cream (see page 25)
½ cup pureed, sieved fresh
    raspberries
¼ cup framboise liqueur
1½ cups heavy cream, whipped to
    soft peaks
4 cups whole fresh raspberries
Confectioner's sugar

YOU'LL FIND A NUMBER OF DIFFERENT FRENCH PASTRIES GOING UNDER the name of *Millefeuille*—the "thousand leaves" of the name referring to the layering of flaky puff pastry in its construction. I consider this classic version, alternating the crisp pastry with layers of fresh raspberries and raspberry-flavored pastry cream, the best of all.

If you like, you can substitute blackberries or strawberries for the raspberries.

Preheat the oven to 325°F.
Divide the feuilletage into 3 equal pieces and, on a cool, floured surface, roll out each piece to a 12 × 5-inch rectangle. Prick the surface of the pastry all over with the tines of a fork. Transfer the rectangles to a baking sheet lined with parchment paper and sprinkle them with the granulated sugar. Bake for about 15 minutes. Remove the baking sheet from the oven and place another sheet of parchment paper over the rectangles; then, grasping both the top and bottom sheets of paper, carefully turn the rectangle over. Lift off the top sheet of paper and bake the rectangles until golden brown, about 15 minutes more. Let them cool to room temperature and, with a large, sharp knife, trim them to neat, equal rectangles.

While the pastry is baking, stir together the pastry cream, raspberry puree, and framboise, and put the mixture in the refrigerator to chill. When chilled, fold in the whipped cream.

Place one pastry rectangle, sugared side up, on a large flat serving platter or pastry base. Neatly arrange a standing row of perfect raspberries all around the rim of the pastry. Then, steadying the outer row with your hand, fill the space inside with a layer of berries. Then, again steadying the outer berries with your hand, spread half the pastry cream–berry puree mixture over the berries. Place the second pastry rectangle on top; repeat with all but 20 of the remaining berries and all the remaining filling. Top with the third pastry rectangle.

Cut 10 strips of heavy paper, each 1 inch wide and at least 8 inches long. Lay them diagonally across the top of the millefeuille, parallel to each other and 1 inch apart. Sprinkle the confectioner's sugar over the top of the pastry; then carefully lift off the paper strips to leave a pattern. Place the remaining raspberries neatly along the unsugared strips of pastry. To serve, steady the top pastry strip and cut crosswise in a sawing motion with a large, sharp, serrated knife.

CHOCOLATE TRUFFLE CAKE

■

FOR ONE 8½ INCH CAKE

FLOURLESS DARK CHOCOLATE CAKE

¼ pound bittersweet melting
    chocolate, such as Valrhona
    Caraque or Tobler Tobamera,
    broken into pieces
10 tablespoons (1¼ sticks) unsalted
    butter, cut into pieces
6 large eggs, separated
½ cup plus 2½ tablespoons
    pulverized almonds (see page 28)
½ cup plus 2½ tablespoons
    granulated sugar

CHOCOLATE TRUFFLE FILLING

2 recipes Ganache (see page 26),
    chilled in the refrigerator until
    semihard
2 large egg yolks
½ cup heavy cream
3 tablespoons framboise liqueur

ASSEMBLY

2 cups fresh raspberries
1 recipe Ganache (see page 26)
¾ cup Praline Powder (see page 26)
Confectioner's sugar
1½ cups Crème Anglaise (see page
    25)

LIKE A GIANT RASPBERRY CHOCOLATE TRUFFLE CUT INTO SLICES, THIS
dessert combines layers of ganache—the basic truffle mixture—along
with fresh raspberries and a flourless dark chocolate cake.

FOR THE FLOURLESS DARK CHOCOLATE CAKE
Prepare, bake, refrigerate, and unmold the cake (do not cut it) as
directed for the Flourless Dark Chocolate Cake on pages 206–207.

FOR THE CHOCOLATE TRUFFLE FILLING
Put the 5 cups ganache in the bowl of an electric mixer and add the
egg yolks, cream, and framboise. Beat on high speed until just thoroughly combined and smooth.

FOR THE ASSEMBLY
Cut pieces of waxed paper to fit the bottom and sides of an 8½ ×
3½ × 2¾-inch metal bread pan. Butter the inside of the pan and line
it with the waxed paper.

Using the bottom of the pan as a guide, cut out 3 rectangles from
the cake. Place one of the rectangles in the bottom of the pan. Spoon
half of the chocolate truffle filling into the pan and spread it evenly.
Place an even layer of the raspberries on top. Repeat with another
layer of cake, the remaining truffle filling, and more raspberries, reserving 5 nice-looking berries for a garnish. Gently press the last layer
of cake on top. Cover with waxed paper and refrigerate until set, at
least 1 hour.

Remove the cake from the refrigerator, take off the top piece of
paper, and replace it with a rectangular cardboard cake base. Soak a
kitchen towel in hot water, wring it out, and wrap it around the pan
on all sides to warm and loosen it. Holding the cardboard in place,
carefully invert the cake and then lift off the pan and peel away the
waxed paper.

Melt the 2½ cups of ganache in the top of a double boiler over
simmering water. Set a wire rack on top of a large platter and place
the cake on the rack. Carefully and evenly pour half the melted ganache over the cake to coat it evenly. Chill in the refrigerator until the
coating sets, about 30 minutes. Return the drips from the platter to
the remaining ganache, melt it again, and coat the cake once more.

With a tablespoon, decorate the bottom edge of the cake with the
praline powder, pressing it gently into the soft ganache. Dip the tops
of the reserved berries in the confectioner's sugar and place them
along the top, gently pressing them into the ganache. Chill the cake
in the refrigerator for at least 1 hour before slicing and serving with
crème anglaise.

BERRY CHOCOLATE MOUSSE CAKE

■

MAKES ONE 9-INCH CAKE

I MAKE THIS ULTIMATE CHOCOLATE MOUSSE CAKE MOST OFTEN WITH raspberries or blackberries. You can also make it plain, without berries, in which case you should substitute rum for the framboise liqueur and decorate with semisweet chocolate flowers, following the technique described for Cinnamon Cake (page 202). Serve the cake with a pool of Crème Anglaise.

CHOCOLATE GENOISE

3 large eggs, at room temperature
½ cup granulated sugar
*5 tablespoons (1½ ounces) all-
    purpose flour*
*5 tablespoons unsweetened cocoa
    powder*

FOR THE CHOCOLATE GENOISE

Preheat the oven to 350°F. Butter and flour a cake ring 9 inches wide and 3 inches deep and place it on a baking sheet lined with buttered parchment paper.

In a metal bowl set over a saucepan of simmering water, whisk the eggs and sugar together until smooth and warm to the touch. Remove from over the simmering water, then, with an electric beater on high speed, beat the mixture until it has tripled in volume and is cool.

Sift together the flour and cocoa powder and, with a rubber or plastic spatula, fold them thoroughly into the egg mixture. Pour the batter into the cake ring and bake until the cake springs back when touched at the center, about 25 minutes. Let the cake cool for about 30 minutes, then remove the ring.

CHOCOLATE MOUSSE

10 ounces bittersweet chocolate

¾ cup Simple Syrup (see page 24)

3 large egg yolks

3 cups heavy cream, whipped to firm peaks

ASSEMBLY

⅓ cup Simple Syrup (see page 24)

3 tablespoons framboise liqueur

6 cups fresh raspberries or blackberries

1 pound semisweet melting chocolate, such as Valrhona or Tobler Velma, broken into pieces

1½ cups Crème Anglaise (see page 25)

FOR THE CHOCOLATE MOUSSE

Melt the bittersweet chocolate in the top of a double boiler over simmering water.

In a saucepan, bring the syrup to a boil.

Put the egg yolks in a metal mixing bowl and beat them lightly with a wire whisk. Add the boiling syrup to the yolks and beat with a wire whisk just until the mixture forms ribbons when the whisk is lifted out. Then beat with an electric mixer at high speed until the mixture is cool and has tripled in volume, 5 to 7 minutes. Then, at medium speed, beat in about two thirds of the melted chocolate. Cover and chill in the refrigerator for about 30 minutes.

FOR THE ASSEMBLY

With a long, sharp, serrated knife, carefully trim the top and bottom crusts from the cake, then cut the cake horizontally into three equal layers. Place 1 layer on a circular cake cardboard and place the cake ring back around it. Stir together the simple syrup and framboise and lightly brush some of it on the first layer of cake.

Whisk the whipped cream into the mousse mixture, then the remaining chocolate. Spoon the chocolate mousse into a pastry bag filled with a #8 tip. Pipe a ½-inch-thick layer of the mousse—about a third of the mousse—on top of the first layer of cake, starting at the rim and working toward the center; spread it even with a narrow spatula. Scatter a third of the berries in a single layer on top of the mousse. (Be sure to save the best-looking berries for the top layer.)

Repeat the two previous steps with another layer of cake, pressing it down firmly but gently, moistening it, and covering it with more mousse and more berries. Add the third layer of cake, moisten it, and cover with the remaining mousse, smoothing it even with the top of the cake ring. Chill the cake in the refrigerator for 30 minutes.

Melt the semisweet chocolate in the top of a double boiler over simmering water. Cut a strip of waxed paper 3 inches wide and about 30 inches long and place it on top of a wider sheet of waxed paper on a cool work surface. With a metal spatula, spread the chocolate evenly over the strip of waxed paper. Carefully lift the waxed paper strip, place it on a cool work surface, and let chocolate set for 1 to 2 minutes, until firm but still slightly wet, shiny, and flexible.

Meanwhile, soak a kitchen towel in hot tap water, wring it out, and wrap it around the cake ring to loosen it. Lift off the ring.

Lift the waxed paper up from the work surface and wrap it, chocolate side in, around the cake. Put the cake back in the refrigerator for about 30 minutes, until the chocolate is hard.

Arrange the remaining berries neatly on top of the cake inside the chocolate band. Before serving, carefully peel off the paper from the chocolate band surrounding the cake. Use a sharp knife to cut the cake into wedges, and serve with crème anglaise.

STRAWBERRY BAGATELLE

■

FOR ONE 8-INCH CAKE

THIS IS ONE OF THE GREAT SHOWPIECE DESSERTS AT THE RESTAURANT, but in a way it's really just my version of strawberry shortcake—light almond biscuit cake, fresh strawberries, and a white chocolate mousse filling.

NOUGATINE

2 tablespoons plus 1 teaspoon glucose syrup
½ cup plus 1 tablespoon granulated sugar
¼ cup plus 3 tablespoons cold water
1 cup slivered blanched almonds, toasted until golden in a 350°F oven

WHITE CHOCOLATE CHARLOTTE MOUSSE

6 tablespoons Simple Syrup (see page 24)
3 large egg yolks
¾ pound white chocolate, broken into pieces
2½ cups heavy cream, whipped to soft peaks

ALMOND BISCUIT

1 cup plus 2 tablespoons confectioner's sugar
1 cup plus 2 tablespoons pulverized blanched almonds (see page 28)
6 tablespoons all-purpose flour (2 ounces)
5 large eggs
5 tablespoons unsalted butter
6 large egg whites
¼ cup granulated sugar

FOR THE NOUGATINE

In a heavy saucepan, boil the syrup, sugar, and water over high heat until they form a dark caramel color, 10 to 15 minutes, watching carefully to make sure that the mixture doesn't burn.

Immediately remove the pan from the heat, add the almonds, and stir with a wooden spoon to coat them.

Pour out the mixture onto a baking sheet and let it cool to room temperature and harden.

Break the mixture into pieces and put them in a processor. Process until pulverized.

FOR THE WHITE CHOCOLATE CHARLOTTE MOUSSE

Prepare the mousse as directed in the Raspberry–White Chocolate Charlotte Cake, short of blending in the remaining white chocolate and whipped cream.

FOR THE ALMOND BISCUIT

Butter a 24 × 12-inch sheet cake pan. Cover it with parchment paper, then butter and flour the paper.

In the small bowl of an electric mixer, put the confectioner's sugar, almonds, flour, and 2 eggs. Mix at slow speed until combined, then turn up to high speed. After 1 minute, add the other 3 eggs. Continue beating for 3 minutes, then set the mixture aside.

Melt the butter in a saucepan and set it aside.

In another bowl, beat the egg whites to soft peaks. Add the granulated sugar and beat until just combined. Set aside.

Preheat the oven to 375°F.

With a rubber spatula, mix a small amount of the sugar-almond mixture with the melted butter. Quickly pour the butter mixture into the rest of the sugar-almond mixture. With the spatula, fold a small amount of the egg white mixture into the almond mixture. Then quickly but gently fold this mixture into the remaining whites.

Pour the batter into the prepared pan and bake until the biscuit is golden and pulls away from the sides, 12 to 15 minutes. Remove from the oven and let cool.

½ cup Simple Syrup (see page 24)

⅓ cup framboise liqueur

6 cups fresh strawberries, stemmed

10 ounces white chocolate, broken
    into pieces

Confectioner's sugar

FOR THE ASSEMBLY

Use a cake ring 8 inches wide and 3 inches high to cut out one circle of the biscuit. Use a 6-inch cake ring to cut out another circle; or cut it out with the 8-inch ring and trim the second circle down to 6 inches.

Place the 8-inch layer of biscuit on a cardboard cake circle and place the 8-inch cake ring around it. Stir together the simple syrup and framboise and lightly brush some of it over the biscuit layer.

Cut about 2 cups of the strawberries in half lengthwise. Place them—stem ends down and cut sides facing out—tightly side by side all around the inside of the cake ring; if necessary, cut a few more berries so you have a neat row all the way around. Then fill the inside of this rim with a layer of whole berries, stem ends down.

At this point, complete the mousse, melting and adding the remaining white chocolate, and whisking in the remaining whipped cream. Pour in enough of the white chocolate mousse mixture to cover the berries by about ½ inch, packing the mousse down and spreading it evenly with a metal spatula. Sprinkle the mousse evenly with a layer of the nougatine powder.

Place the second layer of biscuit, centered, on top and brush it with more of the syrup-framboise mixture. Cover with the remaining mousse, packing it down and spreading it even with the top of the cake ring. Put the bagatelle in the refrigerator to chill until the mousse is thoroughly set, 3 to 4 hours.

Melt the white chocolate in the top of a double boiler over simmering water.

Pour the chocolate on the back of a clean large cookie sheet and use a metal pastry spatula to spread it thinly. Refrigerate for about 2 minutes, until it is almost but not quite hard. Using a wide-bladed painting spatula, make flower petals. Place the blade edge at a 45-degree angle to the chocolate. Pressing down and using one corner of the edge as a pivot, rotate the blade in a 90-degree arc to create a broad curled petal. Set the petal aside on a tray and repeat to make about 10 petals. Put the petals in the refrigerator to chill until hard, at least 10 minutes.

Meanwhile, remove the cake from the refrigerator. Soak a kitchen towel in hot water, wring it out, and wrap it around the cake ring to warm and loosen it; carefully lift off the ring.

Carefully place the white chocolate petals on top of the cake in a flower pattern, gently pushing their narrow ends into the mousse. Sprinkle with confectioner's sugar.

STRAWBERRY
BAGATELLE

RASPBERRY LEMON
TORTE

RASPBERRY LEMON TORTE

■

FOR ONE 8-INCH TORTE

THE FLAVORS OF RASPBERRIES AND LEMON GO TOGETHER SO WELL—
and nowhere better than in this classic cake, which combines fresh
whole berries, fresh lemon curd, a light almond biscuit cake, and a
white chocolate custard tart bottom.

LEMON CURD

4 large eggs
4 large egg yolks
1⅓ cups granulated sugar
⅔ cup fresh lemon juice
15 tablespoons (1⅔ sticks) unsalted
    butter, cut into ½-inch pieces

ALMOND BISCUIT

1 cup plus 2 tablespoons
    confectioner's sugar
1 cup plus 2 tablespoons pulverized
    blanched almonds
6 tablespoons (2 ounces) all-purpose
    flour
5 large eggs
5 tablespoons unsalted butter
6 large egg whites
¼ cup granulated sugar

PÂTE SUCRÉE-CUSTARD SHELL

¼ recipe Pâte Sucrée (see page 40)
4 large egg yolks
1 cup heavy cream
3½ ounces white chocolate, melted
    over a double boiler
Zest of 1 lemon

ASSEMBLY

6 cups fresh raspberries
¾ pound white chocolate, broken into
    pieces

FOR THE LEMON CURD
In the top half of a double boiler, away from the heat, whisk together
the eggs, egg yolks, sugar, and lemon juice until smooth and thoroughly blended.

Over the double boiler on medium heat, add the butter pieces
and cook, whisking thoroughly every 3 minutes or so, until the mixture thickens, about 25 minutes. Remove from the heat, pass the
lemon curd through a sieve, and let it come to room temperature;
then chill it in the refrigerator for at least 1 hour.

FOR THE ALMOND BISCUIT
Prepare and bake the biscuit as directed for the Strawberry Bagatelle
on pages 214–215.

FOR THE PÂTE SUCRÉE-CUSTARD SHELL
Let the pâte sucrée warm and soften at room temperature for about
30 minutes. On a cool, floured surface, pound it with a rolling pin to
flatten it, then roll it out to a circle about 11 inches in diameter and
about ⅛ inch thick. Place a cake ring 8 inches wide and 2 inches high
on a parchment-paper-covered baking sheet. Gently roll the pastry
around the rolling pin, then unroll it carefully into the cake ring.
Gently press the pastry against the bottom and sides and trim the
edges. Refrigerate for about 1 hour.

Preheat the oven to 350°F. Line the pastry with a large coffee filter
or parchment paper and fill it with pie weights or dried beans. Bake
until the pastry turns a light golden color, about 20 minutes. Remove
from the oven and let the pastry cool, then remove the weights and
paper.

Preheat the oven again to 350°F. In a bowl, whisk together the
egg yolks, cream, chocolate, and lemon zest until smooth. Pour the
mixture into the prebaked shell. Bake until the mixture sets and a
knife inserted into the center comes out clean, 20 to 30 minutes.
Remove from the oven and let cool to room temperature.

FOR THE ASSEMBLY
Remove the ring from the custard tart shell and place the pastry shell
on a round cardboard cake platform.

Use a cake ring 5 inches wide to cut 2 round cake layers from the sheet of almond biscuit. Place 1 layer centered on top of the custard tart filling. Spoon about half the lemon curd on top and spread it evenly over the biscuit and beyond its edges up to the inside edge of the pastry shell.

Reserving the best-looking berries to decorate the top later, with your hands or a wooden spoon, crush about 1 cup of the berries. Spread them evenly on top of the lemon curd, staying within the rim of the biscuit layer below. Center the layer of biscuit on top of the berries.

Melt the white chocolate over a double boiler. Cut a strip of waxed paper 26 inches long and 3 inches wide and place it on top of a wider sheet of waxed paper on a cool work surface. With a metal spatula, spread the melted chocolate evenly over the strip of waxed paper. Carefully lift the waxed paper strip, place it on a cool work surface, and let chocolate set for 1 to 2 minutes, until firm but still slightly wet, shiny, and flexible.

Lift the waxed paper strip up from the work surface and wrap it, chocolate side in, around the torte. Put the torte in the refrigerator for about 30 minutes, until the chocolate is hard.

Spoon the remaining lemon curd into the torte, spreading and packing it down evenly with a rubber spatula. Return the torte to the refrigerator to set for about 1 hour.

Before serving, arrange the remaining berries in neat concentric circles on top of the torte inside the rim of chocolate. Carefully peel off the waxed paper from the chocolate band before serving.

FRESH FRUIT PRESENTATION

■

FOR 6 SERVINGS

1½ cups Crème Anglaise (see page 25)
6 Coupes (see page 39)
1½ cups fresh seasonal berries of one or more kinds
6 sprigs fresh mint

FOR THOSE GUESTS WHO SIMPLY WANT FRESH FRUIT FOR DESSERT, WE DEveloped this straightforward, elegant presentation for fresh seasonal berries. The fruit sits in a light crisp cookie coupe atop a ladleful of Crème Anglaise as an alternative to the double cream usually served with seasonal berries in Europe.

In each shallow soup plate, pour ¼ cup of the crème anglaise.
Place a coupe at the center of each plate, on top of the crème.
Arrange the berries inside each coupe. Top with a sprig of mint.

FIGS WITH FIG SORBET, VANILLA ICE CREAM, CRÈME ANGLAISE, AND PORT SAUCE

•

FOR 6 SERVINGS

1¼ cups port

1¼ cups Simple Syrup (see page 24)

1½ cups Crème Anglaise (see page 25)

6 scoops (4 ounces each) Fig Sorbet (see page 236)

6 scoops (4 ounces each) Vanilla Ice Cream (see pages 238–239)

9 fresh, ripe figs, cut into quarters lengthwise

6 sprigs fresh mint

WINE SUGGESTION
SERVE WITH A GOOD PORT TO COMPLEMENT THE FIGS AND THE PORT SAUCE.

THIS IS ANOTHER GREAT DESSERT WHEN FRESH FIGS ARE IN SEASON. THE intense flavor of figs goes fabulously with port.

In a bowl, stir together the port and syrup. Cover and chill in the refrigerator for at least 1 hour.

On one side of each chilled dinner plate, carefully ladle or pour ¼ cup of the crème anglaise, forming as neat and straight a line as you can down the center of the plate. On the other side, carefully ladle or pour the port sauce up to the crème anglaise.

Carefully place a scoop of fig sorbet on top of the crème anglaise, perpendicular to where the two sauces meet. Place a scoop of vanilla ice cream on top of the port sauce, just touching and symmetrical to the sorbet.

On each plate, arrange 6 pieces of fig symmetrically on either side of the sorbet and ice cream. Garnish each plate with mint.

HOT CARAMELIZED FIGS WITH VANILLA ICE CREAM

•

FOR 6 SERVINGS

1½ cups Simple Syrup (see page 24)

12 tablespoons (1½ sticks) unsalted
    butter

9 medium-size, fresh, ripe figs,
    quartered

¾ cup port

1½ cups Crème Anglaise (see page
    25)

6 Coupes (see page 39)

12 scoops (4 ounces each) Vanilla Ice
    Cream (see pages 238–239)

6 sprigs fresh mint

THIS IS ANOTHER OF THE FRESH FRUIT AND VANILLA ICE CREAM COM-
binations I like so much, terrific when fresh figs are in season.

In a medium-size skillet, bring the syrup to a boil over high heat.
Add the butter and simmer until the syrup is thick and bubbly,
about 30 seconds.

Add the figs and simmer for about 30 seconds; then remove the
skillet from the heat and stir in the port. Return the skillet to the heat
and continue simmering, stirring occasionally, until the syrup turns
a light golden color, 1 to 2 minutes more.

Pour ¼ cup of the crème anglaise into the bottom of each shallow
soup plate. Place a coupe on top and place 2 scoops of ice cream in
each coupe. Spoon the hot figs and caramel over the ice cream and
garnish with mint.

WINE SUGGESTION

SERVE WITH QUADY ELLYSSIUM OR
ESSENCIA, WHOSE FLAVORS PERFECTLY
COMPLEMENT THE TASTE OF RIPE FIGS.

CARAMELIZED PEARS WITH VANILLA ICE CREAM

·

FOR 6 SERVINGS

1½ cups Caramel Sauce (see page 32)

1½ cups Simple Syrup (see page 24)

12 tablespoons (1½ sticks) unsalted
    butter, cut into ½-inch cubes

3 firm, ripe pears (Bartlett or other
    good, firm variety), peeled and
    cored, each half cut crosswise
    into 12 slices

1 cup plus 2 tablespoons Poire
    Williams liqueur

6 scoops, 4 ounces each, Vanilla Ice
    Cream (see pages 238–239)

6 tablespoons chopped walnuts

THIS IS MY ADAPTATION OF THE CLASSIC FRENCH DESSERT IN WHICH A whole, peeled pear is completely caramelized. While that recipe is a real pain to make, mine is much simpler—in effect, a simple sauté of pears that's dynamite with vanilla ice cream. In its way, it's also a new twist on that all-American favorite, the caramel sundae.

Prepare the caramel sauce and keep it warm.

In a large skillet, bring the syrup to a boil over high heat. Add the butter and cook until the mixture is thick and bubbly, about 30 seconds. Add the pear slices and sauté, stirring gently, for 3 to 4 minutes. Remove the skillet from the heat and stir in the Poire Williams; then return the skillet to the heat and continue cooking, stirring occasionally, until the pears are lightly browned, 1 to 2 minutes.

Pour ¼ cup of the warm caramel sauce onto each serving plate. Place a scoop of ice cream on top of the sauce on each plate. Carefully arrange the pears in a spiral pattern around the ice cream and sprinkle each serving with walnuts.

WINE SUGGESTION
ANY GOOD DESSERT WINE WILL GO WELL
WITH THE MELLOW FLAVOR OF THE
PEARS.

HOT
BLUEBERRY
FEUILLETÉ
WITH
VANILLA ICE
CREAM

∎

FOR 6 SERVINGS

1½ cups Simple Syrup (see page 24)
6 tablespoons (¾ stick) unsalted
    butter, in pieces
3 cups fresh blueberries
6 tablespoons framboise liqueur
6 Feuilletés (see pages 38–39)
6 scoops (4 ounces each) Vanilla Ice
    Cream (see pages 238–239)

WHAT A GREAT LITTLE COMBINATION—FRESH BLUEBERRIES QUICKLY cooked in syrup, a great scoop of ice cream, and a hot, crisp, flaky pastry shell. It's kind of a sophisticated version of an ice cream sandwich.

In a saucepan, bring the syrup to a boil. Stir in the framboise, then swirl in the butter.

When the butter is melted, add the blueberries and framboise. Let the berries cook just until heated through, about 30 seconds. Remove the pan from the heat.

Split each feuilleté in half horizontally and place the bottom halves on large dessert plates. Place a large scoop of ice cream on top of the bottom half and spoon the blueberries and sauce over the ice cream. Place the top halves of the feuilletés on top.

MICHAEL'S FAMOUS DESSERT

■

FOR 6 SERVINGS

2 firm, ripe freestone peaches
6 scoops (4 ounces each) Vanilla Ice
    Cream (see pages 238–239)
6 scoops (4 ounces each) Raspberry
    Sorbet (see page 237)
1½ cups Crème Anglaise (see page
    25)
1½ cups Raspberry Sauce (see page
    236)
1½ cups each white and red wild
    strawberries (fraises du bois)
6 sprigs fresh mint

WINE SUGGESTION
THIS IS SPECTACULAR WITH A
CALIFORNIA LATE-HARVEST WINE SUCH
AS ONE FROM CHATEAU ST. JEAN, JOSEPH
PHELPS, OR BONNY DOON.

THE ULTIMATE STUDY IN WHITE AND RED, AND A PERFECT COMBINATION of flavors and textures.

Fraises du bois—little wild strawberries—can be found at gourmet markets and produce shops in late spring and early summer; they're usually red in color, but you can also sometimes get ripe white ones. If you can't find either kind, feel free to substitute regular strawberries, raspberries, blackberries, blueberries, or any other berry you like.

Bring a medium-size saucepan of water to a boil. Add the peaches and simmer about 30 seconds; drain well and rinse under cold running water. Then, with a small, sharp knife, nick the skins of the peaches and carefully peel off the skins. Halve and stone the peaches, then cut them into thin slices. Arrange a fan of slices—about one fourth of a peach—at the top of each chilled dinner plate; reserve the remaining half peach for another recipe if you like.

Place a scoop of ice cream and a scoop of sorbet across the middle of the plate, touching at the center.

On the bottom half of each plate, spoon ¼ cup of the crème anglaise on the side touching the sorbet; spoon ¼ cup of the raspberry sauce on the side touching the ice cream.

Scatter the white berries on top of the raspberry sauce; scatter the red berries on top of the crème anglaise. Garnish each plate with mint and serve immediately.

HOT BLUEBERRY
FEUTILLETÉ WITH
VANILIA ICE CREAM

RASPBERRY GRATIN

PEAR GRATIN

BIG MIKE'S SPECIAL
GRATIN

RASPBERRY GRATIN

■

FOR 6 SERVINGS

4½ cups fresh raspberries
¾ cup framboise liqueur, or to taste
¾ cup granulated sugar
3 cups Crème Anglaise (see page 25)
3 cups heavy cream, lightly whipped
    just until thickened
¾ cup Praline Powder (see page 26)

THIS VERY SHOWY DESSERT AND THE THREE OTHER GRATINS THAT FOLLOW it are extremely simple to make. All it takes is great fruit and an excellent crème anglaise. Though all three are rich enough to satisfy anyone's dessert cravings, they're actually very light in concept.

Preheat the broiler until very hot.
    In a mixing bowl, toss the berries with 6 tablespoons of the framboise and a ¼ cup of the sugar. Arrange the berries in individual gratin dishes.
    Stir together the crème anglaise and cream. With a whisk, whip in the remaining framboise. Pour this mixture over the berries.
    Sprinkle each serving with the praline powder and then the remaining sugar. Place the gratin dishes under the broiler until the surface of the cream is browned and bubbly, 20 to 30 seconds. Place each gratin dish on a serving plate and serve immediately.

BLOOD ORANGE GRATIN WITH GRAND MARNIER

■

FOR 6 SERVINGS

3 cups blood orange segments (about
    12 blood oranges)
3 cups Crème Anglaise (see page 25)
3 cups heavy cream, lightly whipped
    just until thickened
6 tablespoons Grand Marnier
6 tablespoons Praline Powder (see
    page 26)
6 tablespoons granulated sugar

THE COLOR OF BLOOD ORANGES, WHICH ARE BEGINNING TO BE AVAILABLE year round, makes for a startlingly beautiful dessert.

Preheat the broiler until very hot.
    Place ½ cup orange segments in each individual gratin dish.
    Stir together the crème anglaise and cream. With a whisk, briefly whisk in the Grand Marnier. Pour this mixture over the oranges.
    Sprinkle each serving with the praline powder and sugar. Place the gratin dishes under the broiler until the surface of the cream is browned and bubbly, 20 to 30 seconds.

PEAR GRATIN

．

FOR 6 SERVINGS

3 firm, ripe pears (Bartlett or other
good firm pears)
3 cups Crème Anglaise (see page 25)
3 cups heavy cream, lightly whipped
just until thickened
¾ cup Poire Williams liqueur, or to
taste
¾ cup granulated sugar
1 cup chopped walnuts

THE MELLOW FLAVORS OF RIPE PEARS AND CRÈME ANGLAISE GO WON-
derfully together.

Preheat the broiler until very hot.
Peel, halve, and core each pear. Place each half cut side
down; with a sharp knife, cut it lengthwise into thin slices, keeping
the slices together to keep the half intact. With a spatula, carefully
transfer each half to an individual gratin dish.

Stir together the crème anglaise and whipping cream. With a
whisk, whip in the Poire Williams. Pour this mixture over the pears,
coming about three fourths of the way up the sides of each pear.

Sprinkle the cream mixture around each pear with the sugar, then
walnuts; do not sprinkle them over the pears. Place the gratin dishes
under the broiler until the surface of the cream is browned and bubbly,
20 to 30 seconds. Place each gratin dish on a serving plate and serve
immediately.

BIG MIKE'S SPECIAL GRATIN

．

FOR 6 SERVINGS

2 firm, ripe freestone peaches
1½ cups each fresh raspberries,
blackberries, and blueberries
¾ cup framboise liqueur
¾ cup granulated sugar
3 cups Crème Anglaise (see page 25)
3 cups heavy cream, lightly whipped
just until thickened
¾ cup Grand Marnier
¾ cup Praline Powder (see page 26)

SIMPLY PUT, MY FAVORITE GRATIN COMBINATION.

Preheat the broiler until very hot.
Bring a medium-size saucepan of water to a boil. Add the
peaches and simmer about 30 seconds, then drain well and rinse
under cold running water. Then, with a small, sharp knife, nick the
skins of the peaches and carefully peel off the skins. Halve and stone
the peaches, then cut them into thin slices. Arrange a fan of slices—
about one fourth of a peach—in the center of each individual gratin
dish, reserving the remaining half-peach for another recipe if you
like.

In a mixing bowl, toss the berries with the framboise and a ¼ cup
of the sugar. Arrange about ¾ cup berries around the peach slices in
each gratin dish.

Stir together the crème anglaise and cream. With a whisk, briefly
whisk in the Grand Marnier. Pour this mixture over the fruit.

Sprinkle each serving with the praline powder and then the remaining sugar. Place the gratin dishes under the broiler until the
surface of the cream is browned and bubbly, 20 to 30 seconds. Place
each gratin dish on a serving plate and serve immediately.

GRAND MARNIER SOUFFLÉ

.

FOR 6 SERVINGS

7 tablespoons granulated sugar,
    approximately
6 large eggs, separated
Pinch of salt
6 tablespoons Grand Marnier
1½ cups Raspberry Sauce (see page
    32)

WINE SUGGESTION

THE BRANDY BASE AND COOKED ORANGE
FLAVOR OF THE GRAND MARNIER IN THE
SOUFFLÉ WILL SHOW OFF A GREAT AGED
SAUTERNES, GERMAN
TROCKENBEERENAUSLESE, OR
CALIFORNIA LATE-HARVEST WINE.

THIS IS A CLASSIC SOUFFLÉ, FLAVORED WITH ONE OF THE WORLD'S GREAT liqueurs. Served with a fresh raspberry sauce, it's a knockout.

Preheat the oven to 350°F. Butter six 2-ounce soufflé ramekins and sprinkle them with sugar, using about 1 tablespoon.

In the small bowl of an electric mixer, beat the egg whites until foamy. Add the salt and continue beating until firm peaks form. Add 6 tablespoons sugar and briefly beat in.

In a separate, larger bowl, whisk together the egg yolks and Grand Marnier. Fold in the egg white mixture.

Pour the soufflé mixture into the prepared ramekins and bake until puffed and golden, about 8 minutes. Serve with raspberry sauce.

CHOCOLATE SOUFFLÉ

■

FOR 6 SERVINGS

¾ *cup plus about 1 tablespoon*
  granulated sugar
6 *ounces semisweet chocolate, such as*
  Valrhona Superior, Tobler
  Velma, or Lindt, broken into
  pieces
6 *large eggs, separated*
Pinch of salt
6 *tablespoons crème de cacao liqueur*
1½ *cups Crème Anglaise (see page*
  25)
1½ *cups heavy cream, whipped to*
  firm peaks

THIS IS ANOTHER FAVORITE SOUFFLÉ AT MICHAEL'S. THE COMBINATION of a good semisweet melting chocolate such as Valrhona Superior, Tobler Velma, or Lindt and crème de cacao liqueur give an intense chocolate flavor. I serve this one with whipped cream and crème anglaise, both of which can be spooned to taste into the top of the soufflé by each guest.

Preheat the oven to 325°F. Butter six 2-ounce soufflé ramekins and sprinkle them with sugar, using about 1 tablespoon.

Melt the chocolate in the top of a double boiler over simmering water, stirring it with a whisk as it melts. Remove the pan from the heat and keep the chocolate resting over the water.

In the small bowl of an electric mixer, beat the egg whites until foamy. Add the salt and continue beating.

While the egg whites are being beaten, in a separate, larger bowl whisk the egg yolks until smooth. Whisk in the crème de cacao and the melted chocolate. As soon as the egg whites form firm peaks, briefly beat in the sugar and fold the egg white mixture into the yolk mixture.

Pour the soufflé mixture into the prepared ramekins and bake until puffed and golden, 8 to 10 minutes. Serve with crème anglaise and whipped cream.

LEMON COOKIES

■

MAKES ABOUT 4 DOZEN

2 lemons
½ pound (2 sticks) unsalted butter,
    at room temperature
½ cup granulated sugar
1 large egg yolk
Pinch of salt
1½ teaspoons vanilla extract
2 cups (9 ounces) all-purpose flour
Confectioner's sugar

THIS IS THE KIND OF COOKIE YOU ALWAYS FOUND IN YOUR GREAT GRAND-mother's stash box.

With a swivel-bladed vegetable peeler, remove the zest from the lemons; coarsely chop the zest. Juice the lemons.

In a large bowl, with an electric mixer on medium speed, cream together the butter and sugar for about 4 minutes. Add the egg yolk, salt, vanilla, and lemon zest; beat for about 2 minutes more. Then beat in the lemon juice until blended. Reduce the speed to low and add the flour, mixing just until blended in. Cover the bowl and refrigerate for 30 minutes to 1 hour.

Preheat the oven to 325°F.

With a tablespoon or 1-inch scooper, scoop the dough into balls about 1 inch in diameter and place them about 2 inches apart on baking sheets lined with parchment paper.

Bake the cookies until their edges are light golden in color, 12 to 15 minutes. Let them cool, then dust them with confectioner's sugar and store in an airtight container.

CINNAMON WALNUT COOKIES

■

FOR ABOUT 6 DOZEN

½ pound (2 sticks) unsalted butter,
    at room temperature
½ cup granulated sugar
1 large egg yolk
Pinch of salt
1½ teaspoons vanilla extract
⅔ cup coarsely chopped walnuts
½ cup firmly packed brown sugar
2 teaspoons ground cinnamon
2 cups (9 ounces) all-purpose flour

A VARIATION ON THE TRADITIONAL BUTTER COOKIE, THIS IS GREAT WITH coffee, sorbets, and ice creams.

In a large bowl, with an electric mixer on medium speed, cream together the butter and granulated sugar. Add the egg yolk, salt, and vanilla, and beat well. Add the walnuts, brown sugar, and cinnamon, and beat until blended. Reduce the speed to low and add the flour, mixing just until blended in. Chill the dough, in the bowl, in the refrigerator for about 10 minutes.

On a cool, lightly floured surface, roll the dough into 3 logs about 2 inches in diameter. Wrap in waxed paper and refrigerate for about 1 hour.

Preheat the oven to 350°F.

Cut the dough into ⅛-inch slices and place them on baking sheets lined with parchment paper, spacing about 1 inch apart. Bake until their edges are light golden in color, about 12 to 15 minutes. Let cool, then store in an airtight container.

CARDAMOM COOKIES

■

FOR ABOUT 4 DOZEN

½ pound (2 sticks) unsalted butter
¼ cup granulated sugar
1 large egg yolk
1½ tablespoons freshly ground cardamom
1½ teaspoons vanilla extract
Pinch of salt
2 cups (9 ounces) all-purpose flour

CARDAMOM, ALONG WITH THE MORE WIDELY USED NUTMEG AND CIN-namon, holds a great place in American cooking. It's a sweet spice, with an exotic, arresting flavor that comes across perfectly in these simple cookies. This recipe was developed from one that was brought to the restaurant by one of my early pastry chefs, Becky Naccarato, who in turn got it from her grandmother.

In a large bowl, with an electric mixer on medium speed, cream together the butter and sugar. Then beat in the egg yolk, cardamom, vanilla, and salt until smoothly blended. Reduce the speed to low and gradually blend in the flour.

Refrigerate the bowl for about 10 minutes to firm up the dough. Then, on a floured work surface, form it into 1 or 2 logs about 2 inches in diameter. Wrap the logs in waxed paper and refrigerate for about 1 hour.

Preheat the oven to 350°F.

Cut dough into ¼-inch slices and place them on baking sheets lined with parchment paper, spacing about 1 inch apart. Bake until their edges are light golden in color, about 12 to 15 minutes. Let cool, then store in an airtight container.

PECAN DELIGHTS

■

FOR ABOUT 4 DOZEN

½ pound (2 sticks) unsalted butter
¼ cup granulated sugar
Pinch of salt
1 cup coarsely chopped pecans
2 cups (9 ounces) all-purpose flour
Confectioner's sugar

A VARIATION ON THE CLASSIC BUTTER COOKIE.

Preheat the oven to 350°F.

With an electric mixer on medium speed, cream together the butter and granulated sugar, then beat in the salt and pecans. Reduce the speed to low and gradually blend in the flour.

With a teaspoon or a 1-inch scooper, scoop out small balls of the dough and place them about 1 inch apart on cookie sheets lined with parchment paper.

Bake the cookies until light golden, about 12 to 15 minutes. Remove from the oven and let cool. Place the confectioner's sugar in a sifter and shake it over the cookies. Store them in an airtight container.

CHOCOLATE CHIP COOKIES

■

FOR ABOUT 4 DOZEN

12 tablespoons (1½ sticks) unsalted
   butter
6 tablespoons firmly packed brown
   sugar
6 tablespoons granulated sugar
1 large egg
1 tablespoon vanilla extract
1 cup plus 2 tablespoons (⅓ pound)
   all-purpose flour
1½ tablespoons salt
¾ cup coarsely chopped pecans
13 ounces semisweet chocolate, such
   as Valrhona Superior or Tobler
   Velma, chopped by hand into
   ¼-inch pieces

I SNEAK INTO THE KITCHEN AND EAT SOME OF THESE EVERY DAY. They're the best, a combination of the dry, crisp variety and the moist, chewy variety of chocolate chip cookie.

In a large bowl, with an electric mixer on medium speed, cream the butter, then cream it together with the brown and white sugars. Then beat in the egg and vanilla until smoothly blended. Reduce the speed to low and gradually mix in the flour and salt. Fold in the pecans and chocolate. Cover the bowl and refrigerate for 1 hour.

Preheat the oven to 325°F.

With a teaspoon or 1-inch scooper, scoop out small balls of the dough and place them about 2 inches apart on baking sheets lined with parchment paper.

Bake the cookies until light golden brown, 12 to 15 minutes. Let cool, then store in an airtight container.

MACAROONS

■

FOR ABOUT 2½ DOZEN

1¼ cups granulated sugar
1¼ cups shredded coconut
6 large egg whites
2 tablespoons unsalted butter, melted
1½ tablespoons apricot preserves or
   applesauce
1½ tablespoons honey

I WAS TURNED OFF FROM COCONUT AS A CHILD, BUT PIÑA COLADAS brought me back as an adult. These rich, chewy macaroons—combining coconut with sugar that caramelizes during baking—take coconut to the ultimate level.

Preheat the oven to 350°F.

In a mixing bowl, combine all the ingredients with your hands until evenly mixed.

With your fingers, form the mixture into cone-shaped mounds about 2 inches high and place them about 2 inches apart on a baking sheet lined with parchment paper.

Bake the macaroons until evenly golden, about 20 minutes. Let cool, then store in an airtight container.

DIPPED STRAWBERRIES

■

FOR 6 SERVINGS

½ pound semisweet or white chocolate, broken into ½-inch pieces

6 large, ripe but firm, long-stemmed strawberries

FOR THE MOST ELEGANT PRESENTATION, LOOK FOR LONG-STEMMED BER-ries; your best bet at finding them is in gourmet produce departments. Needless to say, the berries should be the best, most flavorful seasonal ones you can buy; anything less than a full-flavored berry will pale beside the chocolate. The berries should be ripe but good and firm so they'll hold up well.

Whatever you do, don't wash the berries; that will only bring their juices to the surface and make them difficult to coat properly. Just give them a gentle wipe with a clean, dry cloth or paper towel.

Use the best-quality semisweet or white chocolate you can find; at Michael's, we use Valrhona or Tobler.

Melt the chocolate in the top of a double boiler over barely simmering water. As the chocolate melts, stir with a wire whisk to help it melt evenly and smoothly.

Cover a small baking sheet with parchment paper or waxed paper. Remove the melted chocolate from the heat to a work surface. Holding a berry carefully at the base of the stem, dip it sideways into the chocolate, covering it halfway at a steep diagonal. Turn the berry around and dip it the same way symmetrically on the either side, leaving a V shape of uncoated berry below the stem.

Immediately rest the coated berry on its back side on the paper-covered tray. Repeat with the remaining berries and refrigerate them until the chocolate has firmly set, about 30 minutes. Keep them chilled until ready to serve, then place them in paper candy cups.

CHOCOLATE TRUFFLES

■

FOR ABOUT 20

1 cup Ganache (see page 26), at room
    temperature
6 ounces bittersweet chocolate—
    Valrhona Caraque, Tobler
    Tobamera, or Lindt—for
    coating, broken into pieces
3 ounces chocolate for decoration (if
    required), broken into pieces
¼ cup liqueur or other flavoring (see
    variations)

I LIKE TO THINK OF TRUFFLES AS CHOCOLATE "SHOOTERS"—A PURE,
simple, elegant hit of great chocolate. We've studied all kinds of truffle
variations to arrive at the five perfect ones we like to serve after dinner.
The recipe describes the basic method, and then the specifics of each
variation follow.

In a bowl, stir together the ganache and flavoring. Refrigerate until
slightly set, about 20 minutes.

Using a ½-inch melon baller or a 1-inch scooper, scoop small balls
from the ganache mixture and place on a baking sheet covered with
parchment paper. Chill in the refrigerator about 1 hour.

Melt the coating chocolate in the top of a double boiler over simmering water; melt the decorating chocolate in a second double boiler
or in a metal bowl set over a saucepan of simmering water.

One at a time, place each chilled truffle on top of the end of a
long fork and spoon the melted chocolate over the truffle to cover it
completely. Return it to the parchment paper. If coating with white
chocolate, let the coating set and dip again to coat completely.

If decorating with a chocolate design, fit a small piping bag with
a fine writing tip. Fill it with the other melted chocolate and drizzle
it over the dipped truffles once the coating has set. Chill before
serving.

FRAMBOISE TRUFFLES
Flavor the ganache with framboise liqueur. Place a fresh raspberry in
the scoop before scooping each ball of ganache mixture. Dip in bittersweet chocolate, such as Valrhona Caraque or Tobler Tobamera.
Decorate with a crisscross pattern of melted white chocolate.

POIRE WILLIAMS TRUFFLES
Flavor the ganache with Poire Williams liqueur. Place a ½-inch chunk
of fresh pear in the scoop before scooping each ball of ganache mixture. Dip in bittersweet chocolate, such as Valrhona Caraque or Tobler
Tobamera. Decorate with a dot of melted white chocolate.

WHITE CHOCOLATE COCONUT MINT TRUFFLES
Make the ganache with white chocolate. Flavor it with white crème
de menthe liqueur and ½ cup of shredded coconut that has been
blanched for 1 minute in boiling water, drained, dried, and finely
chopped. Dip in white chocolate, giving it 2 coatings.

WHITE CHOCOLATE PRALINE TRUFFLES
Make the ganache with white chocolate. Flavor it with ½ cup Praline
Powder (see page 26). Dip in white chocolate, giving it 2 coatings,

and decorate with a sprinkling of praline powder before the second coating sets.

KAHLUA TRUFFLES

Flavor the ganache with Kahlua liqueur. Dip in bittersweet chocolate, such as Valrhona Caraque or Tobler Tobamera. Decorate each truffle with a chocolate espresso bean—available in gourmet shops—before the coating sets.

DOUBLE CHOCOLATE BROWNIES

■

FOR 6 DOZEN

6 ounces semisweet chocolate, such as Valrhona Superior or Tobler Velma

6 ounces bittersweet chocolate, such as Valrhona Caraque or Tobler Tobamera chocolate, broken by hand into small pieces

3 tablespoons unsalted butter

¾ cup granulated sugar

3½ tablespoons water

2 large eggs

1⅓ cups (6 ounces) walnuts, coarsely chopped

¾ cup plus 1 tablespoon (¼ pound) all-purpose flour

¾ teaspoon salt

1 tablespoon confectioner's sugar

I WANTED TO MAKE AN *ADULT* CHOCOLATE BROWNIE, WITH A PERFECT, subtle balance of qualities—moist but not too gooey or fudgelike, with a rich but not-too-sweet flavor and a great interplay of textures.

The solution I hit on was to use two different kinds of chocolate, both imported from Europe and available in gourmet stores. Valrhona Caraque or Tobler Tobamera bittersweet chocolate gives the brownie batter a smooth, moist consistency and glossy sheen. Valrhona Superior or Tobler Velma semisweet chocolate forms small, succulent nuggets in the brownies.

Serve the brownies with an excellent vanilla ice cream.

With a large, sharp knife, carefully chop the semisweet chocolate into pieces about ¼ inch in size. Transfer the chocolate to a bowl and put it in the refrigerator.

Combine the bittersweet chocolate with the butter, sugar, and water in a heavy saucepan over the lowest possible heat. Cook, stirring occasionally with a wooden spoon, until the chocolate has melted, 8 to 10 minutes.

Preheat the oven to 325°F. Butter one 9 × 9-inch square cake pan.

Remove the chocolate mixture from the heat and stir in the eggs. Fold in the walnuts, then gradually stir in the flour and salt until the batter is smooth.

Stir the chopped and chilled semisweet chocolate into the batter. Pour the batter into the prepared pans. Bake for 20 to 25 minutes, until a toothpick inserted in their centers comes out clean. Let them cool in the pan for about 30 minutes.

Sprinkle the brownies with the confectioner's sugar and cut them into 1½-inch squares. Transfer the brownies to individual paper candy cups. Store them in an airtight container.

FRESH FRUIT SORBETS

■

FOR ABOUT 1½ QUARTS

⅔ cup granulated sugar
2 cups water
2 to 2¼ cups fresh fruit juice or
    puree (see below)

WE ALWAYS SERVE A SELECTION OF FIVE DIFFERENT FRUIT SORBETS—whatever fruits are fresh in season—scooped onto a chilled plate and accompanied by a plate of cookies.

The trick with any of them is to get the right balance of fruit puree or juice and sugar syrup to highlight the fruit's natural flavor in the sorbet without getting too sweet. The amount of syrup you add will depend on the sweetness of the fruit you buy.

In a heavy saucepan, combine the sugar and water and bring to a boil. Remove this syrup from the heat and let it cool to room temperature.

Stir half the syrup into the puree, then continue adding syrup and tasting until the desired sweetness is reached; very sweet fruit may need only half the syrup.

Place the mixture in a sorbet machine and freeze, following manufacturer's instructions.

Serve a selection of different sorbets, arranged in oval scoops on a chilled plate. Accompany with a selection of cookies.

BLACK CURRANT
Use 2 cups pureed and sieved fresh black currants.

BLUEBERRY-LIME
Use 2 cups pureed fresh blueberries and ¼ cup fresh lime juice.

BOYSENBERRY
Use 2 cups pureed and sieved fresh boysenberries.

FIG
Use 2 cups pureed and sieved fresh figs.

KIWI
Use 2 cups pureed kiwi fruit, with the small black seeds.

ORANGE
Use 2 cups freshly squeezed orange juice.

PASSION FRUIT
Use 2 cups fresh passion fruit that has been scooped out of its skin and pressed through a sieve to eliminate the seeds.

PINEAPPLE
Use 2 cups pureed and sieved fresh pineapple.

POMEGRANATE-GRAPEFRUIT
Press pomegranate seeds in a sieve to get 2 cups of juice and combine with ¼ cup fresh grapefruit juice.

RASPBERRY
Use 2 cups pureed and sieved raspberries.

RUBY GRAPEFRUIT
Use 2 cups freshly squeezed ruby or pink grapefruit juice.

STRAWBERRY
Use 2 cups pureed and sieved fresh strawberries.

SORBET PLATE

CHOCOLATE CHIP ICE CREAM

PISTACHIO ICE CREAM

CARAMEL ICE CREAM

WHITE CHOCOLATE MINT ICE CREAM

PRALINE ICE CREAM

CHOCOLATE ICE CREAM

VANILLA ICE CREAM

■

FOR ABOUT 2 QUARTS

1½ vanilla beans
4 cups heavy cream
4 cups half-and-half
16 large egg yolks
1½ cups granulated sugar

REAL VANILLA ICE CREAM IS KIND OF LIKE SALT AND PEPPER—YOU'VE just got to have it around or you're missing one of life's basics. There's nothing complicated to this recipe; it just uses the best, most basic, richest ingredients—egg yolks, half-and-half, whole milk, sugar, and real vanilla bean.

For vanilla chocolate chip ice cream, stir in ¾ pound finely chopped or shaved semisweet chocolate just before freezing the mixture.

With a small, sharp knife, very carefully split the vanilla beans in half lengthwise. With the tip of the knife, scrape the insides of the beans into a mixing bowl. Place the hulls of the beans in a large saucepan.

Put the cream and half-and-half in the saucepan and place over high heat.

While the cream mixture is heating, put the egg yolks and sugar in the mixing bowl with the vanilla beans. With a wire whisk, beat the mixture until the yolks are pale yellow, about 1½ minutes.

When the cream mixture has come to a boil, very slowly pour it into the yolk mixture, whisking continuously. As soon as they have been combined, return them to the pan and stir over low heat just until the mixture is thick enough to coat a wooden spoon, no more than about 1 minute.

Pour the mixture through a sieve into a metal bowl and set it inside a large bowl filled with ice to chill for about 45 minutes, stirring every 3 minutes or so.

Freeze the ice cream mixture in a commercial ice cream freezer, following the manufacturer's directions.

PRALINE ICE CREAM

Omit vanilla beans from recipe and add 1 cup granulated sugar to the egg yolks. After blending the egg yolk and cream mixtures together and cooking them, stir in ¾ cup Praline Powder (see page 26). Do not sieve mixture.

PISTACHIO ICE CREAM

Omit vanilla beans from recipe. Add 1½ cups shelled, skinned, and roasted natural pistachio nuts, coarsely chopped, to the heavy cream and half-and-half and leave at room temperature for about 1 hour. Then pour the mixture through a sieve into a large saucepan; reserve the pistachio nuts. Continue as for Vanilla Ice Cream recipe. After blending the egg yolk and cream mixtures together and cooking them, stir in the pistachio nuts. Do not sieve mixture again.

Omit vanilla beans from recipe and add only 1 cup granulated sugar to the egg yolks. After blending the egg yolk and cream mixtures together and cooking them, stir in 2 cups Caramel Sauce (see page 32). Do not sieve mixture.

CHOCOLATE ICE CREAM

■

FOR ABOUT 2½ QUARTS

1 pound bittersweet chocolate, broken into ½-inch pieces
4 cups heavy cream
4 cups half-and-half
16 large egg yolks
1 cup granulated sugar

USE THE BEST-QUALITY BITTERSWEET CHOCOLATE YOU CAN FIND, SUCH as Valrhona or Tobler.

For chocolate chocolate chip ice cream, stir in ¾ pound finely chopped or shaved semisweet chocolate just before freezing the mixture.

Put the chocolate in the top of a double boiler over simmering water. As the chocolate melts, stir with a wire whisk to help it melt evenly and smoothly. Turn off the heat but leave the chocolate on top of the water to keep it melted.

Put the cream and half-and-half in a large saucepan and place over high heat.

While the cream mixture is heating, put the egg yolks and sugar in a mixing bowl. With a wire whisk, beat the mixture until the yolks are pale yellow, about 1½ minutes.

When the cream mixture has come to a boil, very slowly pour it into the yolk mixture, whisking continuously. As soon as they have been combined, return them to the pan and stir over low heat just until the mixture is thick enough to coat a wooden spoon, no more than about 1 minute.

Remove the pan from the heat and gradually pour in the melted chocolate, whisking constantly, until it has been smoothly incorporated. Pour the mixture into a metal bowl and set it inside a large bowl filled with ice to chill for about 45 minutes, stirring every 3 minutes or so.

Freeze the ice cream mixture in a commercial ice cream freezer, following the manufacturer's directions.

WHITE CHOCOLATE MINT ICE CREAM
Make the recipe substituting an equal amount of white chocolate and adding only a ¼ cup of granulated sugar to the egg yolks before whisking them together. After you mix the melted chocolate in with the egg yolk and cream mixture, whisk in ½ cup of crème de menthe liqueur.

INDEX

．